KEYNES AND INDIA

Keynes and India

A Study in Economics and Biography

Anand Chandavarkar

M
MACMILLAN

First published 1989

Published by
THE MACMILLAN PRESS LTD
Houndmills, Basingstoke, Hampshire RG21 2XS
and London
Companies and representatives
throughout the world

Printed and bound in Great Britain at
The Camelot Press Ltd, Southampton

British Library Cataloguing in Publication Data
Chandavarkar, Anand, *1925–*
Keynes and India: a study in economics and biography.
1. Economics. Keynes, John Maynard, 1883–1946 — Biographies
I. Title
330.15′6
ISBN 0–333–51333–9

For Tara and Nikhil

Contents

Acknowledgements

The author wishes to acknowledge his grateful thanks to:

- Deena Khatkhate as the prime and most helpful catalyst for this project at all stages;
- I. G. Patel, Paul Streeten and Jagdish Bhagwati for sustained interest and encouragement;
- Dharma Kumar for launching and keeping afloat an unreconstructed central banker in the heady waters of Indian economic history;
- Dr Michael Halls, Modern Archivist, King's College, Cambridge, for invaluable assistance during a delightful working week and thereafter;
- David Bensusan-Butt, Vinayak V. Bhatt, Sir Alec Cairncross, Harold Dunkerley, Polly Hill, the late L. K. Jha, I. G. Patel, Walter Salant and Hans Singer for useful communications;
- Mrs Hilary Corbett and Mrs Sathya Menon for patient and efficient word processing of successive drafts;
- The staff, particularly Patricia Kane, of the Joint Bank-Fund Library, Washington, DC, for ever willing and competent assistance;
- The late Raja Balkishandas Mukandas, the late I. Sitarama Rao, Raja Vallabhdas Bhagwandas, Nawab Mir Nawaz Jung, and Hadi Bilgrami, for opportune and generous assistance towards my tenure as a Hyderabad State Scholar at the London School of Economics and Political Science which laid the foundations of my interest in this genre.

Permission to use copyright material from the respective sources is gratefully acknowledged:

- Unpublished writings of J. M. Keynes, copyright The Provost and Scholars of King's College, Cambridge, 1990, located in King's College Library and other sources indicated in the text.
- Master and Fellows of Trinity College, Cambridge, for the Edwin Montagu Papers.
- D. C. Grigg of Pettiphers Farm, Pebworth, Stratford-on-Avon, Warwickshire, and the Master, Fellows and Scholars of Churchill

College, in the University of Cambridge, for the James Grigg Collection.

- Centre of South Asian Studies, University of Cambridge, for the Malcolm Darling Papers.
- The International Monetary Fund, Washington, DC, for the archives of the Savannah Annual Meeting (1946).
- The Controller of Her Majesty's Stationery Office for unpublished Crown copyright material in the India Office Records.
- Bank of England for quotations from the letters of Lord Norman and Sir Otto Niemeyer.
- The Royal Economic Society and the Macmillan Press Ltd for quotations from *The Collected Writings of John Maynard Keynes*.

Every effort has been made to trace all the copyright-holders, but if any have been inadvertently overlooked the publishers will be pleased to make the necessary arrangement at the first opportunity.

Keynes and India: A Chronology

1883 Born at No. 6 Harvey Road, Cambridge on 5 June.
1897 Scholarship to Eton College.
1902 Entered King's College, Cambridge.
1903 28 February, admitted to the Apostles.
1905 President of the Cambridge Union Society and the Liberal Club. November, speech at the Cambridge Union in support of more popular government for India. Graduated 12th Wrangler in Mathematical Tripos.
Studied economics for the Civil Service Examination.
1906 2 March, guest of honour, Annual Dinner of Cambridge Indian Majlis. Entered India Office on 16 October as a Junior Clerk in the Military Department.
1907 Transferred in March to the Revenue, Statistics, and Commerce Department of India Office.
1908 Resigned from India Office on 5 June on his 25th birthday. 20 July, last day at India Office.
1909 16 March, elected Fellow of King's College, Cambridge (1909–46). 20 May, letter in defence of Indian students, *Cambridge Review*. 20 October, started the Political Economy Club.
1910 May. Invited to give six lectures on Indian finance at the London School of Economics.
1911 Lectures on 'Currency, Finance and the Level of Prices in India', at the London School of Economics and at Cambridge (in place of his Company Finance and Stock Exchange lectures).
January. Appointed Girdlers' Lecturer in Economics at Cambridge to succeed H. O. Meredith.
25 February, guest of honour, Annual Dinner of Cambridge Indian Majlis.
9 May, paper on Indian Currency read to the Royal Economic Society at its quarterly meeting. This was based on his lectures on Indian currency to the London School of Economics and to the Economics Tripos at Cambridge.
October. Editor of *The Economic Journal* and Secretary of

the Royal Economic Society (1911–45).
15 December, signed agreement for *Indian Currency and Finance* for publication by Macmillan and Co.

1913 February. Circulated proofs of *Indian Currency and Finance* to, among others, Neville Keynes, Hartley Withers, and Lionel Abrahams.
May. Appointed Member, Royal Commission on Indian Currency and Finance 1913–14 (Chairman, Austen Chamberlain).
5 May, first meeting of Commission.
9 June, publication of *Indian Currency and Finance* (Macmillan). The preface was dated 12 May.

1914 Report of the Royal Commission on Indian Finance and Currency (signed 24 February and published 2 March).

1915 Joined wartime Treasury. As Secretary of the Cabinet's Wheat Committee organised government purchases of Indian wheat.

1917 Companion of the Order of the Bath (CB). A rare honour for a temporary member of the Civil Service.

1919 Principal Representative of the Treasury at Paris Peace Conference. Resigned in June from Treasury over the Peace Treaty.
July. Gave evidence to the Indian Exchange and Currency Committee (Chairman, Sir Henry Babington Smith).
Published *The Economic Consequences of the Peace.*

1920 Served on Committee to select a Governor for the Reserve Bank of South Africa. Resigned University Lectureship in Economics.

1921 7 October. Appointed Vice-Chairman of the Indian Fiscal Commission on tariff policy.
Published *A Treatise on Probability*.

1922 2 February, passage booked from Venice to Bombay.
10 February, resigned from the Indian Fiscal Commission.
Published *A Revision of the Treaty*.

1923 Published *A Tract on Monetary Reform*.

1924 Bursar of King's College, Cambridge (1924–46).

1925 Married Lydia Lopokova. Visited Russia.

1926 Gave evidence to the Royal Commission on Indian Currency and Finance (Chairman, Hilton Young).

1928 Visited Russia.

1929 Elected Fellow of the British Academy (FBA).

1929–31	Member, Macmillan Committee on Finance and Industry.
1930	Published *A Treatise on Money*.
1930–39	Member, Economic Advisory Council.
1931	The 'Circus' on the *Treatise*.
	Publication of *Essays in Persuasion*.
1933	Publication of *Essays in Biography*.
1936	Opening of the Arts Theatre in Cambridge.
	Publication of *The General Theory of Employment, Interest and Money*.
1940	Fellow of Eton College.
	Publication of *How to Pay for the War*.
	Adviser to Chancellor of Exchequer (Kingsley Wood, John Anderson, Hugh Dalton) with special authority on Indian financial questions.
1941–46	Director of the Bank of England.
	Trustee of the National Gallery.
1942	Chairman of the Committee for the Encouragement of Music and the Arts (later the Arts Council).
	Became Lord Keynes (Baron Keynes of Tilton in County of Sussex).
1943–46	High Steward of the Borough of Cambridge.
1944	June. Chairman, British Delegation Preliminary Drafting Conference, Atlantic City.
	July. United Nations Monetary and Financial Conference, Bretton Woods.
	Washington Negotiations on Stage II of Lend Lease.
1945	Washington Negotiations on US Loan to Britain.
1946	Honorary Doctor of Science, University of Cambridge (Hon. Sc.D).
	Savannah Conference for Inauguration of International Monetary Fund and World Bank.
	Elected Fellow of the Royal Society (FRS).
	Accepted appointment to (but died before receiving) the Order of Merit (OM).
	21 April, died at Tilton, Sussex, aged 62.

1 Prologue

'I want to see Keynes reassessed by another generation. For reassessed he must be.' *Austin Robinson*

Keynes is arguably the most written-about economist. The steady stream of publications on Keynes and Keynesian Economics since his death (1946), has attained the proportions of a massive growth industry, and prompts just the type of question Quentin Bell was moved to ask in the Preface to an exhibition devoted to Bloomsbury: 'Haven't you had enough?'[1] But in responding to such a question on Keynes no author need feel too apologetic. Keynes's protean intellect, his public and private persona, and achievements as an economist, adviser, statesman, author, teacher, policymaker and institutional architect seem to demand almost periodic reappraisals, rather like those of eminent figures like Samuel Johnson, Jefferson, Kipling, Forster, Russell, Kafka, Disraeli, T. E. Lawrence, and Oscar Wilde. There can be no definitive, only revisionist, appraisals of such eternal contemporaries even as of perennially controversial historical episodes like the Industrial Revolution, the Great Depression, or the American Civil War. Biography, like history, is much too complex and many-sided to be written by any one person. Rather, it is like an elaborate edifice to be diligently built up by different authors, who approach the subject from different angles and points of view, and yet are united by a common focus of interest and empathy. Equally, there often seems to be an inevitable dialectic in the biographical treatment of the eminent, with the hagiographic thesis being followed by the antithesis of the negative revisionism leading, in turn, to a synthesis of positive revisionism. The *furor biographicus* gives way at some point to more muted tones. Thus the Boswellisation of Keynes in Harrod's pioneering biography has been followed by the Stracheyesque revisionism of Skidelsky and Hession.[2] There is, however, always room for exploring and interpreting some fresh or neglected aspect of the life and work of a many-sided genius like Keynes. No wonder Keynesian scholarship seems to partake of the inexhaustible quality of the proverbial Widow's Cruse.

The present study has been undertaken as an in-depth historical and biographical appraisal of what is, even today, well after his centennial, perhaps the least researched aspect of Keynes, namely, the crucial formative role of the Indian Connection in Keynes's life and work and its contribution to the development of his economic ideas and its manifestations in his psyche and career. India loomed large in the life and work of Keynes, but, surprisingly, even the prolific symposia published on virtually every aspect of Keynes do not contain a single piece on Keynes's Indian Connection. There are at best passing references to its influence on him.[3] Even the three full-length biographies by Harrod, Skidelsky, and Hession give only fragmentary treatment of this aspect of Keynes's life in the context of his service with the India Office. While Keynes and Indian economic issues have been studied by themselves, there has been no historical and biographical analysis of the fascinating mutual impact of India on Keynes's thought and of Keynes on Indian economic thought and policy. These gaps in the literature prompted the present author to prepare a historical essay on 'Keynes and India' in the year of the Keynes centennial (1983) which was followed by analyses of related facets of Keynes.[4] Still, the intrinsic fascination and significance of the theme and the wealth of untapped source material seemed to merit a systematic treatment in a much wider perspective. Alike in its intensity and range, it could be said that India and Indian affairs ranked second only to Britain in Keynes's intellectual preoccupations, and in some respects even outranked it, as for instance, his contributions to the theory and practice of the gold exchange standard and the formulation of the developmental role of a central bank. It is all too often overlooked that every applied economist is necessarily a country specialist and it only smacks of needless self-flagellation to 'Pity the Poor Country Specialist'.[5] Keynes, the quintessential applied and institutional monetary economist, too was emphatically a country specialist (India) in his most formative years.

Any study like the present one has logically to start with an answer to the basic question: What triggered Keynes's interest in India and led him to making such path-breaking contributions to Indian monetary and economic affairs and monetary economics generally despite the absence of any family tradition of service or other links with India? Keynes never visited India whether on business or pleasure. The only developing countries he ever visited, Tunisia and Egypt, were for a holiday. Admittedly, personal links are not always an assurance of intellectual or emotional interest or involvement in any country, as in the case of Keynes's close friend and fellow Bloomsberry, Lytton Strachey, whose father and his family had served in

India with great distinction.[6] Yet, Strachey was not only himself averse to entering Indian service but was even overtly racialist[7] in discouraging Leonard Woolf and Bernard Swithinbank (an Etonian friend of Keynes's who served as District Commissioner, Pegu, and later as wartime Adviser (1942) on Burma to the Secretary of State) from joining the Ceylon and Indian Civil Services, respectively. 'Have you thought enough of the horror of the solitude and wretchedness of every single creature out there and the degrading influences of the years away from civilization. . . . But go away and be a great man and like the blacks and enjoy yourself among apes and peacocks' (Strachey to Swithinbank).[8] If family links were no assurance of an abiding interest in India, the same was perhaps true of economists who had official links with India like the classic example of Malthus, who, despite his thirty-year tenure (1805–34) as Professor of Modern History and Political Economy (the earliest Chair of Political Economy in England) at the East India college for the cadets of the East India Company, first at Hertford and later at Haileybury, hardly showed any interest in India's economic problems.

Keynes did not share Alfred Marshall's pedagogic interest in India as a case of 'applying contemporary observation of the East to explain the economic past' of Europe.[9] But he 'belonged to a generation to which the Indian Empire and the problems of the British Government of India stood as a great challenge, luring many of the intelligent men of the age into its service, out of all proportion to its economic importance, though this itself was greater than nowadays'.[10] The sheer scale and inherent complexity of Indian society and economy so well captured by Joan Robinson – whatever you say about India the opposite is equally true – have always afforded a constant spur to the enquiring economist. The intellectual challenge of India also derived from the fact that it was 'the only part of the British Empire to which laissez-faire never applied'.[11] India served as a much larger and more complex testing-ground than Ireland for both men and policies on lines which 'the most conventional of Englishmen . . . were not prepared to contemplate or tolerate at home'.[12] India, in effect, functioned as a vast social laboratory where economic and juridical changes and reforms could be implemented and observed with minimal political constraints, despite the unavoidable deference to custom and status in a traditional society. No wonder India was a fertile field for sowing the seeds of various types of Utilitarian philosophy and practice.[13] Several of these policies and institutions were later transplanted to Britain in the light of Indian experience, like Macaulay's reforms of the Indian Civil Service which considerably influenced the British Home Civil Service reforms of 1853–54. The Indian Negotiable Instruments Act 1881, had also a similar impact on the corresponding British legislation, the Bills of Exchange Act 1882.

Keynes's interest in India was no doubt triggered by his two years in the India Office but it was sustained and enlarged even more by the sheer intellectual challenge posed by the uniqueness of India's monetary history during British rule which witnessed practically every variety of monetary standard, passing successively from a silver standard to a managed inconvertible silver currency, gold exchange standard, paper standard, a gold bullion standard, and finally a sterling exchange standard. To Keynes, the core of the challenge derived from the need to devise an appropriate version of the gold exchange standard for India and to create a central bank with a strong developmental orientation removed as far as possible from the Bank of England prototype. Significantly, the issue of the appropriate rate of exchange for the Indian rupee, the celebrated rupee ratio controversy – the King Charles's Head of Indian economic history – did not excite Keynes as much as the more overriding problem of a suitable monetary standard for India.

This then is the backdrop for the present study which combines the historical and thematic approach in studying Keynes's Indian Connection. It may be regarded as a segment of the intellectual biography of Keynes as well as an essay in the history and sociology of economic doctrine and policy in the Indian conjuncture. It draws on the published writings of and on Keynes, the unpublished Keynes papers in King's College, Cambridge and other archives (International Monetary Fund, Malcolm Darling Papers, Centre for South Asian Studies, Cambridge, James Grigg Collection, Churchill College, Cambridge) as well as personal communications from students and associates of Keynes. The assessment of Keynes's work in the Indian context is made in terms of the contemporary state of economic doctrine and the prevailing economic conjuncture as well as, wherever relevant, in the light of subsequent research in economic history and advances in the state of art. The study is a voyage of discovery in some respects and a reappraisal in other respects. But 'any process of reappraisal, if it is honest and not merely a vainglorious attempt to pull down the great to the level of the self-appointed appraiser, will recognize Keynes's greatness'.[14] It is in this spirit that the present study has been undertaken.

It is organised as follows. Chapter 2 reviews Keynes's formative years at the India Office and his first exposure to Indian economic problems as in the nature of an apprenticeship to his future greatness. Even after his resignation from the India Office, Keynes's lectures and writings continued to have a strong Indian content and covered a varied range of topics such as the monetary transmission mechanism, British investment in India, the economic 'drain', the salt tax, protection, free trade, and so on. A major episode was Keynes's appointment and subsequent resignation as Vice-President of the Indian Fiscal Commission (1921–22) (Chapter 3). Keynes's writings, notably his classic *Indian Currency and Finance*, and his work for successive Indian Currency Commissions and Committees, are analysed with reference to three major issues: the appropriate monetary standard for India; the rupee ratio controversy (the rate of exchange of the rupee with sterling); and the role of gold as a private store of value in India and as an official reserve (Chapter 4). This is followed by an analysis of Keynes's pioneering ideas on the regulatory and developmental rationale and institutional set-up of central banking in India and his efforts to create a central bank for India (Chapter 5). Keynes's somewhat subdued but nevertheless meaningful contacts with Indian economic affairs during the thirties were followed by his active contributions to the equitable settlement of the vexed question of India's wartime sterling balances and his prominent role in securing an appropriate quota for India and an appointed seat as a founding member on the Board of Directors of the International Monetary Fund (Chapter 6). The impact of Keynes and Keynesian Economics on Indian economic thought and policy, particularly the influence of Keynesian models and paradigms on planning, development and employment policy, are assessed in Chapter 7. Keynes's interest and involvement with Indian students, which throw rare sidelights on the human aspects of his personality, are analysed in the context of the links of Cambridge and King's College with the Indian Subcontinent (Chapter 8). Keynes's little-known attitudes to Indian politics and self-government and his lack of interest in Indian society and culture are examined in the penultimate Chapter 9. The Epilogue attempts an integrated appraisal of the interface between Keynes and India in the light of the analysis and evidence presented in the study.

Notes

1. George Spater and Ian Parsons, *A Marriage of True Minds: An Intimate Portrait of Leonard and Virginia Woolf* (Harcourt, Brace Jovanovich, New York and London, 1977), p. XIII.
2. R. F. Harrod, *The Life of John Maynard Keynes* (Macmillan, London, 1951); Robert Skidelsky, *John Maynard Keynes, Vol. I: Hopes Betrayed 1883–1920* (Macmillan, London, 1983); Charles H. Hession, *John Maynard Keynes: A Personal Biography of the Man Who Revolutionised Capitalism* (Macmillan, London, 1983).
3. Cf. the series of Keynes Seminars organised by the University of Kent at Canterbury: *Keynes: Aspects of the Man and His Work*, (ed.) D. E. Moggridge (Macmillan, London, 1974); *Keynes and International Monetary Relations*, (ed.) A. P. Thirlwall (Macmillan, London, 1978); *Keynes and Laissez Faire*, (ed.) A. P. Thirlwall (Macmillan, London, 1978); *Keynes and the Bloomsbury Group*, (ed.) Derek Crabtree and A. P. Thirlwall (Macmillan, London, 1980); A. P. Thirlwall (ed.), *Keynes as a Policy Adviser* (Macmillan, London, 1982). The neglect of the Indian Connection is also true of the following publications: *Essays on John Maynard Keynes*, (ed.) Milo Keynes (Cambridge University Press, 1975); *The Keynes Centennial Essays* by Milton Friedman, F. A. Hayek, Sir John Hicks, and Paul Samuelson, in *The Economist* (London) 4, 11, 18, 25 June 1983; *Keynes and the Modern World* (Proceedings of the Keynes Centenary Conference), (ed.) David Worswick and James Trevithick (Cambridge University Press, Cambridge, July 1983). The published Seventh Keynes Seminar on *Keynes and Economic Development* (November 1985) (Macmillan, London, 1987), (ed.) A. P. Thirlwall has a small appendix on 'Keynes and India' by the editor.
4. See Anand G. Chandavarkar, 'Keynes and India', *Economic and Political Weekly*, Vol. XVIII, No. 28, 9 July 1983, pp. 1235–37; 'Keynes Revisited', *Economic and Political Weekly*, Vol. XIX, No. 45, 10 November 1984, pp. 1910–12; 'Keynes and Central Banking', *Indian Economic Review*, Vol. XX, No. 2, July–December 1985, pp. 283–297; 'Was Keynes a Development Economist?' *Economic and Political Weekly*, Vol. XXI, No. 7, 15 February 1985, pp. 304–7.
5. See Martin Bronfenbrenner, 'Pity The Country Specialist!' *Rivista Internazionale di Scienze Economiche e Commerciali*, Vol. 32 (1985), No. 4, pp. 297–303.
6. Lytton Strachey's father, Sir Richard Strachey, served in India, among other assignments, as Finance Member in the Viceroy's Council and as Lieutenant Governor of Bengal. He is known for his pioneering *Memorandum on The Introduction of the Metric System in India* (1865) which was later to prove the foundation for independent India's decimalised currency, coinage, weights and measures. Lytton Strachey's godfather was the first Earl of Lytton, Viceroy of India.
7. Strachey remarked to Moore after Woolf's departure to Ceylon that he was 'absolute Lord there of a million blacks' (p. 214) and was critical (as noted by Holroyd) of Woolf's novel *The Village in the Jungle* in a 'manner that perfectly catches the racialism so prevalent among the

Edwardian upper classes'. Strachey wrote to Woolf: 'my tastes are not at all in the direction of the blacks, etc. . . . the more black they are the more I dislike them. Perhaps really for everybody the blacks are not a very interesting subject. . . . Fortunately there are other things in the world. . . . Whites! Whites! Whites!' (p. 514). Michael Holroyd, *Lytton Strachey, A Biography* (Holt, Rinehart and Winston, New York, 1971).

8. Holroyd, ibid., p. 394.
9. A. Marshall, *Principles of Economics*, Ninth Edition (Macmillan, London, 1961), Vol. 2, p. 737.
10. R. S. Sayers, 'The Young Keynes', *Economic Journal*, June 1972, p. 592.
11. E. J. Hobsbawm, *Industry and Empire* (Pelican Books, Harmondsworth, 1969), p. 123.
12. W. L. Burn, 'Free Trade in Land: An Aspect of the Irish Question', *Transactions of the Royal Historical Society*, 4th Series, Vol. XXI, p. 68.
13. See Eric Stokes, *The English Utilitarians and India* (Oxford University Press, 1959).
14. Austin Robinson, 'John Maynard Keynes: Economist, Author, and Statesman', *Economic Journal*, Vol. 82, No. 326, June 1972, p. 545.

2 India Office: Apprenticeship to Greatness

'The East is a career.' *Benjamin Disraeli*

ENTRY

Keynes's public life and career date back to his appointment to the India Office in 1906 where his two-year tenure was to prove crucial in the transformation of a mathematician civil servant into the quintessential applied monetary economist of eminence. It exposed him at first hand to the Indian monetary and financial system, arguably the most intricate of its kind, and 'eventually through a combination of natural interest, the trust and encouragement of India Office colleagues and a crisis that put the Indian currency situation in the foreground of public discussion, resulted in the writing of his first book, *Indian Currency and Finance*, and his creative role with the Royal Commission on Indian Finance and Currency'.[1]

The background and circumstances of Keynes's entry into the India Office are also of unusual interest. After taking the Mathematics Tripos (Part 1) at Cambridge as Twelfth Wrangler (1905) in 'a good but not exceptional year',[2] Keynes stayed on a fourth year to prepare himself for the Civil Service examination and also attended Alfred Marshall's lectures on economics and read widely in economics. It is not known whether Indian economic issues at all excited the undergraduate Keynes despite Marshall's strong interest in this subject deriving from his lectures at Oxford to Indian Civil Service probationers and his evidence before the Indian Currency Committee (1899). Despite Marshall's importunities and high expectations,[3] Keynes was not inclined to complete the newly-created Economics Tripos (1906) and instead decided, albeit with almost total nonchalance, to appear for the Civil Service examination, which even provoked his London hostess, Philippa Strachey (1872–1968), Lytton Strachey's sister, to ask: 'Really, Mr. Keynes, is this a pose, or do you care whether you get into the Civil Service or not?' But Keynes, as Harrod relates, was quite confident of being among the first ten, and as it turned out Keynes stood second out of 104 candidates, obtaining 3498 marks (out of a maximum possible of 6000).[4] The top candidate, with 3917 marks was Otto Niemeyer, a classical scholar from Balliol College, Oxford. Ironically, Keynes scored his worst marks in the two subjects in which he possessed a solid knowledge, namely mathematics and economics (256 marks out of a possible 600 and 7th in order of merit) whereas he was placed first in Political Science, Logic, Psychology, and in Essay.[5] Keynes was sorely disappointed at his performance in economics (356 marks as against Niemeyer's 370), which provoked him to say, 'I evidently knew more about Economics than my examiners.' But Keynes's overreaction to his performance in the economics paper has to be seen in proper perspective.

> His economics of 1906 were, in fact, mainly self-taught, and it was only after a spell of service in London that he gave anything like the whole of his mind to economic science. Keynes never covered the field or submitted to the full discipline of the Cambridge teaching of Marshall's day. . . . To the end of his days there remained parts of the field into which his interests had never happened to lead him, and in which he was appreciably less sure-footed than in those parts that he had made completely his own.[6]

This seems a more plausible assessment than Harrod's, who disagrees with Sir Austin on grounds of Keynes's 'quick absorptive capacity' and the paucity of fully qualified examiners in economics.[7] Richard Kahn, while recognising that 'Keynes had no systematic education in economics' cites approvingly Harrod's remark that Keynes was 'absorbing Economics through every pore while living with his parents in Cambridge'.[8] But Keynes's excellent performance in the Essay paper makes one wonder what he really thought of its practical utility for a civil servant, a speculation prompted by Keynes's pointed citation of the observation of a Chinese scholar that the chief cause of the 'weakness of China' was 'in the requirement of the "modern essay" in civil service examinations (Class I). The modern essay was of no practical use, and its mastery required long practice. Instituted in 1370, in 1902 it was abolished'.[9] The Essay paper – a natural extension of the Oxbridge tutorials – was always a solid bastion of the British and Indian Civil Service examinations. Critics of the Indian Civil Service might also well argue that generations of successful candidates honed up on essay-writing have tended to be obsessed more with the mandarin niceties of form, style and drafting, than with the imperatives of problem-solving and crisis management.

Successful candidates for the Civil Service were allowed, in order of their examination results, to choose a Department with an available vacancy. The list of vacancies was published only after the examination but it is significant that Keynes decided that there were only two openings he would care to accept – the Treasury and the India Office, putting the two on a par. Traditionally, if there was a vacancy in the Treasury, the top candidate usually opted for it. Otto Niemeyer, the top candidate in Keynes's year, had initially indicated his preference for the India Office but changed his mind at the last minute and finally entered the Treasury, whereupon Keynes took the India Office vacancy. It is noteworthy that

> both these brilliant young men [Niemeyer and Keynes], topping the list considered the India Office second only to the Treasury, and Niemeyer's first thoughts had reversed even this order. They belonged to a generation to which the Indian Empire and the problems of the British Government of India stood as a great challenge, having many of the most intelligent men of the age in its service, out of all proportion to its economic importance, though this itself was greater nowadays. There was in the Keynes family no tradition of service in India, he himself had never visited the country (and never did, but at 23 into the India Office he went). He found there the economic problems that were to exercise him through the remaining years before the 1914 war.[10]

THE ARCANA OF BUREAUCRACY: MILITARY DEPARTMENT

The India Office was one of the British state departments created by the Act for the Better Government of India in 1858.[11] It was the supreme authority of the Government of India in London and was headed by a Principal Secretary of State, assisted by a Council. The India Office was divided into five main departments: the correspondence department, described as 'the India Office proper' by Lord Crewe (Secretary of State, 1910–15), which dealt with the administrative correspondence relating to India; the accountant-general's department; the stores department; the registry and record department; and the auditor's establishment which was to some extent independent of the Secretary of State in Council. The correspondence department (since July 1879) was divided into six branches: Financial; Military; Judicial and Public; Political and Secret; Public Works; and Revenue, Statistics, and Commerce. Keynes entered the India Office on 16 October 1906 as a junior clerk at a salary of £200 a year in the Military Department, which consisted of six Departments run by Secretaries, assisted by six Assistant Secretaries, eight senior clerks, ten junior clerks, and seventy-six second division clerks.

The Permanent Under-Secretary in charge of the India Office (1883–1909) was Sir Arthur Godley (Keynes's superior) and the Secretary of State (1905) was the famous Liberal politician and man of letters, John (First) Viscount Morley (1838–1923). This was the age when the Secretary of State for India was at the apogee of his powers primarily because 'between 1880 and 1905 so little did Parliament concern itself with Indian domestic business that in 1889 and 1891 the Secretary of State was able to disregard resolutions of the House of Commons relating to the opium trade and in 1894, after consulting the Government of India, he declined to take action on another resolution of the same House in favour of simultaneous examinations in England and India for admissions to the [Indian] Civil Service'.[12] Thus Keynes entered the India Office at the height of its power and influence.

The India Office, although 'considered to be organized along the best possible lines to administer the best of the imperial possessions'[13] was in many respects a classic bureaucratic machine, the very embodiment of routine and paperwork reduced to almost an art form.[14] Nevertheless, for Keynes it offered the right blend of working time (11 a.m. to 5 p.m. on weekdays and 11 a.m. to 1 p.m. on Saturday and an hour's break for lunch) and leave privileges (two months a year plus bank holidays and Derby Day). No wonder he was delighted to find 'shorter hours and longer holidays than in any other office' (letter to John Neville Keynes, 17 October 1906). The congenial working hours and Keynes's phenomenal speed in dispatch of his office work left him enough time to work on his fellowship dissertation on Probability and to do extensive personal correspondence.

The Military Department of the India Office was usually headed by a retired Indian army officer of high rank till the appointment of Sir O'Moore Creagh (1907–9) who actually went to India after holding the secretaryship of the Military Department. Keynes was required to assist R. M. Stewart, and in addition to bookkeeping, his assignments covered matters such as leave and leave pay, the Indian Medical Service and Medical Board, medals, decorations, pensions, and prize money. There was an early *contretemps* soon after his appointment when he clashed with a superior official who had questioned the authority of his figures. Keynes was, however, vindicated by higher authority (letter to Lytton Strachey, 31 January 1907). His first official assignment soon after joining duties was the shipment of ten young pedigree stud Ayrshire bulls from Hull to Bombay (draft para. of Military Despatch to the Government of India, dated 18 October 1906 – Keynes Papers). Keynes discharged his office duties very conscientiously and even perceptively. Thus in minuting the shipment of the bulls to Bombay, he noted that 'young bulls will run a better chance of becoming acclimatised' and for the future it might be worth considering 'whether a few heifers should not be bought, preferably in calf, for . . . the foundation of a breeding stock'. In another minute (No. 16420, 1906) Keynes argued cogently on grounds of economy and equity for retaining the prevailing regulations for dating the commissions as lieutenants of candidates for the Indian Medical Service (IMS) as from 'the date on which the course of Instruction commences and they begin to receive pay at the same time'. He was opposed to the War Office's proposal to apply the new Royal Army Medical Corps regulations to the IMS probationers. Commenting on the Instructions to be observed by Marine Courts of Inquiry in India he shrewdly noted that 'this does not make it quite plain that the questions printed are only to show the kind of questions, not the actual questions to be asked' (Minute Register No. 3234 of 2 November 1907).

But, as noted by Neville Keynes in his diary, Keynes did not really have enough work to fill his office time, which led him to utilise the spare time for working on his dissertation on Probability. This had in fact became such a major preoccupation for Keynes that he even declined the offer of a better-paid post of a resident clerk in the India Office, because the evening working hours which it entailed would have interfered with the writing of the dissertation (John Neville Keynes's diary, 8 February 1907). There were, however, moments, when like any research candidate, even Keynes appeared to be so bored with his dissertation that he hardly touched it (letter to Lytton Strachey). This was more like a manifestation of the proverbial research blues and moodiness rather than any studied attempt to slant his letters to 'what he wanted each correspondent to believe'.[15]

TRANSFER TO REVENUE, STATISTICS, AND COMMERCE: THE RITES OF PASSAGE

Keynes was transferred, after barely four months' service in the Military Department, at the beginning of March 1907 to the Revenue, Statistics, and Commerce Department of the India Office, a move which was congenial to him in every way. As Neville Keynes observed: 'he is liking his work much better, does much reading, as he sees all papers that come in the Department' (7 March).[16] Keynes liked the system by which 'everything comes to me to read, and I read it' (to Lytton Strachey, 7 March 1907), an obvious reference to the regulation circulation file, inward and outward. He found the sheer variety of material utterly absorbing – Foreign Office commercial negotiations with Germany, disputes with Russia in the Persian Gulf, regulation of opium in Central India, proposals on Chinese opium, and so on. But Keynes's impressions of the first meeting of the Committee of the Secretary's Council were distinctly unflattering. 'The thing is simply government by dotardry; at least half those present showed manifest signs of senile decay, and the rest didn't speak' (to Strachey). But, as Harrod says, due allowance must be made for 'the frustration of youthful enthusiasm' and 'for his not yet seeing clearly the inherent limitations in any central department of government, discharging administrative duties under parliamentary control' (ibid. p 123). On the other hand, Harrod also exaggerates the extent of parliamentary control over the India Office, considering the previously cited cases where the India Office disregarded the House of Commons.

Keynes preserved the drafts of some of the memoranda that he wrote on a variety of subjects: the proposed grant of a monopoly of bonded warehouses in Cyprus; the prevention of smuggling of liquor from Portuguese India into British India; imposition of a low fixed licence fee to combat illicit distillation of country liquor in the Punjab. All these minutes are notable for their shrewd eye for detail and a rare feel for the subtle interplay of economic and social factors. Thus in his minute (R and S No. 3659, 21 December 1907 – *Keynes Papers*, King's College) on the liquor problem in the Punjab districts of Amritsar, Jullundar, Ludhiana, and Ferozepore, Keynes, while noting the increase in drinking, particularly amongst the youth and the lower classes due partly to higher wages and fear of plague, cautioned against any ill-advised attempts at direct prevention of private distillation by *Jats* [the principal peasant caste of the Punjab] 'for their own use on festive occasions'. Such attempts, Keynes argued, might also 'stimulate immensely the odious trade of the informer' and only accentuate police corruption and oppression. He favoured a low fixed licence fee to combat illicit distillation. In another interesting minute (R and S Register No. 1502, 24 May 1907) Keynes argued against the grant of a monopoly of bonded warehouses and stores in Cyprus to the Anglo-Egyptian Land Allotment Company as being unnecessary, as well as prejudicial to the interests of Indian traders whose trade with the Levant for 'a large part goes indirect'. Of more human interest was Keynes's lengthy memorandum on what he thought was the unwarranted censure of an official in charge of the stamp office in Rangoon, Burma. He wrote to Lytton Strachey (13 September 1907) in anger and disgust.

> I have demonstrated quite clearly that he is wholly innocent of X, but that if he had been charged with a quite different offence Y, and if he had been allowed to reply and the thing had been investigated, he would probably have deserved censure for Y. But it seems to me that, whatever else is done, censure for doing X should be cancelled. They say – No, he deserves censure, and therefore censure must be maintained.

Keynes's reactions to this incident are very revealing of his innate sense of justice and fair play in a case concerning an unknown official in a remote country, a trait which was to surface so often on different occasions in Keynes's career.

A COMMODITY PROBLEM: THE INDIAN JUTE TRADE

Keynes's 'reforming zeal' and 'impatience with bureaucratic procedures' were further manifested in an extensive draft memorandum on 'The Position of the Jute Trade' of 19 March 1907, which apart from its cogent blend of facts, analysis, and policy elucidation, is notable for its characteristic heterodoxy and percipience.[17] Keynes was concerned about the peculiar position and vulnerability of the Indian jute trade because, despite possessing a practical monopoly, the Indian producer had not been able or willing to increase the area under cultivation to keep pace with the increasing demand for jute, the bulk of which was manufactured into sacks. This demand was projected to increase with the opening of the wheat-growing regions of America and also the general increase in the world carrying trade. Keynes noted that the Eastern Bengal jute specialist, Mr Finlow, had issued a favourable report on the extension of the area of cultivation in Bengal and also of introducing jute into other parts of India. But Keynes was also properly sceptical of the prospects of expansion not only because of the general conservatism of the Indian *ryot* (farmer) but of the unavoidable risk in the conditions of abnormal prices and profits, with the attendant 'exceptional opportunity to the cupidity of dishonest merchants', which might well lead to the discovery of some efficient substitute for jute, or else its successful cultivation in foreign countries before India was in a position to supply the 'normal demand at a normal price'. Keynes recognised that India's monopoly in the past had rested on, first, the excellent quality of Indian jute at a relatively low price which had enabled it to compete with possible substitutes like flax. Secondly, India's comparative cost advantage had enabled it to keep its market position at a price that 'has not stimulated the necessarily speculative attempt to grow it elsewhere'. Both these advantages were being eroded by a combination of high prices and deterioration of quality and Keynes thought there was a real danger of a breakdown of India's jute monopoly either by substitution or rival production. Experimental cultivation was already afoot in several countries, and the Colonial Office had asked for seed for West Africa, and the British South Africa Company for Rhodesia. The German and Austrian trade representatives dwelt on the deterioration of quality due to large-scale adulteration, which Keynes attributed to the enormous profits to be made at prevailing prices, and the intense competition amongst dealers 'which prevents their picking and choosing too carefully from fear lest they should be boycotted by the whole trade' (ibid., p. 8). Keynes adduced statistics to show the decline in jute exports to the USA and Germany and to support the presumption, in the light of India's monopoly and the rising demand for jute, that jute-substitutes were already being used in considerable quantities.

Keynes noted, with great insight, that it was more important to deal with the export trade separately since the bad quality of exported raw jute was most likely to encourage its cultivation outside India and, in any case, local manufacturers were better able to protect themselves. Moreover, insofar as excessive moisture damaged the jute this was largely a question of the time elapsing before its manufacture. Consequently, foreign manufacturers were more hard-hit by adulteration than were local manufacturers. The jute trade, while alive to the dangers of adulteration, was not strong enough to cope with it voluntarily because although it was 'plainly opposed to the interests of the trade as a whole, it [was] nevertheless to the interest of every individual to practise it' – a classic case of the Prisoner's Dilemma. Consequently, the trade unanimously asked the Government of India for appropriate inspection and legislative procedures.

Keynes concluded that 'if the legislation proves a failure, it can easily be repealed. The request of the great jute buyers that there should be a penal clause against themselves is, as the Lt. Governor notes, remarkable proof of the desire for legislation in the trade. It is greatly to be hoped that the question will not be allowed to drop'. Keynes, addressing the draft to his superior, Thomas Holderness (later Sir Thomas Holderness) said that, subject to Holderness's agreement, the Lt Governor be urged to follow up his suggestion of legislation for the export trade and that he was 'inclined to agree with the unanimous opinion of the trade that legislation might do something'. Holderness's response was that 'without agreeing with Keynes's final recommendation [legislation] for the export trade' he was disposed for the present to agree with Keynes that 'action might be taken as regards exported jute. But one has still to hear what the Government of India says and they may consult the trade as to confining action to exports before committing themselves' (19 March 1907).

While Keynes's analysis was perceptive particularly on the consequences of adulteration and the threat of competition from substitutes like flax and foreign sources, it had one serious analytic flaw. Keynes overlooked that in Bengal, jute (a cash crop) and rice (a cash-cum-subsistence crop) were highly competitive, as evidenced by the cobweb type of cyclical fluctuations in the cultivation of jute attributable to variations in the price of both jute and rice. Notwithstanding this omission, the memorandum on the Indian jute trade is of particular interest as Keynes's first systematic analysis of commodity problems which regrettably did not engage his attention till much later when he addressed the question of government storage of raw materials and commodities in the pre-Second World War years and thereafter.

A BUREAUCRATIC EPISODE: THE SEARCH FOR A DIRECTOR OF STATISTICS

Keynes reacted very strongly in a memorandum (9 February 1908) to the Government of India's startlingly insouciant suggestion for filling the post of a Director of Statistics by a chartered accountant. He thought that this was an 'admirable opportunity for supplementing his [the present Director General of Commercial Intelligence] ignorance by the appointment of a real trained statistician'.[18] Keynes substantiated the charges of ignorance by pointing to the 'extremely unscientific character of the official index number' published by the Director General's office and his erroneous account of India's balance of trade. Subsequently Keynes had occasion to comment on 'the extreme unreliability of many Indian statistics after leaving India Office.[19] He wrote,

> It is a good general rule that where detailed figures are collected for a definite administrative purpose they can be relied on; but where their sole purpose is to satisfy the simple but legitimate requirements of the merchant, or the troublesome and often trifling curiosity of the academic statistician neither speed nor accuracy can be looked for . . . the commercial departments laboriously collect estimates, and publish them after their practical value is lost. . . . We can hardly ask the Indian Government to spend large sums at the present time on the collection of such facts, but they do not, perhaps quite realise to what an extent accurate and easily accessible information oils the wheels of commerce. We have already called attention in these columns to the inefficiency of the machinery for collecting and disseminating the crop forecasts. The great bulk of the statistics relating to agriculture, prices, and wages is open to similar criticisms. The apologist of our Indian administration still asks in vain for the simple statistical data which would upset the statistical fiction of an India declining under British rule.

It would be hard to fault the eminent good sense of this critique of Indian statistics, even if Keynes overestimated the reliability of Indian statistics with an administrative purpose. Ironically, in the mid-1980s yet another Cambridge economist, Miss Polly Hill – Keynes's niece – recited the same litany.[20] Keynes rightly pointed out that it was no longer possible to prepare and present statistics without special knowledge of mathematics and economics. Such a professional class of statisticians now existed and since this was still a 'precarious and ill-paid trade' in England, 'it ought to be possible to secure a good man at the salary proposed – not . . . one of the leading experts, but at least one of their best pupils'. Keynes therefore suggested that this would be easy to find by enquiries from the Director of the London School of Economics (the LSE has had a strong Department of Statistics since its inception in 1895), or Karl Pearson (the eminent statistician who was then Professor at the University College, London), or C. P. Sanger[21] (also a Lecturer at University College). Keynes also suggested sounding out the Board of Trade as they were constantly employing outsiders for their statistical work, or else inserting an editorial note in the Journal of the Royal Statistical Society. It is noteworthy that of all these sources, Keynes said that he would 'trust the judgement of Mr. C. P. Sanger by far the most', not only because of his wide knowledge of theoretical statistics and experience as director of large scale practical operations but even more as an 'exceptionally good judge of ability' even though he was not of the professional standing of others like Pearson. Sanger's long service as Lecturer in Statistics had made him particularly well acquainted with the up-and-coming younger statisticians.

There is no evidence of whether this memorandum was sent to Keynes's immediate superior, Sir Thomas Holderness, who was not only regarded as a most accessible official but as one who was inclined to react favourably to even the most provocative of Keynes's memoranda. Nevertheless, the memorandum is of intrinsic interest in not only revealing Keynes's appreciation of the proper role of a technocrat, which was well ahead of the contemporary climate of thought and opinion, but in his unerring judgement and assessment of the distinction between professional and administrative ability, in identifying Sanger's qualities as a superior judge of ability even though he was not in the top league of statisticians. Equally noteworthy is Keynes's emphasis on the distinction between commercial intelligence and statistics and their complementary role in the data base of policy. The fact that the first Director of Statistics of the Government of India was an economist of distinction, George Findlay Shirras,[22] who served in this post from 1914 to 1921, could be reasonably attributed to Keynes's expressed views on the matter, a *dénouement* that happily refutes his own observation that Adam Smith's ideas took half a century to reach the floor of the House of Commons! Keynes in an appreciative review of the Trade of India in 1913–14 (Calcutta, Government Printing Office, 1914) wrote: 'This issue . . . is the first which has appeared under the editorship of Mr. G. F. Shirras, who has been appointed to the newly created office of Director of Statistics. Mr. Shirras has revised its form in a good many respects, and has taken the opportunity to introduce several improvements. He is to be congratulated on one of the first fruits of his new appointment'.[23] The subsequent Directors-General of Commercial

Intelligence have included statisticians like Dr R. L. Meek. The first Indian incumbent of the post was an economist Dr John Mathai (LSE and Oxford) who later became Finance Minister of the Government of India. Keynes must also have been particularly gratified that another subsequent incumbent of the post was one of his star pupils at King's, J. V. Joshi.

THE LAST EXIT

But life at the India Office, after nearly two years, was clearly beginning to pall on young Keynes as is evident from his letter of 13 September 1907 to Lytton Strachey:

> I'm thoroughly sick of this place and would like to resign. Now the novelty has worn off, I am bored nine-tenths of the time and rather unreasonably irritated the other tenth whenever I can't have my own way. . . . It's maddening to have thirty people who can reduce you to impotence when you are quite certain you're right. Then the preoccupation, which seems characteristic of officers, to save their own skin, is fatal. Drake's [Assistant Secretary of the Revenue and Statistics Department] dread of taking any responsibility is almost pathetic . . . it prevents any original or sporting proposal ever being made. With this machine . . . the risk to India of free speech in the India Office is nil. . . . All my thoughts are on probability.[24]

Not surprisingly, Keynes once again declined the offer of a resident clerkship and wrote to the Permanent Secretary, Sir Arthur Godley as follows (3 October 1907):

> I am still most unwilling to take up the resident clerkship. My fellowship work does not finish until December. But – apart from this special and temporary reason – now that I have settled down in London, I find the idea of sacrificing any of my out of office freedom repellent. I am, for instance, almost always away from London for weekends; and I should not like to have to give this up. I shall be very grateful if you find it possible to make another arrangement.[25]

It should, however, be noted that Keynes, on obtaining the Fellowship, would not necessarily have been required to give up his job at the India Office. A Prize Fellowship would not have involved residence in Cambridge and could have been held concurrently with a

Civil Service post. Keynes finally decided to resign and his resignation letter to Sir Thomas Holderness (dated 5 June 1908) was submitted, as he confessed, 'after a great deal of doubt and hesitation. But the desire for scientific and theoretical work and for life here [Cambridge] is so great that I think I am probably right in giving way to it'. Keynes was, however, careful to stress 'please do not think that I have disliked my work in the Revenue Department, or have been discontented. I have liked it very much and have learnt a great deal from it and from you. But the choice has been between two quite opposed ways of life, and on the whole I think, now at any rate, that the way here is better'.[26] The resignation was consequent upon the very timely offer of a lectureship in Economics at Cambridge from Pigou, who had succeeded Alfred Marshall as the Professor of Political Economy. Keynes's resignation was accepted with great regret by both his superiors, Sir Arthur Godley and Sir Thomas Holderness. Godley firmly believed that had Keynes stayed on he would 'have been very soon in one of its highest places' but added graciously that 'the choice is between the two careers, and I personally am one of the last to quarrel with your decision'.[27] Holderness had hoped to have Keynes at least until such times as 'Godley should annex [him] for Private Secretary work'. However, he fully appreciated 'the motive which urges you to strike for intellectual freedom and leisure for research . . . a government office . . . is a comfortable means of life . . . but it is rarely exciting or strenuous'. But Holderness concluded with typical bureaucratic ambivalence: 'I suppose I ought to counsel reflection before you plunge, and paint the possible successes of official life in attractive colours. . . . But I won't do this, because I take for granted that you have fully weighed the cost'.[28] On the other hand, Neville Keynes did not share his son's enthusiasm for quitting the India Office and for 'throwing up a certainty and taking risks' which 'fits in with his scheme of life, not mine'. He recorded ruefully in his diary, 'I had reconciled myself to Maynard's giving up the India Office, for he seems so thoroughly to have set his heart on returning to Cambridge and a student's life'.[29] On 17 July Keynes wrote to his mother, 'But I have no regrets – not even now that it has come to it – not one'. The die was cast and Keynes left the India Office on 20 July 1908. He took a holiday with Duncan Grant in the Orkneys, during which he worked on a revised version of his Fellowship dissertation on Probability. He went over to Cambridge in time for the opening (Michaelmas) term of 1908. Years later, in 1914, Edwin Montagu, then Under-Secretary of State for India, wrote to

Holderness, 'If freedom of expression had been allowed to Keynes, should we have ever lost him'. But then Keynes clearly did not intend, and nor was he carved out to be a permanent civil servant.

What then was the role and significance of his short spell of service at the India Office? Was it a passing episode or a necessary apprenticeship to a memorable life and career? There have been various assessments of the role of his India Office spell in the formation of Keynes's mind-set and range of interests. According to Harrod:

> In these two years, he had gained the knowledge of how a Government Department works. One might almost say that such knowledge should be regarded as an essential part of an economist's education. He had acquired an interest in Indian affairs: the problem of the rupee was the liveliest issue in the field of money in those days, and Keynes was to make his debut as an economist by his treatment of that subject. His brief spell at the India Office had a consequence which was more important than either of these. He had made his abilities known to the officials of the Office. That knowledge was a necessary link in the chain of events which brought Keynes into prominence in public affairs early in life. He might well have achieved prominence in other ways, but his path would necessarily have been more devious.[30]

This appraisal is well supplemented by that of Austin Robinson:

> His short period . . . in the India Office was not wasted. He had learned there a great deal about the way the machinery of government operated, and in particular to see the problems of economics from the angle of the administrator, who must make the decisions, as well as from that of the academic, who must discuss the principles that must underlie the decisions. He had formed an abiding interest in the problems of Indian currency and finance. Above all, he had attained a maturity unusual at the age of twenty-five.[31]

But both Harrod and Austin Robinson overlook a paradoxical feature of Keynes's work at the India Office. It concerned all subjects except monetary matters.

Keynes's 'experience and previous contacts with senior officials like Sir Robert Chalmers and Basil Blackett at the India Office and on the Royal Commission on Indian Currency and Finance proved to be of great value' when he joined the Treasury in January 1915 as assistant to Sir George Paish, special adviser to the Chancellor of the Exchequer.[32]

But life for Keynes at India Office was not all economics and Probability! He browsed diligently among English-language Indian periodicals and newspapers during a period of considerable political turmoil in India, and amused himself by copying out select quotations from the flowery nationalistic editorials.

> Mr. Morley [the Secretary of State for India] is a mountain in labour which has produced a huge monstrosity, a thing of shreds and patches. He has brought out only a small rat by boring a hill (Akhber (sic)-e-Soudagar, which translates as Trader's Journal) *Keynes's Papers*, IA/31).

One can well imagine the reactions of Keynes, always the fastidious prose stylist, to such sonorous effusions of contemporary Indian leader writers. This delectable pastime doubtless gave him some feel and sensitivity for Indian national *amour propre* which surfaced later in his spirited defence of Indian students at Cambridge. Keynes even found time to sign an appeal, together with J. L. Hammond, the historian and social reformer, circulated by Edward Carpenter (1844–1929), the leading exponent of Whitmanism in England. The appeal 'urged the establishment of a British Academy to promote a simpler way of life'.[33] Shades of Gandhism!

Notes

1. *The Collected Writings of John Maynard Keynes*, Activities, 1906–14, *India and Cambridge*, Vol. XV, (ed.) Elizabeth Johnson (Macmillan, London, 1971), p. 1.
2. '(J. E. Littlewood, now [1947] Rouse Ball Professor of Mathematics at Cambridge, was first) – a satisfactory result, but a little disappointing to those who had formed high hopes of his mathematical abilities. This confirmed his decision not to go to Part II of the Mathematics Tripos'. Austin Robinson, 'John Maynard Keynes', *Economic Journal*, March 1947, Vol. LVII, No. 225, p. 11.
3. 'I trust your future career may be one in which you will not cease to be an economist. I should be glad if it could be that of an economist' (Marshall's remark on one of Keynes's essays). '. . . if you went in for the Economics Tripos . . . you would probably get a first class' (Marshall's letter to Keynes), *Collected Writings*, Vol. XV, pp. 1–2.
4. 'Yes I am a clerk in the India Office – having passed the medical with flying colours. . . . My marks have . . . left me enraged. Really knowledge seems an absolute bar to success'. Keynes to Lytton Strachey, 4 October 1906.

5. *Oxford Magazine*, Supplement, November 1906, Civil Service Competition, 1906.
6. Austin Robinson, 'John Maynard Keynes', ibid., p. 12.
7. Harrod, *Life*, op. cit, pp. 121–2.
8. Richard F. Kahn, *The Making of Keynes's General Theory* (Cambridge University Press, 1954), p. 50.
9. Keynes's review of Huan-Chang Chen, *The Economic Principles of Confucius and His School*, 2 Vols, Columbia University Studies (New York, Longmans, 1911), *Economic Journal*, December 1912, Vol. XXII, No. 88 pp. 584–8, cited in *Collected Writings*, Economic Articles and Correspondence: Academic, (ed.) Donald Moggridge, Vol. XI, (Macmillan, London, 1983), p. 522.
10. R. S. Sayers, 'The Young Keynes', *Economic Journal*, June 1972, Vol. 82, No. 326, p. 592.
11. See Syed Anwar Husain, 'The Administrative Departments of the India Office, 1858–1919', *Indian Journal of Public Administration*, New Delhi, XXVII, No. 2, April – June 1981, pp. 430–43.
12. Sir Verney Lovett, 'The Home Government 1858–1918' in *The Cambridge History of India*, Vol. VI, The Indian Empire 1858–1918, edited by H. H. Dodwell (Cambridge University Press, 1932), pp. 216–17.
13. Syed Anwar Husain, ibid., p. 443.
14. 'The logistics of moving papers to their proper destination was complex, requiring a large subordinate staff. The extensive network of offices and departments – almost $3\frac{1}{2}$ million cubic feet – filled three floors in its half of Whitehall'. Arnold P. Kaminsky, 'The India Office in the Late Nineteenth Century' in Robert I. Crane and N. Gerald Barner (eds), *British Imperial Policy in India and Sri Lanka 1958–1912 – A Reassessment (1981)*, p. 30.
15. Skidelsky, *Keynes*, op. cit., p. 178.
16. *Collected Writings*, Vol. XV, ibid., p. 3.
17. *Collected Writings*, Vol. XV, pp. 5–11.
18. *Collected Writings*, op. cit., p. 12.
19. In his unsigned review in *The Economist*, 3 July 1909 of the India Office's Annual Statement on the Moral and Material Progress and Condition of India during 1907–8 reproduced in *Collected Writings*, Vol. XV, pp. 34–8.
20. Polly Hill, 'The Poor Quality of Official Socio-Economic Statistics Relating to the Rural Tropical World: With Special Reference to South India', *Modern Asian Studies*, Vol. 1.8, Part 3, July 1984.
21. Sanger was a Fellow of Trinity College, Cambridge and a frequent contributor to the *Economic Journal*. In his obituary Keynes wrote of his 'acute and critical mind'. *Collected Writings*, Vol. X, Essays in Biography, 1972, p. 324.
22. G. Findlay Shirras (1885–1955), after a distinguished academic career at the University of Aberdeen, also served as officer on Special Duty, Finance Department, Government of India (1910–13) and in the Indian Educational Service as a Professor of Economics (1905 – Dacca) and in

the Gujerat College, Ahmadabad (1926–39). He wrote numerous books on Indian economic problems and policies.

23. *Collected Writings*, Vol. X, p. 36.
24. Skidelsky, Keynes, op. cit., p. 181 and Harrod, *Life*, op. cit., pp. 123–4.
25. *Collected Writings*, Vol. XV, ibid., pp. 3–4.
26. Ibid., p. 15.
27. *Collected Writings*, Vol. XV, p. 16.
28. Ibid.
29. Skidelsky, *Keynes*, op. cit., p. 183.
30. Harrod, *Life*, op. cit., p. 130.
31. Austin Robinson, 'John Maynard Keynes, 1883–1946', op. cit., pp. 12–13.
32. N. H. Dimsdale, 'Keynes and the Finance of the First World War' in Milo Keynes, *Essays*, op. cit., p. 143.
33. Hession, *Keynes*, op. cit., p. 110. See also C. Tsuzuki, *Edward Carpenter 1844–1929, Prophet of Whitmanism* (Cambridge University Press, 1980).

3 Varied Passages to India

'In your economic studies don't forget the field for observation which India offers'. *Sir Thomas Holderness*

INTERIM

Keynes left the India Office in July 1909 and took a busman's holiday in the Orkneys with his friend Duncan Grant, during which he revised his dissertation on Probability. Following the holiday he settled down in Cambridge for the Michaelmas term of 1909. Since his first lectures were not due to be given until January 1910, he utilised the time to finish his dissertation (5 December 1908) which secured him the coveted Fellowship of King's College (1909). Around this time Sir Arthur Godley wrote to him sincerely hoping that Keynes would 'continue to keep an eye on Indian affairs, and to write about them as opportunities occur' (letter dated 30 March 1909).[1] This aspiration of one of Keynes's senior superiors in the India Office was more than fulfilled both by design and circumstance. In fact, Keynes's departure from the India Office, far from breaking his involvement with Indian affairs, seems to have strengthened and enlarged it. The bulk of his writings and public activities in the period 1909–11 related to India as did a fair proportion of his lectures for the Cambridge Economics Tripos. Keynes wrote extensively for the *Economic Journal* on Indian economic themes, both monetary and non-monetary, a combination which he never equalled or even approached subsequently. Significantly, his first major article and book both related to Indian economic affairs. Keynes's former colleagues at the India Office were especially supportive of Keynes's work through discussions and correspondence and supplied him steadily with information. The most notable among Keynes's former colleagues was Sir Lionel Abrahams (Financial Secretary and later Under-Secretary of State for India), who has been aptly described 'as the moulder and manipulator of India's involved but efficient financial system'. Keynes regarded him as his mentor on Indian matters, and in fact used to submit to him virtually everything that he wrote on Indian finance and arranged for Abrahams to bring some of his staff to Cambridge to discuss Indian currency and prices with Alfred Marshall. Keynes when lecturing later at Cambridge 'went out of his way to pay tribute to the perception and originality of Abrahams',[2] an extraordinary civil servant whose life and work still awaits systematic research.

THE QUANTITY THEORY OF MONEY AND PURCHASING POWER PARITY – THE INDIAN EXPERIENCE

Keynes submitted to Abrahams the proofs of his first major article after leaving the India Office, 'Recent Economic Events in India' (*Economic Journal*, March 1909) and also his first one in the *Economic Journal*.[3] It is noteworthy, among others, for what Neville Keynes called 'surprising statistical confirmation' of the quantity theory of money since Keynes was able to correlate price movements in India with the inflows and outflows of gold and foreign capital rather than to the 'drain' through which the Government of India met its liabilities in England. Even more significant was Keynes's pregnant statement in this article, 'Apart from the practical side of the matter, India's intricate and highly artificial system presents problems of special interest to the student of the theory of currency',[4] which was in the nature of a prolegomena to an abiding intellectual and practical interest in Indian monetary affairs.

The rise of prices in India which began in 1903 approached famine levels in 1907 and affected all commodities and the cost of living in all parts of the country. Keynes, while recognising the limitations of the index numbers, analysed the possible causes as follows: (1) decreased productivity due to poor harvests or lessened area of cultivation; (2) increased consuming power following on an increased demand for Indian exports in world markets; (3) fluctuations in world gold prices; and (4) working of the Indian currency and credit systems.

(1) Keynes did not substantiate the decrease of productivity, which he thought was plausible given the growth of population and of demand, although he regarded much of the statistical evidence relating to the area under cultivation as unreliable. Also, taking food grains as a whole, there was not sufficient ground for believing that high prices were, prior to the famine, wholly or even largely due to shortage of supply. He also questioned the view often expressed by Indian politicians that the increased cost of living was due to the substitution of non-food crops for food crops. While this explanation did possess some value, he did not regard it as the predominant influence since there was no tangible evidence that the area under

food crops had been significantly reduced. In fact, in Bengal the high price of rice, had, if anything, led to its encroachment on areas previously under jute cultivation, an aspect which Keynes had overlooked when discussing the problems of regulating the jute trade.

(2) Keynes agreed that there was a rise in purchasing power, particularly in the jute districts of Bengal, consequent upon the extraordinarily high prices of jute in 1906–7 which led to a clear profit of £10 million to the cultivators. (This figure, whose derivation is not explained, certainly seems too precise!) The consequential increased consumption of rice should have also led to higher prices all round, but there was no evidence of analogous conditions in other parts of India.

(3) The rise in rupee prices in India was much larger than could be explained by external factors and might have been partly due to the harvests which, leaving aside the famine conditions of 1907–8, were neither specially unfavourable nor specially abundant, partly to exceptional prices in world markets for some of India's exports, and partly to changes in the gold price which were not peculiar to India. Although Keynes hesitated to quantify these factors, he doubted whether they could together account for the observed results.

(4) Keynes was therefore led, by elimination, to monetary factors as the most influential ones in the rise of prices, particularly since causes (2) and (3) could only have come into operation by 'aiding an expansion of the circulation'. The monetary factor had also been noted, as Keynes said, in an unsigned article on 'India's present monetary condition' (*Economic Journal*, March 1907) and by Mr Gokhale 'in a moderate and well-reasoned speech' in the Budget debate (March 1908) in the Imperial Legislative Council. According to Gokhale the excessive issue of rupee coinage (the rupee being no more than a note printed on silver) was mainly responsible for the rise in prices.[5]

More importantly, Keynes noted that the rise of prices was nearly proportional to the increase of currency, even allowing for the limitations of the index number of prices, the element of estimation in the volume of currency, and the possible fortuitous balancing of unconnected causes.

Keynes summarised the causal mechanism of rising prices as follows. A large increase of coinage and currency, followed by an increase of imports relative to exports, first by unprecedented sales of Council bills (due to a prosperous export trade and an influx of capital into India) and then by a collapse which would have led to a fall in the exchange value of the rupee but for the drastic corrective action of the Secretary of State. The encashment of Council bills led to an increase in the volume of currency and permitted the rise in prices, due to a variety of causes, to continue. Finally, the failure of harvests precipitated what might have occurred later in any case. Keynes also noted that the flow of capital into India was always likely to be followed by rising prices, contrary to the views of Indian politicians who were 'fond of ascribing high prices in India to the "drain" through which the Government meets its liabilities in England'. As Keynes pointed out, the Secretary of State's need for remittances tended to keep prices low and it was in fact the inflow of foreign capital, the 'drain' from England into India, which drove prices up. Altogether, 'Indian experience during the years which followed the closing of the mints served to show that there are no peculiar circumstances in the monetary customs and organization of the country which tend to hinder the natural operation of the quantity theory of money, and that the influence, which we should expect the volume of currency to exert upon the relative value of exports and imports, is actually present.'[6] In fact, Keynes's analysis of the price rise, as also Gokhale's, was far more comprehensive and cogent than that of the Government of India's Prices Enquiry Committee (The Datta Committee) 1910, which made a serious analytic error in rejecting currency inflation as the major cause of the rise in prices. There was, in fact, a striking correlation between the general index number of prices in India and the estimated total of currency for each of the years between 1903 and 1907.

In sum, Keynes's analysis of the causes of rising prices in India was very instructive but he disclaimed any attempt 'to propose remedies' in the light of the analysis. As Harrod notes: 'The reasoning was solid and the statistics used with caution. I do not think that there is anything in the paper of which he would have been ashamed thirty years later, although the technique of analysis is naturally different.'[7]

Keynes reverted to this theme in his early lectures at Cambridge. In his lectures on the Quantity Theory of Money, he noted, very significantly, that the 'theory differs in detail according to the stage of economic organization which exists in the countries to which it is applied'[8] and considered, what he then regarded, as four typical cases, namely, seventeenth-century Europe, England thirty years ago and at the present day, and India at the present day. Keynes also remarked that the best and clearest statements of the Quantity Theory were to be found in Marshall's evidence before the Gold and

Silver Commission of 1888 and the Indian Currency Committee of 1898.[9] Keynes regretted that Marshall 'never published his theory in a full and complete form' and acknowledged handsomely that what he had to say was 'entirely derived from him [Marshall] either from his printed evidence . . . or in conversation'.

THE TRANSMISSION MECHANISM IN INDIA

Keynes's lectures are also notable for their perceptive exposition of the channels through which an increase in the quantity of money affects prices. Keynes recognised that not all commodities would be affected equally, in timing or magnitude, by an increase in the quantity of money. The initial impact of an increase in the stock of money will be on those commodities whose prices are most sensitive to changes in the money market, whereas some other commodities would not feel the effect until long after. At this point Keynes emphasised the differences between the case of contemporary England and England twenty years ago or India. In all these three cases the first impact of new money is felt through the 'greater willingness of lenders to lend' but thereafter the similarity between these three cases becomes less. Keynes recognised that the order of events in contemporary India was 'of a complexity which would require more detailed knowledge than I possess for its unravelling' (p. 780). He took the view that a good deal of speculation was stimulated by new money in directly consumable articles – jute and cotton too received their share of speculative attention – and that speculation in food grains was probably a much more important factor than in contemporary England. Easy money conditions stimulated 'the natural tendency of Indian grain dealers to hold up and speculate for the rise'. Keynes had an uncanny perception of the role of speculation in Indian commodity markets, particularly in food grains. If he had followed closely the subsequent gyrations of speculation in Indian commodity and stock markets, compounded by the ease of cornering and insider trading in thin markets, he might have well wondered whether the Indian speculators' calculations did not go well beyond the insights which he attributed to the financial wizards of western markets in the General Theory! Keynes's most important conclusion was that 'the effect in India of new currency on the prices of many important articles of direct consumption is therefore unexpectedly rapid' (p. 780) and that the 'primitive manner by which new money raises prices is probably partly operative in India at the present time as well as the modern manner' (p. 781). Keynes, using the apparatus of Cairnes, traced the impact of newly-mined (or imported) gold on prices as follows:

> Those who possess gold must, if they do not hoard it, increase their purchases. As there is no reason, so long as prices have not risen, why other people should diminish theirs, there is, on the whole, an increased demand [which] will raise the prices of those articles for which it exists. Those who have obtained no share of the new gold will then have to diminish their purchases; and we shall have even eventually the same volume of purchases as before at a higher level of price. But this process may move slowly from commodity to commodity, and very slowly from district to district. I have heard Professor Marshall say that the higher level of prices caused by the new bullion from South America did not move from the European receiver of the new supply at the rate of more than 30 or 40 miles a year. (Ibid., p. 781)

Keynes, in a review of a German book on Indian economic geography, specially noted that the prices of wheat and rice steadily rose with their movement from the districts where each is grown and that food grain prices were generally higher in Southern India during the period under review than in Bengal. Keynes also noticed the influence of railways in levelling prices in different parts of India with the decade beginning 1881 compared with the decade beginning 1871,[10] a conclusion well substantiated by subsequent research.[11]

However, Keynes overlooked the impact of uneven distribution of new and old liquidity between different types of producers and middlemen, and its consequences for the spending and speculative propensities of different groups of economic agents. It is more meaningful to treat liquidity as a pattern rather than as a quantity or a ratio. Keynes's presentation underplayed the effects of gold hoarding, and the generally more pronounced liquidity preference in the Indian economy, in restraining the rise in prices following an increase in the quantity of money. Given the undeveloped character of the Indian banking system and the absence of a central bank, the response of prices to new gold differed from the pattern of response in England where the mechanism, as outlined by Keynes, was as follows. New gold raises prices by making borrowers more eager or willing to borrow by lowering the rate of discount below the normal or 'by raising an expectation of higher prices in the future more than in

Table 3.1 India: prices

	Indian prices	*English prices*[1]	*Value of rupee in sterling*	
			Purchasing power parity	*Actual exchange*
Average 1919	100	100	100	100
Highest 1920	112	129	115	152
Lowest 1921	95	65	69	72
Average 1922[2]	90	64	71	74

Source: Keynes, Review of H. Stanley Jevons *The Future of Exchange and the Indian Currency* (Oxford University Press, India, 1922) in *Economic Journal*, reprinted in *Collected Writings*, Vol. XI, p. 46.
[1] *Statist.*
[2] First ten months.

proportion to any momentary rise in the rate of discount – which may take place' (ibid., p. 783). Keynes was positive that, apart from seasonal fluctuations, the Indian level of prices was most influenced by the influx of foreign capital.

Although he refrained from any policy inferences in this particular analysis, in another context he was categorical that 'in the interests of the peace and contentment of India I believe that no problem [that is, price stability] is more important, and I should be strongly disposed, if I were in their [Government of India] place, to subordinate currency policy to price policy'.[12] In the same vein, Keynes was critical of Stanley Jevons for overestimating 'the advantages of exchange stability as against stability of the internal price level in the case of such a country as India'; and for not being sufficiently 'aware of the important antithesis between these two aims, although the latter aim much influenced the recommendations of the Indian Currency Committee of 1919'.[13] Keynes also pointed out that Jevons did not conclude from his cited data that the relative stability of Indian prices around 1919–21 was largely due to the policy of a fluctuating rupee-sterling exchange rate. Keynes, in fact, compiled a table (Table 3.1) of approximate values which showed the remarkable stability of Indian prices during 1919–20 and 'the accuracy with which the purchasing power parity theory has worked, apart from the temporary and unsuccessful aberration of the rupee for a brief period in 1920, as between India and England, indicating considerable stability in the real ratio of exchange between the two countries'.[14] Clearly, Keynes was more concerned about India's economic welfare in terms of insulating the economy from extreme price fluctuations than worshipping the icon of the appropriate exchange rate.

BRITISH INVESTMENT IN INDIA: A STATISTICAL CONUNDRUM

One of the main contemporary political issues in Britain around 1909 was the movement of the Tariff Reform League for a 'scientific tariff' and the contention of the tariff reformers that too much British capital was being invested abroad thereby depriving British industry. Thus the issue was one of both statistics – the magnitude of British foreign investments – and policy; that is, whether its size was optimal in relation to its possible benefits for the British economy, a classical problem of political economy. Keynes encountered a similar statistical problem in his research for an article on British investment in India, which was triggered by an article in *The Economist*, 20 February 1909, on 'Our Investments Abroad'.[15] This latter article attempted to determine the total of British investments abroad using two estimates, one by 'a correspondent' (£470 million) and the other by H. Beaumont (£500 million), a member of the London Stock Exchange. Keynes questioned both the estimates as being too high, while conceding that there had been a rapid inflow of capital into India, and provided the following alternative estimates:

1.	Rupee and sterling government debt held in London (1906)	£160 million
2.	Ordinary and debenture capital of Indian companies registered in London (1905), the bulk of which was accounted for by railways, tea plantations, and mines	£96 million
3.	Capital of joint stock companies registered in India	£28 million
4.	Debt of municipalities and port trusts	£20 million
	(Keynes estimated that the bulk of this total of £48 million was held in India)	
5.	Foreign banking capital employed in India (outside estimate)	£50 million

Source: Keynes's estimates in letter to the Editor of *The Economist* 27 February 1909, reprinted in *Collected Writings*, Vol. XV, pp. 20–21.

Keynes thought that, 'even allowing for the unknown resources of foreign merchants and private firms trading in India, it would be difficult to account for foreign investments in excess of some sum between £300 million and £350 million'. Further, he provided an additional argument, based on the analysis of India's balance of trade, 'against any estimate which approaches £500 million. For allowance being made for probable new investment and other known items on both sides of the account, the sum left over is quite insufficient to pay the interest on so large a sum.' Keynes concluded with a plea for more accurate data on British capital and interest transactions with foreign countries 'if any safe deduction is to be made from the figures of foreign trade regarding the financial position' of Britain.

In his reply (*The Economist*, 6 March 1909) Beaumont maintained that Keynes had underestimated the volume of British capital involved by using figures for 1905 and 1906. He cited the present market value of Indian railway securities (c. 1909) listed on the London Stock Exchange at £137 million. 'If British investors held £160 million of Indian Government stocks in 1906, and account was taken of subsequent borrowings, the total present British holdings of Indian and Ceylon Government and railways securities must be "fully £325 million". The remaining £175 million in his estimate of £500 million he accounted for by the considerable volume of floating Indian railway debentures held in London.' Beaumont added that he failed 'to see how any analysis of India's trade balance could settle the point at issue, as it is difficult to ascertain how far payments due for interest are cancelled by fresh borrowing at the time. India's yearly debt to us is largely settled by her trade balance of £35 million due to her from the United States and Europe.'

Keynes (*The Economist*, 20 March 1909) argued that Beaumont had only partially explained the discrepancy between his estimate and that of Keynes. It did not fully account for Beaumont's total of £500 million even if he intended 'India' to include Ceylon. Secondly, Keynes attributed the discrepancy between his total for the capital of private railways and Beaumont's entirely to the latter's inclusion of the capitalised value of the annuities paid by the Secretary of State and also certain Government railway debentures 'by means of which the companies have been from time to time bought out.' However, Keynes argued that a deduction ought also to be made from the capital of private companies on account of the recent purchase of the Madras Railway. He also doubted whether the unascertained banking and private trading capital employed in India could be reasonably assessed at much more than £50 million, which about made the estimate of £350 million for India (excluding Ceylon).

Keynes added that, due allowance being made for Government transactions, virtually the whole of the net balance of India's exports over imports was required to meet various liabilities of the Secretary of State for India, and the balance of private trade between 1903 and 1908 would be almost equal on the average to the drawings of Council Bills. From this Keynes inferred that 'the new capital annually loaned to India and remitted by private persons, together with any small miscellaneous amounts which may be due to her, must equal the payment due from her on account of interest, freight, insurance, banking charges, and other remittances. If . . . the foreign capital in India, exclusive of Government debt, is not far short of £300 million, the fresh capital annually loaned to India, exclusive . . . of Government borrowings, to enable her to pay the interest on this and the charges for freight, etc. must exceed £15 million. There is no visible trace of so large an amount of new investment . . . '.

In his rejoinder (*The Economist*, 27 March 1909) Beaumont argued that if, as Keynes maintained, practically the whole of India's balance of trade was required to meet the liabilities of the Secretary of State, it was difficult to see how the annual interest on investment in India was to be met. Even assuming that the £8 million of new capital submitted in 1908 was the yearly average, it would still not cover the total interest bill. Beaumont also criticised Keynes for using an average of only five years of Council bills and transfers sold in London when the annual fluctuations were so considerable. Finally, Beaumont gave his own rough estimates as follows:

1.	Representing the part of the £245 million Government debt of India and Ceylon held in the United Kingdom	£180 million
2.	Sterling railway debt (involving £20 million of floating debentures)	£160 million
3.	Tea plantations	£30 million
4.	Investment in all other British enterprises in India	£100 million

Source: Beaumont's letter to *The Economist*, 27 March 1909, reprinted in *Collected Writings*, VOL XV, p. 21.

At this point the anonymous correspondent whose figures *The Economist* had originally quoted with Beaumont's, entered the fray with an article on 'British Investments in India' (*The Economist*, 10 April 1909) furnishing the basis of his estimates of £470 million. His estimate covered more items than either Beaumont's or Keynes's since they also included government stock and rupee paper, market value of Indian railways with the capitalised value of their annuities and Ceylon stocks, commercial enterprises located in India (assuming them to be wholly British), the total capital of Indian registered joint stock companies and Indian local authorities. He also argued that the available balance of trade figures were unreliable and not inconsistent with his estimate of a capital sum of £470 million. 'Using figures for the year ending March 31, 1908, he added the net balance of India's exports over its imports of £2,626,000 (including Government transactions) to the net amount subscribed in Britain for investment in India – £15,200,000 – and arrived at the sum of £17,826,000. This . . . capitalized at 25 years purchase represented a total sum of over £445 million.'

Keynes returned to the debate with a reply (*The Economist*, 8 May 1909) in which he ascribed the difference between his and the correspondent's estimate to 'allowing in every case of doubt . . . a total excessively generous to his own view'. He added that 'if we take the market value of annuities and railway trade, we must be consistent, and deal with Government stock similarly, deducting an appreciable sum from the total nominal value'. Keynes was particularly critical of the correspondent's assumption that the 'invested savings of the inhabitants of India are of no account' and cited the case of the Bombay cotton mills which operate with rupee capital and are, to all appearances, purely Indian concerns. Likewise Keynes did not think it natural to suppose that a sum of £25 million belonging to miscellaneous Indian registered companies and trusts, was held abroad, considering that no appreciable part of it was quoted on any foreign stock exchange. Keynes's own estimates were based on the reasonable assumption that sterling companies are owned in England and rupee companies in India and that 'the errors in which might be fairly taken in the present state of our knowledge to balance one another'. But Keynes's most decisive rebuttal rested on the balance of trade argument which he thought was peculiarly apposite to India's circumstances, because of the availability of precise information regarding a large part of the total transactions mediated through the Secretary of State. Moreover, it could be safely assumed that the miscellaneous payments due to India were smaller than those due from her.

Keynes devised an ingenious method to arrive at a plausible estimate for private transactions, which were the prime source of controversy. After deducting all Government transactions, he found by comparing the volume of Council bills and the balance of private trade during the last five years, that the source of remittances to England arising out of the latter was almost wholly absorbed by sales of the former (Council bills). The proceeds of Council bills, together with the Secretary of State's borrowings in London, went to service interest on the public debt, and for expenditure on railway materials, government stores, silver bought in England, the gold standard and currency reserves, and other miscellaneous charges. Also, he was categorical 'that during the last few years the fresh capital annually loaned to private companies in India must almost equal the sum of the interest on capital previously loaned to them, plus the payments due from India on account of freight, insurance, banking charges, etc.'[16]

Keynes noted very perceptively that while the year 1908 was specially favourable to the correspondent's argument in respect of capital investment, it was, on the whole, unfavourable to him on account of the unprecedentedly small trade balance of that year. His choice of a year unfavourable to his argument was counterbalanced by his omission of the Secretary of State's home charges, beyond those for treasure, stores and interest, of the growth of his reserves, and of the sums due from India for freight, and so on. 'His example does not do his argument justice, but the argument is for these reasons bad.'[17]

The controversy is revealing of Keynes's flair for applied statistics and the deft interplay of analysis and figures. There was no doubt that the honours rested with Keynes. As Sir Thomas Holderness wrote to Keynes (23 March 1909) 'It seems to me that you have [the] facts on your side. . . .'[18] Three years later, Keynes reverted to this subject in his letter (22 February 1912) to Sir Thomas Holderness after receiving a copy of Holderness's letter to Percy Ashley, a correspondent, who had requested Holderness for an estimate of the relative magnitudes of Indian and non-Indian capital invested in India. Holderness himself took the following view:

> In most cases the bulk of the capital is European. But there is probably not a single company in which many native names do not figure in the list of shareholders; and it is impossible to say what proportion of the total capital their aggregate shareholding represents. . . . Broadly speaking, . . . in the Bombay Presidency

> possibly the Parsis and other non-Europeans own a half or more of the mills and other industrial concerns; but that elsewhere in India the non-European share is less than one-fourth and may not exceed one-sixth or even one-eighth. (Ibid., p. 28)

Keynes, while agreeing with the general tenor of Holderness's reply, confessed that he had 'never yet hit upon a method of making a really accurate estimate' (ibid., p. 28). At the same time, Keynes was critical of George Paish's estimate (in his papers to the Royal Statistical Society) which, among others, did not distinguish India and Ceylon. This misaggregation particularly affected the estimate for plantation capital since a considerable part of capital invested in tea and coffee would have been accounted for by Ceylon. Keynes also argued that in countries where the bulk of the foreign investment goes into public companies it is easier to estimate its amount than in India where much of the foreign capital is in banks and private businesses. Consequently, this made any inferences from the statistics of public companies 'peculiarly unreliable'. Keynes therefore preferred to rely more on calculations based on the balance of trade like those which he attempted in his review of Sir Theodore Morison's book on 'The Economic Transition in India', (*Economic Journal*, March 1909). Keynes concluded from an analysis of the balance of trade that during the ten years 1899–1909 the interest payable abroad on private capital previously invested in India was approximately balanced by the private capital newly invested during the same period, but he did concede that the value of each of these two items is 'very conjectural'. Keynes estimated that part of the foreign capital in India on which interest is not paid through the Secretary of State would be between one hundred million and 140 million pounds, with the latter figure 'being an absolutely outside limit'. But he conceded that 'calculations arrived at in this manner are necessarily vague'. It is, however, noteworthy that even to this day analysts have not been able to improve upon Keynes's conjectural estimates and have conceded that 'it is difficult to find out the exact net amount of foreign investment in India during this period [1870–1913]'.[19]

THE ECONOMIC 'DRAIN' FROM INDIA

The so-called economic 'drain' from India to Britain, defined as a unilateral unrequited transfer of capital and economic resources, was one of the most hotly debated issues of Indian economic history, particularly in the second half of the nineteenth century. This theory, which was vigorously advanced by Indian analysts and economic historians like Dadabhai Naoroji and Romesh Chunder Dutt was also supported by radical British observers like John Strachey, as well as by some British officials like Richard Wingate and historians like John Stuart Mill.[20] The estimates of the 'drain' have ranged from over £20 million and £34 million (the latter figure was Naoroji's estimate for 1905) annually to about 2–3 per cent of India's national income 1757–1939.[21]

Keynes touched upon the question of the 'drain' somewhat peripherally but positively in his review of Theodore Morison's book which contained the 'most detailed and perhaps the best exposition of the point of view of the critics' of the 'drain' theory.[22] Morison defined the 'drain' as the amount of India's exports in goods and or money for which in that year it receives no material equivalent.[23] Keynes agreed with Morison's exposition 'of the correct theory governing the relation between India's exports and imports' which, he thought, 'ought to be of great assistance in finally dispelling the mistaken view on this subject, once so widely held but now repudiated by an increasing number of Indian economists of the younger school'.[24] Here Keynes misinterpreted Indian views on the 'drain' insofar as Indian critics of the extreme position such as Ranade did not favour making the 'drain' the central issue of nationalism like Dadabhai Naoroji and the newspaper *Amrita Bazaar Patrika*. It was thus more a question of degree of emphasis among the Indian economists rather than a sharp polarity of views. Keynes, however, thought Morison's statistics were not 'altogether reliable when he attacks the very interesting and difficult problem of the amount which would be due from India to foreign creditors, supposing no part of this were liquidated by fresh loans of capital'. However, Keynes's estimate of the so-called annual potential claim (£24.24 million) was almost the same as Morison's (£21.20 million). The statistical substantiation of the 'drain' hypothesis is, of course, exceedingly complex and, arguably, even indeterminate since the question of whether India received adequate value for the 'Home Charges' (payments by the Secretary of State in London on behalf of the Government of India and the provinces) 'or whether it was forced to pay too much can only be meaningfully discussed item by item'.[25] The nationalist writers have tended to treat the entire export surplus as a net drain, but without deducting the cost of producing the exports (that is, their import content), from their final sales value. 'This difference, insofar as it was paid for through internal taxation, represents the real income leakage. In the long-run it was not so much the capital payments as the absence of active measures for economic development which was probably most responsible for the continuing poverty of India.'[26] This perhaps is the most meaningful interpretation of the concept of 'drain'. It is best regarded as a counterfactual hypothesis rather than a historical unilateral transfer of capital. But the 'drain' did not excite Keynes's interest which was always in specific policy issues rather than in grand themes like metropolitan exploitation of the colonies or of class and regional conflict and he never revisited the theme.

INDIA (1907–8): THE CONDITION OF THE PEOPLE

Keynes's (unsigned) review of the India Office's Annual Statement exhibiting the Moral and Material Progress and Conditions of India[27] is a remarkably percipient and objective analysis of the classical 'condition-of-the-people problem' in one of the 'most trying periods in the history of India, when plague, famine and political unrest quickly followed one another, revenues fell, prices rose to an unprecedented level', and 'the currency system seemed at one moment to be in danger'. Keynes was rightly critical of the 'too rigid economy of statement upon many interesting and controversial subjects, which is somewhat characteristic of the India Office' and cautioned the authorities that 'they must not be surprised that the public sometimes derive their information from less trustworthy sources, or complain of British ignorance respecting the peculiar difficulties of Indian administration.' Thus Keynes noted that the document did not mention political unrest, and that the account of bubonic plague did not refer to the abnormal mortality in certain areas, particularly the Punjab. The account of the famine was 'admirable, if rather colourless'. The reference to political unrest demonstrates Keynes's sensitivity to Indian politics. However, his analysis of the famine emphasised only the extraordinary depletion of food grain stocks (7 million tons in the United Provinces alone valued at £28 million, equal to nine months' food supply and of cash crops like cotton, and oil seeds at £10 million) and its role in explaining the slow movement of the Indian wheat crop for export. Keynes did not take into account the basic economic feature of Indian famines, namely, that they indicated a famine of purchasing power and a general erosion of people's capabilities to acquire food and of their exchange entitlements rather than of crop failures and reduced availability of food grains.[28] Such views were known and expressed not only by influential analysts like Dadabhai Naoroji and R. C. Dutt but also widely disseminated in the contemporary Indian press.[29] Yet, Keynes, reputedly a diligent reader of Indian newspapers since his India Office days, did not show any awareness of this aspect of famines in India.

Keynes also noted that there was 'probably much local distress where wages are not paid in kind', which suggests that the monetisation of the Indian economy was a mixed blessing. But Keynes did not follow up on this interesting line of enquiry. Keynes also observed that wages had risen even more than prices where the ravages of the plague had been worst. The consequent decimation of the working population had also created the paradoxical situation in the affected districts where the standing crops could not be harvested for lack of labourers. The labour shortage had also affected the operations of the North-Western Railway and new canal works as reported by the Indian newspaper, the *Pioneer*. Keynes was, however, constrained to note that the 'great bulk of the statistics relating to agriculture, prices, and wages' was 'open to criticism' and that 'the apologist of the Indian administration still asks in vain for the simple statistical data which would upset the statistical fiction of an India declining under British rule'.[30] But Keynes never explained why he regarded the decline of India under British rule as a 'statistical fiction', an uncharacteristically dogmatic assertion for someone usually meticulous in drawing inferences from data. The question whether India suffered an economic decline during British rule has always been a strongly debated issue, on which the differences of view have not always been on political and nationalist lines. Thus there were contemporary British commentators like William Digby who were supportive of the views of Dadabhai Naoroji and other Indian commentators on the growing immiserisation of India. Subsequent research (by M. Mukherjee and A. Heston) suggests that for the period 1860–1920 per capita income grew by at least 35 per cent, or under 0.5 a year.[31]

Keynes recognised that the Report also contained adequate material 'for a just appreciation of the steady advance in nearly all departments, notably the great expansion of scientific departments since the inception of new schemes since Lord Curzon, the explanation for the first time of the currency system and the composition of the gold standard reserve, and the separate chapter on manufactures and industrial development'. The expansion of the scientific and technical services in India around this time is well attested by subsequent research which shows that 'the period 1900–14 witnessed the first stages in several very slow movements away from a complete domination by the perspectives of British and European science as influenced by the interests of Imperial development towards programmes and policies conditioned by the increasing desire of India to develop indigenous industrial techniques, and a growing determination that science in India should be cultivated without direction from London'.[32]

Keynes noted with particular interest the progress of the agricultural cooperative credit movement (which began in 1904) from 41 in 1905 to 1358 in 1908, with a membership of nearly 150 000 and resources totalling about £300 000 with a good number of the loans (at 9–12 per cent as compared with 15–75 per cent charged by local lenders on ordinarily good security) being used for repayment of old debts bearing exorbitant rates of interest. Also, an increasing number of loans was being made for cultivation and the purchase of cattle. But Keynes missed out the crucial importance of consolidation and liquidation of the huge mass of existing rural indebtedness in India, as a necessary precondition for the success of any type of agricultural financial institutions, an aspect which was well understood by contemporary Indian economists like Ranade, Gokhale, and G. V. Joshi. Several official inquiries like the Deccan Riots Commission (1875) and the Famine Commission (1901) had highlighted the problem of chronic rural indebtedness, but it was not till the 1930s that a concerted effort was made to tackle this problem by setting up Provincial Debt Conciliation Boards. Keynes thought 'a good beginning has been made in what may prove to be a powerful agency for the emancipation of the peasant from the village moneylender and for much-needed direction of new capital into agriculture'. Keynes's somewhat Panglossian faith in the potential of cooperative credit in India has not been fulfilled to date. But could even Keynes have anticipated the host of problems such as factionalism, poor management, overdues, and bureaucratisation that have subsequently plagued and hampered the cooperative movement in India?

THE SALT TAX

In contrast, Keynes in the same article made one of the most perceptive observations on Indian economic policy in his little-known recommendation – not touched upon in any of the standard biographies of Keynes – for abolition of the salt tax in India, a major issue during the British regime. Keynes observed: 'Never before, probably, has taxation sat so lightly on the people of India. The reduction of the salt tax by successive stages from Rs 2 $\frac{1}{2}$ per maund of 82 $\frac{2}{7}$ lb in 1902 to Rs 1 in 1902 has benefited the consumer to its full extent, as returns of retail salt prices throughout India clearly show, and has led to an increase in consumption of 20 per cent. Let us hope it may soon be abolished.'[33] Keynes's reasoning was a perceptive invocation of the price-elasticity argument but more important was his belief that it was not necessary to tax an essential item of mass consumption like salt in a poor country. The salt tax in India, which was the very first excise duty levied by the Government of India (1833) proved a major source of revenue until the Second World War because as the Finance Member of the Government of India remarked in 1865, 'No tax can be collected more cheaply and with less annoyance to the people than the salt tax.' In the nineteenth century the excise duty on salt varied between Rs 2 and Rs 2–8 annas per maund. It was reduced during the prosperous years before the First World War and by 1907–8 it was Rs 1 per maund. It was the third largest source of revenue for the Government of India between 1858 and 1870–71 and the second most important source from 1880–1904. In the year before its abolition on 1947 after independence its share of total revenue (at Rs 1–9–0 per maund) was only about 3 per cent. The salt tax was levied flexibly; it was raised only in emergencies and was also among the first taxes to be reduced when revenues were buoyant. The decline in the fiscal importance of the salt tax reflected not only the considerable development of direct taxation and of other excise duties but also perhaps the relative saturation of demand for human consumption and the still undeveloped industrial and agricultural demand for salt. However, the inferences which Keynes and various Finance Members of the Government of India attempted to draw about the price elasticity of demand for salt from fluctuations in salt tax receipts cannot be regarded as very conclusive.[34]

Indian opinion was not always opposed to the salt tax *per se*, as was pointed out by the official historian of the Indian National Congress:

> On eight other occasions did the Congress virtually repeat this prayer [for remission of the tax], only on one occasion it asked for the restoration of the rate of 1868 and on another the rate of 1888, and the last time it dealt with the question (1902) the Congress

> cited the causation of disease by insufficient salt consumption as an additional ground. Thereafter 'Salt' was promoted from the Congress to the Councils and became the special concern of Mr. Gokhale.[35]

In fact, there were prominent Indian politicians who did not demur to even raising the salt tax if the proceeds could be spent on education, health and agriculture.[36] It was not merely the human consumption of salt that was at issue. The Government of India also recognised, as early as 1885, the bearing of salt consumption on agriculture and industry, as is evident from the following official resolution in the *Gazette of India*, 30 December 1885.

> One of the chief objections taken to the salt duties is that, owing to the resulting high prices, cattle are stinted in their supply of salt, while manufacturers and agriculturists are required to pay duty on salt employed in industry and agriculture. The attention of the Government of India has been given to the matter for some years in the hope that an unobjectionable method of freeing from duty salt required for the purposes above indicated might sooner or later be discovered. No satisfactory way of effecting this object and at the same time of protecting the State from risk of fraud has as yet been found.
> (Quoted in the *Times of India*, Bombay, 30 December 1985, p. 8)

Although Keynes's analysis did not take into account the industrial or agricultural uses of salt, the position of the indigenous salt industry, or the fiscal implications of the abolition of the salt tax this does not detract from his uncanny political percipience in hoping for the early abolition of the salt tax in India. Curiously, in contrast to his analysis of the salt tax, Keynes was less perceptive in his discussion of the economic incidence of land revenue in India, which accounted for about 40 per cent of net government revenue. Keynes regarded land revenue 'as the most economical and least oppressive of all forms of taxation'. His interpretation of Indian land revenue as a tax, as maintained by Indian opinion, was economically valid in contrast to the general official view of it as a rent paid by landholders or cultivators to the state which was treated as the ultimate owner. But Keynes overlooked that the essentially regressive character of land revenue as a tax was further accentuated by the increasingly unequal distribution of both agricultural land and incomes. The decline in the effective rate of the only direct tax on agriculture 'resulted in the creation of a specially privileged class of taxpayers, those who derived large incomes from agriculture' whereas 'the small landholder may have paid more than non-agriculturists with the same income'.[37]

INDIAN TRADE (1913–14)

Alongside his interest in issues of Indian economic policy, Keynes continued to give the most meticulous attention to Indian economic statistics. His reviews of two basic official papers of the Government of India on India's trade and India's commercial relations with Germany and Austria-Hungary are aptly illustrative of this.[38]

Keynes was naturally gratified that the *Annual Review of the Trade of India* (1913–14) was the first to appear under the editorship of G. F. Shirras, the first appointee to the newly-created office of Director of Statistics, Government of India, a post which Keynes had strenuously argued earlier should be held by a professional economist-statistician. He noted 'the several improvements' in the publication and congratulated Shirras on 'one of the first fruits of his new appointment'. However, he regretted that Shirras had compiled separate index numbers for exports and imports instead of combining them in a single index number, without a clear indication of the relative weights of the commodities entering foreign trade. Keynes took this view on the ground that it is much more importnt when the international position of India was being considered, 'to know whether a given quantity of exports is buying more or less than before in the way of imports, than to know the actual average price for the two combined in terms of money'. Consequently, the new index was not reliable for expressing changes in the purchasing power of money in India generally. Likewise, Keynes was critical of Shirras for not stating the evidence for the figures of remittances (Rs 45 crores) and new capital (Rs 24 crores), adding that such estimates 'ought hardly to appear in an official publication without more warning as to their dubious character. . .'. But Keynes found the data on wage trends of great interest; among others, they indicated that the supply of factory labour in India seemed to be 'extraordinarily insensitive to even considerable increases in the prevailing level of wages'.

Keynes also noted that Indian trade with Germany and Austria was particularly important as Germany was an important market for Indian exports of raw cotton, raw jute, raw hides, and rice, and the outbreak of war meant serious cessation of demand from these markets.There was, however, some compensation for this in the cessation of German imports of cotton manufactures into India ('which competed rather with the products of Bombay than those of Manchester) and of synthetic substitutes for indigo. Keynes also made a perceptive analysis of the burden on the Indian consumer of the cutting off of Austrian and German beet sugar, given the large consumption in India (the largest producer of cane sugar in the world) and the inadequacy of domestic supplies. However, Keynes thought that the diminution of sugar imports from Java would stimulate India to imitate the 'example of successful sugar cultivation in Java'. One more unfulfilled hope, like Keynes's aspirations for the cooperative credit movement.

PROTECTION vs FREE TRADE

Keynes's next major stab at Indian economic policy was in the highly topical contemporary debate of the merits of free trade as against protection. Keynes, an ardent free-trading liberal and the Secretary of the Cambridge University Free Trade Association, addressed the Cambridge Majlis, the Indian students' society (c. 1909–10) on 'India and Protection'. On this occasion Keynes espoused the free trade position which was diametrically opposed to the strongly protectionist sentiment in India. This was also the time that Cambridge economists took the issue of free trade versus protection seriously 'to the point of going out on the hustings to advocate free trade'.[39] For instance, Pigou ardently 'defended free trade in writings and speeches thirty years before his presidential address to the Royal Economic Society in 1939' which was 'a scathing description of the abandonment of free trade in 1931'.[40] Keynes's advocacy of free trade for India was based on a wholly static concept of the comparative cost advantage of India in agriculture which also led him to oppose India's industrialisation.[41] He conceded the comparative cost advantage of India in respect of the jute and cotton industries but not in respect of iron and steel. Even in regard to jute and cotton, Keynes thought they will have 'an insignificant influence on the general level of economic well-being in the country'. This line of thought is surprising considering that the infant industry argument on the basis of a dynamic comparative cost advantage had been propagated much earlier by Alexander Hamilton (Report on the Subject of Manufactures, 1791) in the USA and later by Friedrich List (*National System of Political Economy*, 1841) in Germany. John Stuart Mill too had approved of protection for India. In India, as early as 1877, K. T. Telang in his paper on 'Free Trade and protection – From An Indian Point of View' had set out a very sophisticated economic rationale of protection for India, based on the infant-industry argument and a dynamic view of India's industrial potential.[42] Telang had also warned against the risks of monoculture for India and argued the merits of protection for limited periods of time as a necessary instrument of economic diversification. He and others maintained that free trade could operate only among equal nations.

Even in the Cambridge tradition Marshall's analysis of the issues involved was much more nuanced than was Keynes's. Marshall in his correspondence with B. Mukherjee (Lucknow University) observed: 'I have no objections on principle to the "Protection" of Nascent Indian Industries. But a customs tariff is an expensive method to this end; and under existing circumstances it would – as you partly hint – enrich European capitalists rather than India.'[43] Keynes's intellectual stance on the tariff question throughout his life was influenced by the British situation and he was only prepared to mitigate the free trade position by a revenue tariff as 'an iron ration which can be used once only in emergency'.[44] He was, however, consistent in believing that tariffs cannot be a substitute for a sound international currency policy. But could such a policy posture have been valid for a developing economy with industrial potential like India?

Keynes, however, agreed with Morison's view that custom was gradually giving way to competition as an economic force in India, although it was not always easy to identify the role of competition in 'conditions where a money economy was the exception rather than the rule', a movement akin to the notion, advanced by Sir Henry Maine, of modernisation of societies as a transition from status to contract. In this respect Keynes did have a more dynamic view of the Indian economy than when dealing with matters of comparative cost, infant industry protection and industrialisation.

THE ABORTED PASSAGE TO INDIA (THE FISCAL COMMISSION EPISODE)

Keynes had a splendid first-hand opportunity to revert to the age-old question of free trade *vs* protection for India around 1921–2. Soon after his work for the Reparations Commission Keynes received simultaneously offers from three different newspapers, the *Manchester Guardian*, the *New York World*, and the *Baltimore Sun*, asking him to be their special representative at the Disarmament Conference to be held in Washington, DC. Keynes rejected these offers. For one thing, he had no expertise or even interest in naval affairs which were likely to be the main concern of the Conference, and he also wished to confine his journalistic interests to economic and financial matters. But there was a more specific and substantial reason for his rejection of these offers, namely, the invitation of Edwin Montagu, Secretary of State for India to Keynes to become Vice-Chairman of the proposed Indian Fiscal Commission, which was to advise on India's tariff policy.[45] Keynes, responding to C. P. Scott, editor of the *Manchester Guardian*, pleaded the Indian invitation in turning down the Washington offer: 'The Commission will, I think, represent a last effort, almost certainly doomed to futility, to save India for modified Free Trade. But, though there is little hope of success, I expect you will agree that it is an enterprise which is worthwhile.'[46] (14 September 1921) This earlier sentiment of Keynes is rather hard to reconcile with his subsequent expression of regret that he had 'agreed to take up [the appointment on the Fiscal Commission] in a moment of imprudence' which he could not 'now very well get out of'. (Letter to Carl Melchin, 5 January 1922)[47]

Nevertheless, it seemed as though India and Indian affairs continued to exercise a singular gravitational pull on Keynes. After the usual preliminary feelers, the Viceroy of India, Lord Reading, wrote to Edwin Montagu:

> Keynes' presence [in India] for first two months will permit him to hear only the early part of the evidence and will result in our losing his services at the time of discussing the reports, when his special qualities will be invaluable. Would it be possible for him to come out after instead of before the Michaelmas term and to be here for completion of evidence and report finishing about July. (From Montagu's letter of 8 August 1921 to Keynes – *Keynes Papers*, King's College)

To this Keynes replied, 'I could leave at beginning of January returning from India at end of March. The Viceroy's proposal I cannot undertake' (Letter to Montagu dated 8 September 1921). The Indian authorities were particularly keen on getting Keynes's services for the Commission at any cost and the India Office was unusually accomodative considering that although officially Keynes was supposed to be a full-time member of the Commission he was in fact to function part-time. The India Office therefore made a further approach to Keynes, suggesting that in case he could not be in India all the time his services 'would be of the greatest value . . . after the evidence has been collected and when it has to be sifted and weighed and the report prepared.'[48] It was also suggested that Keynes could proceed to India 'at the end of the last term and stay till the report is ready' with a promise that the evidence would be made available to him as soon as it was printed.

Keynes finally accepted the membership of the proposed Indian Fiscal Commission on the terms suggested by him, particularly the clear understanding that 'he could not undertake to be away for more than three months in India while assuring that he would do his best to see the business through'.[49] The terms of reference and personnel of the Commission were announced on 7 October 1921 after consultation with His Majesty's Government. The terms were 'to examine with reference to all the interests concerned the tariff policy of the Government of India, including the question of the desirability of adopting the principle of Imperial Preference, and to make recommendations'. The personnel consisted of Sir Ibrahim Rahimtoola, a distinguished Indian non-official from the Bombay Presidency, with a strong business and public affairs background, as the Chairman, Mr J. M. Keynes (Vice-Chairman), and ten Members: Messrs T. V. Sheshagiri Ayyar, Ghanshyamdas Birla, Jamnadas Dwarkadas, Narottam Morarjee, Sir Maneckjee Dadabhoy (non-official Indians), Professor J. C. Coyajee (Marshall's Indian pupil at Cambridge and the only other economist member), Sir Edgar Holberton, C. W. Rhodes, R. A. Mant and Sir Montague Webb (Europeans).

Keynes's appointment was widely welcomed in India. It seemed as though all knowledgeable and concerned Indians were agog with excitement at the thought of the legendary Keynes's long-awaited visit to India. A typical reaction was beautifully expressed by Mr R. P. Sabnis of the New Poona College, and a member of Fitzwilliam Hall, Cambridge (1913–16), in his letter of 21 March 1921 to Keynes, 'It will be for an expert like you to supply scientific reasons for their [Indians'] conclusions, that is your trust as a member of the Fiscal Commission, which, I hope, you will faithfully discharge' (*Keynes Papers*, King's College). Similar hospitable sentiments in a different vein were touchingly echoed by a distinguished British Indian civil servant and Kingsman, Malcolm Darling, who wrote to Keynes from Lahore, India on 15 March 1921 as follows:

> it would give both my wife and myself the greatest pleasure if you would stay with us during the visit of the Fiscal Commission to Lahore. Ever since I read your great work I have been hoping I might run across you again. I fear, however, that you will be going to Government House where you will certainly be more comfortable though hardly more welcome. (*Keynes Papers*, King's College)

Keynes's appointment had raised the somewhat unjustified expectation among the Indian intelligentsia that he would provide an intellectual foundation for Indian protectionism and for Indian economic nationalism generally, despite his position as the only known free-trader in the Commission.

Keynes's other stipulation, that, in addition to normal travelling expenses and subsistence allowance, he be remunerated at the rate of 500 English pounds for three months as compensation for loss of earnings, was also confirmed by the India Office. Keynes also requested permission to travel overland, which cost an additional six pounds, to Venice to catch the Lloyd Triestino's *SS Tevere* sailing to Bombay on the 2 February 1922 and to be assigned a single cabin on one of the higher decks – this latter a charmingly importunate theme in his correspondence. These too were willingly acceded to by the India Office.[50] The passage was confirmed by the Mercantile Marine Department of the Board of Trade in January 1922. Keynes was thus all set to finally visit the country which was so much at the heart of his professional concerns.

Keynes's arrangements had been made and accepted on the stipulation that he should not be away for more than three months in India given his many commitments and interests in England, which, apart from King's College, included the *Manchester Guardian* and the National Mutual Life Insurance Company of which he became Chairman in 1921. In the same year, C. P. Scott, the editor of the *Manchester Guardian,* had asked Keynes to be general editor of a series of special supplements on the economic and financial problems of postwar Europe. It was at this point that a most unexpected development occurred which completely thwarted Keynes's schedule of visiting India. This was the fateful telegram of 18 January 1922, from the Viceroy, Lord Reading, indicating that the work of the Commission was expected to last six months and possibly even two months longer. Predictably, Keynes wrote (10 February 1922) to Edwin Montagu, regretting his total inability to comply with the revised schedule for the Commission.[51]

> I have always had to stipulate that I should not be away for more than three months, and by the time this telegram [of 18 January from the Viceroy] arrived I had made arrangements which put it out of my power to be longer than that. I am very sorry to have failed Lord Reading and I appreciate very much what he says about his strong wish that I should have helped the Commission. But these Indian Commissions which spread their work over the best part of a year make it very difficult for anyone to attend from this side. . . . the whole question of dates has become quite different from what I contemplated when I first dramatised the question of forming the Commission. All this does not affect my guiltiness in having approached you for release the day before the Viceroy's telegram of the 18th had been received. But that telegram nevertheless clinched the matter.

The disappointment was, of course, mutual as is evident from the telegram of 4 February 1922 from the Viceroy, Lord Reading, to Edwin Montagu. 'Keynes's inability to join the Fiscal Commission. I am intensely disappointed as I regarded Keynes largely as the pilot to steer the ship into safe waters. I am very concerned as to the report without his guidance' (CW, Vol. XVII, p. 332). This recital of a sorry and tangled episode should finally dispel the longstanding myth, propagated by Harrod's biography, that Keynes's resignation from the Indian Fiscal Commission had to do with his burgeoning interest in the ballet and his growing involvement with his future wife Lydia Lopokova.[52] The truth was that Keynes, like a true genius, could compartmentalise his professional and personal interests. His personality and lifestyle would assuredly not have allowed even the charms of Lydia Lopokova, and her enchanting performances in *The Sleeping Princess* and the *Boutique Fantasque* to override matters of state and to prevent the acceptance of the singular intellectual challenge that the Vice-Presidency of the Indian Fiscal Commission represented.

The Commission's Report, which was presented in July 1922 and published in the following September was, predictably, not a unanimous report. The majority consisted of all the four European members and two Indian members, J. C. Coyajee, and Sir Maneckjee Dadabhoy. The minority of five members consisting of the President and the remaining Indian members appended a Minute of Dissent recommending rapid industrialisation through protection. The Government of India accepted the policy of 'discriminating protection' and created a Tariff Board to consider the case of every industry that might put forward a case for protection. It is significant that the policy of discriminating protection (1923–39) was largely confined to eleven existing import-substitution industries (cotton textiles, matches, sugar, paper, salt, heavy chemicals, plywood and tea chests, sericulture, magnesium chloride, and gold thread) but not to prospective or nascent non-traditional industries like machine tools or heavy engineering.

Keynes's inability to join the Commission prompts the question: How would Keynes have reacted to the age-old question of protection for India given his advocacy of free trade before the Cambridge Indian Majlis nearly a decade ago and of 'modified' Free Trade in 1921? There is no indication in his published writings of what he meant by modified free trade. Would he have resiled from his free trade position after hearing the many persuasive and articulate witnesses? Keynes had also argued that tariffs were one of the recognised methods of increasing the foreign balance of a country in addition to rationalisation of production and differential interest rates through subsidies.[53] In contrast to the Indian Fiscal Commission's total neglect of revenue aspects of the tariff, and the recommendations of the majority for abolition of import duties on machinery, coal, hides, and skins, and so on, involving a loss of about Rs 300 million without proposing alternative sources of revenue, Keynes would, as part of 'the recantation of an avowed free trader', probably have strongly argued the merits of a comprehensive tariff as a revenue and employment promotion measure.[54] On the other hand, the Keynes of the General Theory had also cautioned against the beggar-my-neighbour consequences of immoderate trade restrictions compounded by 'private interest, administrative incompetence and the intrinsic difficulty of the task'.[55] Would he have finally signed up with the minority since he was 'not unaccustomed to being in a minority' or reverted to his earlier 'limited' free trade position for India considering his avowed lack of enthusiasm for Indian industrialisation, soon after his India Office days? But one can reasonably conjecture that, given his wide-ranging intellect and persuasive skills, Keynes would certainly have transformed the Commission Report into an enduring *tour d'horizon* of the Indian economy instead of a now-forgotten Report in the Indian Archives. Keynes doubtless read the published Report of the Indian Fiscal Commission and, as one of his pupils vaguely recalls, even recommended it as required reading to students for some aspects of fiscal policy (Mr Harold Dunkerley, c. 1942, King's College, in a personal interview to the author)

Keynes's aborted passage to India, despite all the efforts of the Secretary of State for India to facilitate acceptance of his modest and very reasonable stipulations, meant an aborted classic of economic literature which might well have emerged from Keynes's work for the Commission given his traditional penchant for turning official work to intellectual account (just as his spell with the India Office germinated *Indian Currency and Finance*). This will always be counted as an irreparable loss alike for India and the discipline of economics since Keynes did not have another chance, or even the possibility of addressing such issues, given his characteristic intellectual stance of not reverting to themes which ceased to be matters of pressing policy. Indian tariff policy did not pose the same sort of recurring intellectual challenge for Keynes as Indian currency and banking issues. The unwitting, but not untypical, gyrations of the British Indian bureaucracy deprived Keynes of his last chance of visiting India, as it turned out, and of making a lasting contribution to an understanding of the non-monetary aspects of Indian economic policy. Keynes had also hoped that on his Indian visit he would try to 'get something about the Indian market [for Manchester cotton] and propose to ask Mr. Gandhi to write an article explaining why he hates Manchester so much' (letter to A.P. Wadsworth of the *Manchester Guardian*, 9 January 1922, CW, Vol. XVII, pp. 329–30). This sorry episode will, however, be long remembered for Keynes's unhesitating willingness to serve under a non-official Indian Chairman in the heyday of the Raj – an unparalleled gesture in British Indian history which only serves to enhance Keynes's moral stature.

Notes

1. *Collected Writings*, Vol. XV, p. 17.
2. R. S. Sayers, 'The Young Keynes', *Economic Journal*, Vol. 82, No. 326, June 1972, p. 593. Sayers has drawn on his own full notes of Keynes's lecture on 26 November 1928 to substantiate this.
3. Chapter I of *Collected Writings*, Vol. XI, Economic Articles and Correspondence, Academic, (ed.) Donald Moggridge (Macmillan, London, 1983), pp. 1–22. Subsequent quotations in this section are from this Chapter unless otherwise indicated.
4. Ibid., p. 1.
5. Gokhale indeed made a masterly statement of the quantity theory of money (without calling it that) in the Indian context. 'During the last ten years [1898–1908] the Government have made a net addition to this stock

[of rupees] of over 100 crores. Such a sudden inflation is bound to result in a general rise in prices. . . . The rupees issued in response to the demands of trade go into the interior and spread themselves among those from whom purchases have been made. But they do not flow back quickly to centres of trade, or to banks, and thus new rupees have to be obtained for transactions for which the old rupees might have sufficed. Meanwhile, the melting of rupees having ceased (as a result of the token character of the rupee since the closing of the mints in 1893 and its artificial higher exchange value) every issue becomes a net addition to the volume of currency.' Speeches by G. K. Gokhale, p. 150, cited in G. B. Jathar and S. G. Beri, *Indian Economics* (University Press, London, 1952), p. 299.

6. *Collected Writings of John Maynard Keynes*, Vol. XI, Economic Articles and Correspondence, Academic, (ed.) Donald Moggridge (Macmillan, London, 1983), p.18.
7. Harrod, *Life*, op. cit., p. 146.
8. For details see *Collected Writings of John Maynard Keynes*, Vol. XII, Economic Articles and Correspondence: *Investment and Editorial*, (ed.) Donald Moggridge (Macmillan, London; Cambridge University Press, 1983), Chapter 5.
9. See *Official Papers by Alfred Marshall*, (ed.) J. M. Keynes, (Macmillan, London, 1926).
10. Review of Engelbrecht, Von Th. H., *Die geographische verteilung der Getreidepreise in Indien von 1861 bis 1905 (Berlin, Paul Parey, 1908)*. (From the Journal of the Royal Statistical Society, March 1909) cited in *Collected Writings*, Vol. XI, p. 23.
11. Michell McAlpin in 'Price Movements and Fluctuations in Economic Activity, 1860–1947' in *The Cambridge Economic History of India*, Vol. 2 c.1757–c.1970, edited by Dharma Kumar (Cambridge University Press, 1983) gives statistical evidence to substantiate that the increase in rail mileage reduced 'the spread between prices in different places', p. 885.
12. Review of Findlay Shirras, *Indian Finance and Banking* Third impression (London, Macmillan, 1920) in *Economic Journal*, September 1920, reprinted in *Collected Writings*, Vol. XI, p. 42.
13. J. M. Keynes, Review of H. Stanley Jevons, *The Future of Exchange and the Indian Currency*, (Oxford University Press, Indian Branch, 1922), in *Economic Journal*, March 1923, in *Collected Writings*, Vol. XI, p. 46.
14. Keynes, ibid., p. 47.
15. *Collected Writings*, Vol. XV. The subsequent citations in this section are from this volume, pp. 21–30.
16. *Collected Writings*, Vol. XV, pp. 26–7.
17. Ibid., p. 27.
18. *Collected Writings*, Vol. XV, p. 28.
19. K. N. Chaudhuri, 'Foreign Trade and Balance of Payments', *Cambridge Economic History of India*, Vol. 2, c.1757-c.1970 (Cambridge University Press, 1983), p. 873.
20. Mill wrote in his *History of India*, Vol. VI, 'It is an exhausting drain upon the resources of the country, the issue of which is replaced by no reflex . . .' p. 671. Cf. Bipan Chandra, *The Rise and Growth of Econ-*

omic Nationalism in India (People's Publishing House, New Delhi, 1966), Chapter XIII, 'The Drain', pp. 636–708.

21. Bipan Chandra, ibid., p. 644–9.
22. Bipan Chandra, ibid., p. 676.
23. Theodore Morison, *The Economic Transition in India* (London, 1911; reprinted 1916), p. 193, cited by Bipan Chandra, p. 677.
24. *Collected Writings*, Vol. XI, p. 30.
25. Dharma Kumar, 'The Fiscal System', in *The Cambridge Economic History of India*, Vol. 2, *c*.1757–*c*.1970 (Cambridge University Press, 1983), p. 937.
26. K. N. Chaudhuri, 'Foreign Trade' op. cit., p. 877.
27. From *The Economist,* 3 July 1909 in *Collected Writings,* Vol. XI, p. 34.
28. 'The supply of food is almost the least of the difficulties with which the Indian Government have to contend. There is always a sufficiency of food in the great continent of India even in years of drought.' George Hamilton, Secretary of State for India in the House of Commons, 26 July 1900, Hansard (Fourth Series), Vol. LXXXVI, c.1346, cited by Bipan Chandra, 'Economic Nationalism', op. cit., p. 50. This shows that Indian officials were fully aware of the problems of acquirement and entitlement analysed much later by Amartya Sen, *Poverty and Famines* (Oxford University Press, 1981), who has proved systematically that famines can occur even without any decline in food output or per capita availability.
29. See numerous citations by Bipan Chandra, ibid., p. 49–53.
30. Ibid., p. 36.
31. A. Heston 'National Income' in *The Cambridge Economic History of India,* Vol. 2, c.1757–c.1970 (ed.) Dharma Kumar (Cambridge University Press, 1983).
32. Roy M. MacLeod, 'Scientific Advice for British India: Imperial Perceptions and Administrative Goals, 1898–1923,' *Modern Asian Studies,* Vol. 9, No. 3, 1975, p. 345.
33. Ibid., p. 37.
34. See Pramathnath Banerjee, *A History of Indian Taxation* (London, 1930), pp. 249–313.
35. Dr Pattabhi Sitaramayya, *The History of the Indian National Congress,* Vol. I, 1885–1935 (Padma Publications, Bombay, 1946), p. 50.
36. G. K. Gokhale, observed in the Imperial Legislative Council (1910), 'If . . . every other resource fails . . . I shall be prepared to advocate an extra 8 annas on salt because I think it is a smaller evil that my countryman should eat less salt than their children should continue to grow up in ignorance and darkness . . .'. Cited by V. V. Bhatt, *Education and Economic Development,* Commerce Pamphlet 57 (Vora and Co. Bombay, 1972), p. 9.
37. Dharma Kumar, 'The Fiscal System of India', in *The Cambridge Economic History of India,* Vol. 2, c.1757–c.1970 (Cambridge University Press, 1983), p. 930.
38. *Review of the Trade of India in 1913–14* (Calcutta, Government Printing Office, 1914) and *Memorandum and Statistical Tables relating to the Trade of India with Germany and Austria-Hungary* (Calcutta, Govern-

ment Printing Office, 1914). (From *Economic Journal,* December 1914, reprinted in *Collected Writings,* Vol. XI, pp. 36–42.)

39. Harry G. Johnson, 'The Early Economics of Keynes' in *The Shadow of Keynes,* (ed.) Elizabeth S. Johnson and Harry G. Johnson (Basil Blackwell, Oxford, 1978), p. 109.
40. Harry Johnson, ibid., p. 177.
41. Keynes in his review of Sir Theodore Morison, *The Economic Transition of India* (1911) was critical of Sir Theodore for his 'agreement with much current opinion in India, where a considerable part of the educated class seem to desire, with patriotic fervour, the industrialization of their country . . . such a change is not, in the future, which none can foresee, either desirable or likely. It is an unfortunate consequence of the English connection, that industrialism should present itself to India as the royal road to prosperity and to a dignified position among nations' (p. 27). . . . 'every diversion of indigenous capital from agriculture, where her relative advantage is great, to industries, where . . . the relative positions of coal, iron, and the sea place her at a disadvantage, will be to the detriment of her economic prosperity' (p. 29). John Maynard Keynes, *The Collected Writings of John Maynard Keynes*, Vol. XI. (Macmillan, London, 1983).
42. Bipan Chandra, 'Free Trade vs Protection', op. cit., pp. 725–35.
43. (Letter of 22.x.10), *Memorials of Alfred Marshall,* edited by A. C. Pigou (Macmillan, London, 1925), p. 472.
44. *The Collected Writings of John Maynard Keynes,* Vol. IX, 'Mitigation by Tariff', in *Essays in Persuasion* (Macmillan, London, 1972), p. 238.
45. *The Collected Writings of John Maynard Keynes,* Vol. XVII, Activities 1920–22. Treaty Revision and Reconstruction, Elizabeth Johnson (Macmillan, London; Cambridge University Press, 1977), p. 317.
46. *Collected Writings,* Vol. XVII, p. 319.
47. Ibid., p. 326.
48. Letter of A. Hurtzel of the India Office, India, September 1921 (IE/1) to Keynes, which ended on the somewhat plaintive note, 'It is the only alternative that I can see to abandoning the hope of seeing you.' (*Keynes Papers*, King's College).
49. Letter dated 22 September 1921, to E. J. Turner of the India Office confirmed by Turner in his letter of 26 September 1921 to Keynes (*Keynes Papers*, King's College).
50. Keynes to E. J. Turner of the India Office (dated 1 and 23 March 1921), *Keynes Papers.*
51. *Collected Writings,* Vol. XVII, pp. 332–3.
52. 'On May 26, 1921 Diaghilev opened a new season in London. It was marked by an event of considerable interest, the return to the company of Lydia Lopokova. . . . Keynes went often. . . . He was spellbound by this Princess [Lydia]. . . . How he adored the Ballet! . . . He certainly lacked something to give personal significance to his multitudinous stirrings. Some more vital motive was needed than the general good. This was certainly a very big idea. It was much more important than Indian Free Trade. He already knew Lydia . . . He began to pay her

attention. . . . He had clearly a long way to go before he could achieve what he wished. He decided to abandon the Indian project.' Harrod, *Life*, op. cit., pp. 307–9.

53. Cf. Keynes, *A Treatise on Money, Collected Writings,* Vol. VI, pp. 166–7.
54. See his 'Mitigation by Tariff' (Chapter 6 in *Essays in Persuasion, Collected Writings,* Vol. IX, Macmillan, London, 1982) where he clearly argued for a tariff which 'would include no discriminating protective taxes, but would cover as wide a field as possible at a flat rate or perhaps two flat rates . . . I do not believe that a wise and prudent budget can be framed today without recourse to a revenue tariff. But this is not its only advantage. Insofar as it leads to the substitution of home-produced goods for goods previously imported, it will increase employment in this country' (pp. 236–7). Keynes had first published these 'Proposals for a Revenue Tariff' as an article in the *New Statesman and Nation,* 7 March 1931.
55. *The General Theory,* Vol. VII, *The Collected Writings of John Maynard Keynes* (Macmillan, London, 1973), pp. 338–9.

4 Reforming the Rupee

'He even understood the Indian Rupee.' *Paul Samuelson*

'He began life as a monetary economist.' *Joan Robinson*

THE CHALLENGE OF INDIAN CURRENCY

The sheer complexity and uniqueness of Indian monetary experience have invested the history and problems of Indian currency and finance with a distinctive intellectual appeal and even an indefinable element of mystique.[1] No wonder Indian monetary experience since the advent of British rule seems to have exercised a singular fascination for some of the most acute contemporary economists. It is no accident that some of the major contributions of eminent economists like Alfred Marshall and Keynes to monetary thought have stemmed from a close analysis and observation of India's monetary history. In his very first publication after leaving the India Office, Keynes noted that 'Apart from the practical side of the matter, India's intricate and highly artificial system presents problems of special interest to the student of the theory of currency.'[2] In a subsequent review Keynes for the first time specifically addressed the problems of the Indian rupee.[3] Almost a decade later Keynes remarked that 'Indian currency can always find some new thing with which to interest and instruct the student. More numerous and more skilled Commissions have sat over it than over any other currency in the world; yet no sooner does a Commission rise than this currency presents some further problem, which no one had contemplated in advance, to perplex its official custodians.'[4] The frequency of official enquiries into Indian currency was true not only of the historic period referred to by Keynes but also of developments since then as will be readily obvious from the following list.

1892 Herschell Committee on Indian currency.
1893 Act closing the Indian mints to the coinage of silver on private account. Notification of fixing of the rate of exchange of rupees or notes for tender of gold at the equivalent of 1s 4d to the rupee.
1898 Fowler Committee on Indian currency. Exchange value of rupee touched 1s 4d.

1899 Act declaring the British sovereign legal tender at 1s 4d to the rupee.
1900 Gold standard reserve constituted out of profits of coinage.
1904 Secretary of State for India's notification of his willingness to sell Council bills on India at 1s $4\frac{1}{8}$ d without limit.
1905 Act authorising the establishment of the currency . . . of earmarked gold at the Bank of England as part of the currency reserve against notes and the investment of a specified part of the currency reserve in sterling securities. (Similar temporary Acts had been enacted in 1898 and 1900.)
1906 Withdrawal of notification directing the issue of rupees against tender of gold (as distinguished from British gold coin).
1907 Establishment of rupee branch of the gold standard reserve.
1908 Sale of sterling drafts on London in Calcutta as 1s $9\frac{29}{32}$ to the rupee and cashed out of the gold standard reserve.
1910 Act declaring currency notes of Rs 10 and Rs 50 as unlimited legal tender (Rs 100 in 1911) and directing issue of notes in exchange for gold coins.
1913 Royal Commission (Chamberlain) on Indian Currency and Finance.
1919 Indian Exchange and Currency (Babington Smith) Committee.
1926 Royal Commission (Hilton Young) on Indian Currency and Finance.
1929 Indian Central Banking Enquiry Committee.

Keynes's observation in his review of Stanley Jevons's *The Future of Exchange and the Indian Currency* ('Sir Basil Blackett, the new Finance Member of the Viceroy's Council, has gone to a problem not quite so thrilling as some of those he has left behind him, but of purer *intellectual* quality [Keynes's emphasis] perhaps')[5] once again reiterated the perennial intellectual challenge of Indian monetary problems which Keynes found so peculiarly compelling.

The origins of Keynes's sustained interest in Indian monetary problems are of particular interest considering that during his India Office service he seems to have touched on all varieties of Indian economic problems and issues, except Indian currency. There is no indication whether Keynes's initial interest in Indian monetary problems could be traced to Alfred Marshall, who had been interested in Indian economic problems since his appointment as a Fellow (on the premature death of Arnold Toynbee) of Balliol College, Oxford and Lecturer in Political Economy to the selected candidates of the Indian Civil Service. It is, however, on record that Keynes agreed

Table 4.1 Keynes's lectures at Cambridge 1908–13

Subject	*Years taught*	*Number of terms (terms = 8 weeks)*	*Number of hours per week*
Money, Credit and Prices	1908/9 –1909/10	2	2
The Stock Exchange and the Money Market	1909/10–1913/14	1	1
The Theory of Money	1910/11–1913/14	1	2
Company Finance and the Stock Exchange	1910/11–1912/13	1	1
Currency and Banking	1910/11–1913/14	1	2
The Currency and Finances of India	1910/11	1	1
Money Markets and Foreign Exchanges	1910/11–1912/13	1	1
Principles of Economics	1910/11–1913/14	3	2
The Monetary Affairs of India	1912/13	1	1

Source: Keynes's Lecture Notes, reprinted in *Collected Writings*, Vol. XII, p. 689.

with Marshall on the more important Indian monetary issues. Just as Marshall was Keynes's mentor on economics at Cambridge, Abrahams 'the moulder and manipulator of India's involved but efficient financial system' fulfilled a similar role as Keynes's mentor on Indian finance. Keynes submitted to Abrahams for critical review everything that he wrote concerning Indian financial matters.[6] It is noteworthy that Indian monetary affairs also figured prominently in Keynes's lectures on the Theory of Money and his reading lists for Cambridge undergraduates. (See Table 4.1) In fact, this appears to have been the only regional and institutional subject outside the conventional ambit of British and European economic history and institutions in the syllabus for the Cambridge Economics Tripos. Keynes's lecture notes on Money (Elementary) contain the following entry: 'Explain briefly the nature of the currency system now existing in each of the following countries: France, Germany, U.S.A. and *India*' (emphasis supplied).

Keynes's lectures (1910–11) on Indian Finance in the course on 'Indian Institutions' in the Department of Sociology at the London School of Economics[7] provided the material for his paper on Indian currency to the meeting of the Royal Economic Society on 9 May

1911, which was later developed into his first book, *Indian Currency and Finance.* Around this time Abrahams made a copy of Keynes's draft for the use of the India Office and the Government of India which was later printed at its summer capital, Simla, by the Government of India for internal use. This draft, entitled '*Recent Developments of the Indian Currency Question*' was the first systematic study of Indian monetary problems by Keynes. It had also benefited from Keynes's correspondence with Sir James Wilson, a former finance commissioner of the Punjab, whose major concern was to strengthen the rupee by putting more gold and prewar rupees in circulation and to hold the gold standard reserve entirely in gold in India.

Keynes's ideas and contributions to the analysis of Indian monetary problems are most usefully studied in the framework of four principal topics: (1) the problem of the appropriate monetary standard for India; (2) the rupee ratio (that is, the rate of exchange between sterling and the rupee); (3) the rationale and type of central bank suitable for Indian conditions and (4) problems of Indian commercial banks. The subsequent analysis draws on Keynes's published writings and also on his work as a member of the Royal Commission (Chamberlain) on Indian Currency and Finance, 1913–14; his evidence as an expert witness to the Indian Exchange and Currency Committee, 1919 (Babington Smith); and the second Royal Commission (Hilton Young) on Indian Currency and Finance, 1926.

THE QUEST FOR AN IDEAL MONETARY STANDARD

Although India was not the first country to lead the way to a gold exchange standard, she was, as Keynes stressed so often, the first to adopt it in a complete form on a large scale.[8] As Keynes noted, since the Indian version of the gold exchange standard was perfected and widely known, it had been widely imitated in part of Asia (Straits Settlements), Indo-China, Philippines and Thailand and elsewhere (Mexico and Panama). A similar system was in operation in Java and Japan and a 'powerful body of opinion, led by the United States', favoured the immediate introduction of a gold standard on the Indian model' (CW, I, p. 25). Keynes regarded this variant as 'being something much more civilized, much more economical, and much more satisfactory than a gold currency . . . out of it . . . will be evolved the ideal currency of the future' (CW, XV, p. 69). This judgement of Keynes was based on the 'one essential element' of the gold exchange standard 'as the ideal currency of the future' – 'the use of a cheap local currency artificially maintained at par with the international currency or standard of value (whatever that may ultimately turn out to be)' (ibid., CW, I, p. 25). This form of the gold exchange standard was effectively operative in India from 1898–9 to 1915–16. Its intellectual origins go back to Ricardo's listing of its advantages at the time of the Bullionist controversy. It was also known as the Lindsay scheme (after A. M. Lindsay, the Deputy Secretary of the Bank of Bengal who had advocated it as early as 1876 down to the Fowler Committee of 1898).

The gold exchange standard, as defined by Keynes, could be said to be operative: when gold did not circulate within a country to any appreciable extent; when the total currency was not necessarily redeemable in gold; when the government or central bank made provision for foreign remittances in gold at a fixed maximum rate in terms of the local currency. The gold sovereign was the legal tender in India at 15 rupees to the pound with the Government offering, as a rule, to exchange rupees for sovereigns at this rate. But it was under no legal obligation to do so and did not in fact exchange large quantities at all times. But it was the rupee, a token coin, and virtually a note printed on silver, with the status of unlimited legal tender, which was the principal medium of exchange. The sterling value of the rupee was supported by the Secretary of State for India's willingness in practice, but not in law, to sell bills in London on India in unlimited amounts at a maximum rate of 1s 4 $\frac{1}{8}$ d and to sell bills in India (Calcutta) on London at 1s 3 $\frac{7}{8}$ d.

The monetary reserves were distributed as follows:

(1) Coined rupees were held partly in the currency reserve, and partly in the gold standard reserve.

(2) The gold reserve was held wholly in the currency reserve.

(3) The reserve in the form of loans at call or short notice was held wholly in the gold standard reserve.

(4) The reserve in the form of sterling securities was held partly in the currency and partly in the gold standard reserve.

The rationale of the reserve system was that the reserve of rupees required to meet a reduction in the volume of notes was kept in the currency reserve, while the reserve of rupees required to meet unexpectedly heavy sales of Council bills in London was kept in the gold standard reserve. Strangely, Keynes, without assigning any reasons, hoped that the Government of India's decisions to divert half of the future profits of coinage to capital expenditure on railways 'will be reconsidered before the time comes' (ibid., p. 75). This was, however, in keeping with Keynes's consistent reluctance to divert seigniorage and note issue profits to industrial or other uses. On the other hand, Keynes was also of the view that existing facilities for the use of gold 'ought to be abolished' even though 'public opinion has not yet reached the point when this is practically possible'. India, according to Keynes,

> already wastes far too high a proportion of her resources in the needless accumulation of the precious metals. The Government ought not to encourage in the slightest degree this ingrained fondness for handling hard gold. By import taxes on both precious metals and by their elimination, to the utmost extent that public opinion will permit, . . . from amongst the circulating media of the country, they ought to counteract an uncivilized and wasteful habit (ibid., p. 81).

Keynes argued that when gold does flow to India, a loss is involved. 'If it leaves the Indian reserve, it goes either into circulation or into the hands of the bullion dealers for hoarding or for ornament. If the sovereigns go into circulation, they must displace rupees or notes, and thus reduce the profits on coinage. But . . . relatively few find their way into circulation and that the majority go to the bullion dealers' (ibid., p. 82). Keynes also supported the maintenance of sterling reserves in London since it was 'plainly much more economical to keep in London where, eventually, they will be wanted'. In opposing the proposals of Sir Guy Wilson, Sir Vithaldas Thackersey, and others for the introduction of a larger quantity of gold into the Indian circulation, Keynes argued that 'for obvious reasons of convenience and economy the greater part of the Indian circulation must continue in any case to consist of rupees'. He made the telling point that the gold sovereign, by reason of its high value, was unsuitable for a poor country like India and, as borne out by the Currency Department figures relatively few sovereigns found their way into circulation and the majority were absorbed by bullion dealers. The Chamberlain Commission estimated that, apart from imports of gold bullion, the absorption of gold sovereigns by the public for hoards, circulation, and the melting pot, during the twelve years ended 31 March 1913, (that is, the excess of net amount imported over the amount retained by the Government) somewhat exceeded £60 million, a little less in value than the new coinage of rupees in the same period. The Commission also noticed the increased use of the sovereign as currency in certain areas, such as parts of the Bombay Presidency and of the United Provinces, the Punjab, and Cochin, and that 'speaking generally, no district which wanted gold seems to have experienced in the last four years any difficulty in obtaining it' (CW, XV, p. 223). A greater infusion of gold into the currency would dissipate part of the Government's sterling reserves over the country and put it 'in a weaker position to meet a crisis than if they are concentrated in its own chests.' Keynes refuted the uncritical support of Sir Edward Holden (Chairman, London City and Midland Bank) for the recommendation of the Fowler Committee for the establishment of a gold currency in India, which according to Keynes, 'would plainly increase rather than diminish the drain of gold thither' (Letter to the Editor, *The Times,* 26 October 1912).[9] Keynes therefore endorsed the policy of the India Council as being more economical in the use of gold in India than any alternative policies. This only reflected Keynes's constant emphasis in the Indian context that 'one of the chief objects of a good currency is to combine cheapness with stability.' (See his letter to the Editor of *The Times*, 14 November 1912, ibid., p. 91.)

It was just at this juncture that a whiff of scandal and impropriety rose from certain bullion transactions of the Council of India and sparked off a public discussion of the eternal Indian currency question in which Keynes also joined as a disinterested expert analyst. This episode was the so-called Indian 'silver scandal' which surfaced at the beginning of November 1912 as a fall-out of the more notorious Marconi scandal raging at the time which also involved high-placed members of the British Government. It was alleged that Messrs Samuel Montagu and Co., bullion-brokers, were purchasing silver secretly on behalf of the Government of India for its gold standard reserve. As it happened, Sir Stuart Samuel, a partner in the firm, was too well connected with high-ranking official figures. His younger brother, Herbert Samuel, was the Postmaster General in Asquith's Cabinet and his uncle, Lord Swaythling, a senior partner in the firm, was the father of Edwin Montagu, the Under-Secretary of State for India. All this was grist to the rumour mill. There were dark hints of public men misusing their political positions for private profit by diverting government contracts to firms in which they had a financial interest. Actually, the sole reason for the secrecy surrounding the purchase of large amounts of silver by the Council of India through their regular bullion-brokers, Messrs Samuel Montagu and Co., was the wholly justifiable consideration of avoiding speculation. Moreover, the transactions were fully in accord with the customary procedures of the India Office. Nevertheless, parliamentary critics made great play with the purely fortuitous circumstance that a member of the House of Commons was a partner in the firm and that the senior partner was the father of the Under-Secretary of State for India. 'A rash of questions erupted in the House of Commons concerning the cash balances of India, the selling prices of the securities held in the Indian gold standard reserve, the borrowers from the Indian Office balances, etc.' (CW, XV, p. 90). Around this time *The Times* (1, 2, 4, 6, and 7 November 1912) carried five anonymous articles, referring to 'a state not only of affairs but of opinion which calls for thorough and immediate consideration'. Keynes was curious as to the identity of the anonymous author of the articles and asked Lionel Abrahams, who suspected, but was not at all sure, that someone on the staff of the *Times of India*, Bombay, possibly inspired by Montagu de P. Webb (Chairman of the Karachi Chamber of Commerce and a chronic critic of the Indian currency system) might have written the articles. Abrahams, while welcoming Keynes's forthcoming book on Indian currency, was particularly keen that Keynes 'send a letter to *The Times* as well. There is so little said on our side. I should be most grateful' (CW, XV, p. 91). Keynes readily rose to the defence with a letter to the editor of *The Times* (14 November 1912) which was later reproduced by the *Times of India*, (Bombay) 13 December 1912. First, he supported the centralisation of gold reserves, as one of the guiding principles of the Government of India's policy in opposition to the policy recommended by the Fowler Committee and supported by the correspondence. According to Keynes, the trend of currency policy was rightly to encourage the use of a cheaper medium of actual exchange such as token silver, notes, cheques, etc., and to ensure stability by centralising the reserve of gold to the utmost so that the local currency could be immediately changed for gold when gold was needed to external obligations. Keynes also argued that in assessing the adequacy of the reserves and the suitability of the forms in which they are held 'the only sensible course is regard them as a whole' (ibid., p. 93). Since reserves are accumulated to meet foreign demands in case of need, it is more productive to hold them, within proper limits, in interest-earning liquid balances in some foreign country with a stable money market than as gold whose remission from a distant country also involves delay and expense. Furthermore, India's policy in this regard was also in accord with the best foreign practice. Countries such as France, Russia, Austria-Hungary, Holland, Sweden and Japan had all in varying degrees a gold standard but with a small amount of gold in circulation and the bulk of foreign reserves held in foreign bills and balances. If anything the Government of India's policy was 'more complete, more systematic, and compared with some of them, more public' and 'they have established their currency in a position of almost unassailable stability; and have managed at the same time to save considerable sums for the taxpayer' (p. 94). Keynes's cogent and spirited defence of the Government of India's currency policy evoked lavish encomiums on all sides. William Robinson of the India Office (31 December 1912) acclaimed it as 'the best statement on our side that has yet appeared' and only regretted that '*The Times* did not print it in letters of gold and silver and issue it as a special supplement'. Even *The Times* acknowledged that 'the views of our Anglo-Indian correspondent have altogether failed to secure widespread support' (20 January 1913). This, however, did not inhibit *The Times*'s successful editorial campaign for the appointment of a Royal Commission to inquire into the whole financial management of India Office. Meanwhile, Keynes, amidst the continued parliamentary discussions and questions on Indian currency matters, made steady progress with his book on Indian currency, whose proofs were submitted for criticism to, among others, Hartley Withers, financial journalist with *The Times*, Neville Keynes, and Lionel Abrahams. Abrahams faulted Keynes for regarding the Secretary of State's balances primarily as a loan fund whereas they were really meant to serve as a working balance for the India Office. He also thought that Keynes was a little too harsh in his description of the Government of India's London broker as 'a worthy, harmless man' whose income, rivalled only by that of the Viceroy of India, Keynes felt was excessive for the amount of work he did!

PUBLICATION OF *INDIAN CURRENCY AND FINANCE*

Keynes was in Alexandria, Egypt for his Easter vacation in March 1913 when he was offered through Sir Thomas Holderness of the India Office (dated 11 March 1913) the Secretaryship of the forthcoming Royal Commission on Indian Currency. There was a flurry of cable exchanges between Keynes and Holderness largely to resolve Keynes's initial hesitation to accept the offer because he wanted a clear assurance that his freedom to publish *Indian Currency and*

Finance would not be compromised by his membership of the Commission. In the event, this matter was most happily resolved for Keynes who was offered, instead of the secretaryship, membership of the Commission; 'this is considered in view of the book more suitable than secretaryship' and will give 'greater scope' (Holderness's cable of 3 April 1913 to Keynes at Alexandria, XV, pp. 97–8). In fact, Lord Crewe, the Secretary of State for India, who had seen the proof-sheets of the book 'thought that the character of the work and its subject were a qualification and [the] method of treating the subject [was] no bar to [his] appointment' (Austen Chamberlain, Chairman-designate in his letter of 21 April to Keynes, ibid., p. 99). Chamberlain went even further to say that Keynes should feel 'obviously at liberty to publish it forthwith' and that he as Chairman would 'not wish to interfere in any way with your judgment . . . the point would be that you should not seem to prejudge questions which you are now to judge'. Later, when the Commission had adjourned, Chamberlain, having read the book in proof form, cover to cover, was lyrical in his appreciation of it as being 'admirably lucid' and saw no difference between Keynes's and the Commission's thinking 'except possibly as to the terms in which we should write of a State Bank'. Even this latter issue, Chamberlain was 'hopeful that even if [the Commission] should lay a different stress on the importance and feasibility of this proposal in future conditions, we shall be able to agree as to what should be said about it in the present' (confidential letter to Keynes, 12 August 1913, ibid., p. 100). Equally, Chamberlain was no uncritical reader and asked why Keynes in his book thought that 'for purposes of export at times of depression the 10 rupee price would be worth less than $\frac{2}{3}$ rds of a sovereign'. This, incidentally, was a point on which more than one witness had agreed with Keynes.

It is specially noteworthy that Keynes's projected book on India currency, despite its sensitive character and controversial policy implications, acted as a strong and positive recommendation for his nomination to the Commission, and his elevation from Secretaryship to Membership. It is not often that bureaucracies and politicians take so kindly to published work by economists, much less give it official recognition! Certainly this must rank as an exceptional episode in intellectual history. Keynes was offered the membership of the Commission when all but its last chapter was in type. On his own admission, he would have delayed its publication until the Commission had reported, but in the circumstances he decided to publish immediately what had been already written without the projected additional chapters. The book, *Indian Currency and Finance*,[10] was therefore published in June 1913 as it stood and thus wholly predates the work of the Commission and its Report. Most reviewers, except for a couple of dissenting voices, acclaimed the decision to publish Keynes's *Indian Currency and Finance* and 'the appointment of one so obviously well qualified' (ibid., p. 99). Even knowledgeable witnesses before the Commission were obviously mesmerised by the book. The Secretary-Treasurer of the Bank of Bengal, when questioned about the flow of capital between India and England replied:

> 'It is all explained in Mr. Keynes's book.'
> 'What have you got to say to that?'
> 'I entirely agree with what Mr. Keynes says.'

Keynes's *Indian Currency and Finance*, although a classic which has stood the test of time as an authoritative exposition of the gold exchange standard and the highly complex Indian monetary and banking system, did not specify any criteria for domestic monetary policy. Its principal policy guideline was the maintenance of an adequate level of international reserves by India while economising the internal use of gold as a monetary metal. It also had some analytic gaps in its treatment of gold hoarding. For instance, Keynes overlooked the fact that the main cause of the increased absorption of gold by India was the greater demand for either gold ornaments or sovereigns as against silver consequent upon the artificially appreciated value of the rupee, which imposed a heavy loss on turning silver rupees into ornaments.[11] Likewise, although Keynes was concerned to forestall the mintage of gold coin in Bombay, he did not adduce any reasoning or evidence to prove that this would in itself increase the absorption of gold in India. The mint could serve as a substitute for the goldsmith or for the imported sovereign.[12]

KEYNES AS A COMMISSIONER: THE ROYAL (CHAMBERLAIN) COMMISSION ON INDIAN CURRENCY AND FINANCE, 1913

Keynes's appointment as member of the Commission, which marked his first entry into public affairs, was widely acclaimed and most of all by Alfred Marshall who was 'delighted to know the youngest member of the youngest Commission . . . almost the youngest of any [and] the right man for the place' (Marshall to Keynes, letter of 12 April, 1913 ibid., p. 98). Although the youngest member of the Commission, he was in no way overawed by his vastly senior fellow members, among whom were his old chief at the India Office, Sir Arthur Godley (now Lord Kilbracken) and Sir Robert Chalmers, who was later to be Keynes's superior at the Treasury.

The Commission's terms of reference were to study the financial organisation and procedures of the India Office; the management of the balances of the Government of India and the India Office in London; the sale of Council drafts by the Secretary of State in London; the gold standard reserve, the paper currency reserve, and the mechanism of maintaining the exchange value of the rupee. In the course of its work the Commission realised that it was not possible to ignore two proposals even though they were not part of its terms of reference: the provision of a gold mint in India and the establishment of a central or State Bank.

Keynes's examination of Lionel Abrahams and the latter's replies (Minutes of Evidence taken before the Royal Commission on Indian Finance and Currency, Vol. I cd 7068, Appendix III, paragraph 7, pp. 88–9) helped to illumine many a dark corner of the Indian gold exchange standard except for one important detail. Abrahams's response, when asked by Keynes ('whether it was not rather confusing to the public that the gold standard reserve should hold silver') was uncharacteristically obfuscating.[13] This leading question was never answered satisfactorily either in the evidence or in the subsequent Report. Among the other witnesses examined by Keynes was the Honourable Montagu de P. Webb, President of the Karachi Chamber of Commerce, and an unreconstructed champion of the back-to-the-Fowler Committee school of thought. Reportedly, his speeches and writings had played a major part in inspiring the appointment of the Chamberlain Commission. It is said that although several members of the Commission had questioned Webb rather severely, it was Keynes 'who pressed hard on arguments which did not seem to be based on solid calculations or precise information, came the nearest to discomfiting him' (CW, XV, p.110). Keynes's questions to Webb related largely to policies and procedures underlying sales of Council bills by the Secretary of State. He also questioned closely two representatives of exchange banks doing business in India, J. A. Toomey and T. Fraser, on the proposal for the establishment of a state bank in India.

The central issues facing the Commission were the relative merits of gold as currency in circulation and gold in reserve as a means, among others, of supporting the exchange value of the rupee. It is, however, hard to know from available evidence how far Keynes redrafted the 'Gold Currency in India' part of the Report, which had three subsections: 'Gold in Internal Circulation', 'Proposal Gold Mint for India' and 'Conclusions'. The Commission did not accept Keynes's redraft of 'Conclusions', and preferred to retain the original draft. Keynes's 'Conclusions' stressed the point that a gold currency was not only uneconomical as stated by the Commission, but was positively harmful. According to him,

> India does not require greater facilities for the supply of gold coins than exist at present, that the most suitable media of internal circulation in India in the immediate future are rupees and notes, and that the Government should do all they can to encourage notes, while providing – and this is the cardinal feature of the whole system – absolute security for the convertibility into sterling of so much of the internal currency as may at any moment be required for the settlement of India's external obligations (CW, XV, pp. 233–34).

Keynes had also well-reasoned views on the size, composition, and location of the gold standard reserve. He rightly hesitated to prescribe any precise size for the aggregate reserves but argued against unnecessarily high reserves, because for a country with 'such large and unsatisfied claims, as India has, for further capital development, it would be a great misfortune if more wealth were accumulated in a barren form than is absolutely necessary' (ibid., p. 236). Possibly this is one of the earliest statements of the developmental arguments against excessive accumulation of reserves, i.e., beyond the need to maintain the exchange, which later figured so prominently in the post-Second World War debate on the merits and demerits of the cent per cent foreign reserves system of the colonial Currency Boards. However, its heterodoxy also affords a paradoxical contrast to the orthodoxy of Keynes in objecting to the productive use of seigniorage and note issue profits for capital development. But the Commission, while acknowledging that the aggregate foreign reserves might grow in the future to an unnecessary size, recommended the continued accumulation of gold but with no diversion for developmental purposes.

Equally, Keynes was concerned to maximise the advantages and uses of the paper currency reserve and 'it was in the treatment of the paper currency reserve that he left his mark on the Report' (ibid., p. 237). The Indian paper currency reserve, modelled on the British system of a fixed fiduciary issue, was so low that the 'maximum available for lending had become in effect a minimum of permanent investment'. There was no free money, in the absence of a central bank, for temporary short-term loans to satisfy the periodic public demand for money in the busy season following the slack season. Theoretically, this demand could be satisfied by releasing the idle balances in the government Treasuries and this was possible only through the sale of Council bills in London. But there was no mechanism for making these funds available in India, a situation which was further aggravated by the annual movement of money through taxes and land revenue from public circulation into the Reserve Treasuries just at the time of the peak demand for credit.

Keynes was also critical of the division of India's foreign reserves into the gold standard reserve, the paper currency reserve, the reserves of the Presidency Banks, and Government balances, whereas in other countries a unified note reserve served jointly the separate purposes of all these reserves. The Commission had, at the draft stage, attempted to fix a fiduciary requirement in proportion to the net circulation (one-third), with discretionary lending from the balances, and provision for an increase of the permanent investments to Rs 20 crores through transfer of rupees from the gold standard reserve. But, in effect, the attempted flexibility was nullified by the 20 crores specification which precluded any temporary loans from the paper currency reserve until the net circulation reached a very high figure. Keynes's suggested amendment, as follows, was accepted by the Commission, which recommended: 'that the fiduciary portion of the paper currency reserve be increased at once to 20 crores . . . the maximum of the fiduciary portion should be fixed at the amount of the notes held by the Government in the Reserve Treasuries plus one-third of the net circulation [that is, gross circulation less the amount of notes held in the reserve Treasuries] for the time being . . . the invested portion of the reserve will be at once increased by a transfer (at market value) of sterling securities to that amount from the gold standard reserve in exchange for six crores of the gold now in the paper currency reserve in India. So long as the gross circulation exceeds 60 crores . . . the Government should have power not only to make further permanent investments [of the reserve] but also to make temporary investments or to grant loans either in India or London' (ibid., pp. 263–4).

These final amendments conceded Keynes's points. The stipulation 'so long as the gross circulation is above 60 crores' overcame the constraint set by the 20 crores of permanent investment and enabled the immediate commencement of temporary loans. Similarly, the criterion of 'the amount of the notes held in the Reserve Treasuries plus one-third of the net circulation' gave the necessary latitude and discretion in lending from the combined paper currency reserve and balances. Keynes had an addendum in favour of regarding the paper currency and gold standard reserves as a joint fund. His other suggestion that the India Office, if obliged to sell Consols from the gold standard reserve at a loss, should be allowed, as an alternative, to pledge them as collateral against an advance, was also accepted.

Chamberlain's draft of the Report had favoured regular purchases of silver for rupee coinage to satisfy large fluctuations in demand while, concurrently, reducing the risks in having to purchase large amounts of silver at short notice. This was deleted but it is difficult to say whether this was wholly or partly due to Keynes's criticism of the proposal in his 'Note on Purchase of Silver' (ibid., pp. 266–7) which was based on the expectation that the demand for silver would level off. In the event this expectation was upset by the abnormal absorption of silver by India during the First World War.

Keynes's personal experience of service with the India Office was also turned to productive account inasmuch as his two principal suggestions on the financial reorganisation of the India Office became a part of the Report of the Chamberlain Commission (CW, XV, p. 265). In his memorandum, dated 11 November 1913, Keynes, citing Lionel Abrahams's experience, pointed out that the Financial Secretary had become overburdened with the increase in the financial business of the India Office. His responsibilities involved important decisions and these 'required freedom from the pressure of routine work'. He therefore suggested the creation of two posts of Secretaries for the Financial Department to deal, respectively, with the routine of Treasury control and specialised technical financial affairs. Second, Keynes also opposed the proposal of the Secretary of State for India to 'replace the Finance Committee (five members of the India Council attached to the Financial Department as advisers) by a single member of Council, because it would sacrifice the different kinds of business experience offered by the individual members of the Committee'. Keynes, of course, also shrewdly noted that in the event of the proposed State Bank of India having a London office, with a London Board, the rationale for a Finance Committee would substantially disappear. These ideas show Keynes's customary concern about the need to reflect different varieties of business experience and views as inputs in official decisions in the financial sphere, as well as his insight into the implications of prospective concurrent institutional changes – aspects of Keynes which surfaced constantly in his thinking on the organisational structure of central banking for India.

Keynes was truly the moving spirit of the Chamberlain Commission. Although one of ten commissioners, he asked about one-sixth of all the questions during the hearing of witnesses. While an urbane and sympathetic questioner he could also be 'needlessly provocative', unawed by eminence and authority, as in his examination of Alfred Clayton Cole, the then Governor of the Bank of England. Doubtless, Keynes's earlier service at the India Office and his close association and friendship with Lionel Abrahams, then Assistant Under-Secretary of State for India, conferred an immeasurable advantage on Keynes inasmuch as Abrahams was not only the architect of the system under scrutiny, but was also the first and most important of all the witnesses. This in no way detracts from the range and quality of Keynes's work for the Commission whose proceedings and Report bore a heavy impress of his thought and writing. Keynes's role and influence on the Commission also received the highest possible intellectual accolade – an unusually laudatory letter from Alfred Marshall on 9 March 1914 as follows:

> But I dipped in here and there and then read the conclusions: and finally turned negligently to the Annex. But that held me. I had had no idea you had written it. Much of it, as of the Report itself, deals with matters beyond my knowledge and judgment. But there is quite enough of it within my understanding for me to have been entranced by it as a prodigy of constructive work. Verily we old men will have to hang ourselves, if young people can cut their way so straight and with such apparent ease through such great difficulties. (Ibid., p. 268)

Marshall, however, had some very perceptive comments on at least two important gaps in the Report. The first related to what Marshall regarded as the rather generous treatment of the shareholders of the Presidency Banks who seem to have 'none of the obligations of a State Bank, and yet some of its sources of profit' (ibid., p. 268). Marshall also suggested that the State Banks should consider incorporating elements of the Bank of England Parlour, as described by Bagehot, and nominate assessors from other financial authorities with perhaps the right at least for some of them to subscribe for a few shares of the bank at par. Marshall's second point was even more insightful at least by inference. Referring to his conversations with India experts in 1898 in connection with his own evidence before the Fowler Committee, Marshall hinted 'that the work of the native financiers (Banyans I fancy they were called) was not fully understood' as also 'the extent of native hoarding'. These two subjects had, of course, hardly engaged the attention of the Commission.

KEYNES AS A WITNESS: THE INDIAN EXCHANGE AND CURRENCY (BABINGTON SMITH) COMMITTEE, 1919

The Chamberlain Commission's recommendations could not be implemented because of the First World War, and the monetary situation in India underwent a dramatic change under the combined impact of British war expenditure and the export boom which together expanded the rupee circulation. India also absorbed a considerable amount of silver as a result of the favourable balance of trade, amounting in one year to almost twice the world's annual output of silver. The high international price of silver raised the cost of the rupee until the value of silver in the token rupee exceeded its face value. The exchange rate of the rupee which had been stable at 1s 4d for about twenty years rose to 1s 8d. The shortage of silver threatened the convertibility of the expanded rupee note issue but then this posed the question of what the rupee was to be convertible into, since the pound sterling itself had been delinked from the gold sovereign and turned into the Bradbury note. All these events converged to bring about the appointment of the Indian Exchange and Currency Committee, under the chairmanship of Sir Henry Babington Smith, in May 1919 to examine the working of the Indian monetary system under the new conditions and to make appropriate recommendations to maintain monetary and exchange stability. The Committee comprised, besides the Chairman, the following members: Lord Chalmers, Sir Marshall F. Reid, Sir James Brunyate, F. C. Goodenough, Sir Charles Addis, Sir Christopher Needham, Mr M. M. S. Gubbay, Sir Bernard Hunter, Mr D. M. Dalal (the only Indian member), and two secretaries (C. H. Kisch and H. Denning ICS).

Keynes's role as a witness before this Committee (Friday, 25 July 1919) is of two-fold interest. Hitherto Keynes had focused largely on issues relating to the appropriate monetary standard for India. He was now obliged to address himself to the important related issue of the appropriate level of the exchange rate of the rupee. His testimony before the Committee demonstrates his skills as an expert witness even as the Chamberlain Commission had allowed full play for display of his talents as a Commissioner. Keynes's credentials, apart from his recognised technical proficiency as a monetary economist, to be an expert witness were most impressive indeed. Following his two years at the India Office, the publication of his book on Indian Currency and Finance, and membership of the Royal Commission (Chamberlain) on Indian Currency, he had four-and-a-half years of Treasury service, where his duties largely consisted in supplying the currency to finance the needs of the Allies. During the Paris Peace Conference he acquired firsthand knowledge of the relief and reconstruction problems of war-devastated countries. In his first appearance before the Committee Keynes, with due scholarly modesty, made it clear that although he had not followed closely the developments relating to Indian exchange and currency since the date of the Chamberlain Commission he had 'followed it in a general way'.[14] The Chairman also made it clear that the Committee was not interested in historical aspects of the question and wanted Keynes to give the Committee 'the benefit of [his] opinions on questions of policy and of future development' beginning with 'the general question of the economic effects on India of different levels of value for the rupee – whether a high rupee or a low rupee is advantageous in the general interest of India' (ibid., p. 273).

Keynes's testimony related to the following broad themes: exchange value of the rupee and its impact on India's foreign trade, industrial development and general economic welfare; the Indian price level; and the role of gold and silver in the monetary system. It is particularly noteworthy that Keynes did 'not believe that in the long run the establishment of any one level [for the rupee] has any different effect from that point of view [the industrial development of India] to that of any other level . . . what is disadvantageous is *a great change of price* [emphasis provided]. If you take a view of the next twenty-five years, I do not think it matters to Indian industrial development whether the rupee is 2s or 1s' (reply to question by Mr Gubbay, ibid., p. 286). Keynes's primary concern was to avoid large movements of internal prices in India. However, given the prevailing condition of world prices (whether measured in sterling or gold) he attached 'more importance to fixing the rate at a high level than to the particular means of ensuring the stability of the level, whatever it is' and thought 'it better to fix the rupee at 2s than at 1s 8d or 1s 10d and even higher, if it is practicable' (Reply to Chairman, ibid., p. 273). The rupee was still at 1s 8d when Keynes appeared before the Committee on 25 July 1919 but had reached 2s 4d in December 1919. Keynes pinpointed the crucial issue as 'the prevention of too high a level of prices in India', 'which seems to me quite to transcend any of the other issues – which, however, are also important and must be considered by the Committee' (ibid., p. 274). Keynes viewed with apprehension any rise in internal prices in India and its social and political consequences. He believed that a high-value rupee would act as a corrective to price rises, ease the burden of the external obligations of the Government of India and also help avoid any increase in taxation. Accordingly, he suggested an exchange value of 2s for the rupee, irrespective of any movement in the price of silver in order to keep the standard of value in India more stable in relation to commodities. He favoured for historical reasons a round figure agreeable to sentiment as being 'about as high as you can go without provoking protests from various people who might feel that you were rather overdoing it if you go beyond that' (p. 277). Keynes agreed that if in the event silver rose above the parity of a 1s 8d rupee it would be necessary to move the rupee up to correspond. However, he added that it was not 'impossible to contemplate it [a rupee with a bullion value higher than its exchange value] but . . . it would be very inconvenient and anomalous' (ibid., p. 277). In such a situation, Keynes argued, there would not be a massive melting of rupees but 'a constant dribble of an irregular and illegal character' (p. 278). The world silver market could not be expected to 'absorb anything approaching the entire volume of Indian silver rupees'. If the rupee was fixed at 2s the risk of silver rising to that price could 'be neglected'. Keynes firmly believed, 'subject to the limitations of the necessity of having gold coin or silver coin in India', in 'keeping Indian prices stable in relation to commodities rather in relation to any particular metallic or particular foreign currency . . . in considering at some remote date the possibility of putting down the rupee I should be influenced by the effect it had on prices rather than by its relation to a particular metal' (p. 281). Keynes favoured fixing the rupee in relation to the gold sovereign and allowing it to fluctuate in terms of sterling so long as sterling fluctuates in terms of the gold sovereign, 'hoping that a day would come when they would come together again' (ibid., p. 281). To achieve this objective, Keynes suggested that the Government of India should accept gold in Bombay in exchange for rupees at the rate of 10 rupees to the sovereign. Under his scheme, it would always be open to the exchange banks to purchase Council drafts or to export gold to India. According to whatever was in excess of what could be obtained by Council drafts, they would purchase gold in London and export it to Bombay for exchange into rupees at the rate of 10. At the prevailing rate there was no substantial advantage in shipping gold to India as compared with buying Council drafts. The Government of India should sell on open tender Council drafts of a value equal to their requirements. Keynes did not elaborate on why he wished to confine these transactions to the exchange banks. Once the gold came into India, Keynes suggested that the Government should make it available for circulation in the usual way by coining it or selling it, say through the exchange banks who 'would sell it best' since they would obtain 'their funds as readily by selling gold in bazaars as by turning it over to the mint' (ibid., p. 283). Keynes, however, suggested alternative modes of gold sales depending on the objective. If it was not to alter the relation of the sovereign to the rupee the gold could be sold to the bazaars out of the Government resources and the Government should endeavour to maximise profits consistently with bringing down the bazaar price to parity. If, however, the sovereign–rupee relationship was sought to be changed, he saw advantages in postponing the open market sale until after the change had been made and due notice given.[15]

However, Keynes added that while he did not favour 'artificial means of preventing gold from going into circulation', he was equally concerned to 'stimulate in every possible way other means of effecting payments' so that gold is circulated in the reserves as much as possible. And when the reserves reached a satisfactory level the sales of Councils should be increased and the Government should then revert to the prewar practice of accumulating external reserves in foreign countries as against an increased fiduciary issue. The Government should not encourage a gold currency and should limit the circulation of gold to the actual demands for social purposes (in the arts, for instance), if necessary through taxing it as a luxury item like diamonds, or pearls, or silver, but definitely not by allowing a fluctuating premium as a result of controls and restrictions. If enough gold was sold to prevent the emergence of a premium, that would be a good measure of social demand for gold. Keynes, evidently a somewhat uncritical votary of sumptuary taxation, supported the taxation of gold and silver 'on the same grounds as duties on alcoholic liquors, as tending to cause economy in a wasteful habit.' Keynes mistakenly believed that the non-monetary demand for gold and silver in India reflected a demand for luxuries rater than a portfolio choice for a consumer durable which also served as a store of value in an environment of high risk and uncertainty. He overlooked that any reduction in the elastic demand for hoarding of gold and silver in India would depend more on general economic and social security and confidence than on any official measures to restrict the non-monetary use of gold or silver.

Keynes was also somewhat ambivalent on the desirable proportion of the gold reserve to the note issue. Thus, while on the one hand he expressed surprise at the alarm expressed by the Indian authorities at the prevailing figure of one-third, he also thought 'that for any other country than India I should regard one-third as very much on the safe side!' While he endorsed the policy of the Government in encouraging notes and discouraging coin, he did not 'see any special reason for not putting sovereigns into circulation' if for any reason coin had to be put into circulation. At the same time he wanted the authorities to avoid a situation of bringing about a substantial premium on coin in a particular district by reducing or suspending Government facilities for encashment into coin or by restrictions on private dispatch of coin by rail. It was highly undesirable, he thought, to have a difference of value to the public between two forms of legal tender (notes and coins) but the Government should maintain the existing deterrents to the excessive use of coins by limiting the centres of encashment or else not put sovereigns into circulation at all or only exceptionally. Keynes stressed that the shortage of silver to maintain convertibility was a 'technical difficulty' but the real danger was 'the high level of world prices extending itself to India' (p. 287). He was also opposed to reducing the silver content of the rupee because of the political and practical difficulties in a country like India with a large volume of silver coins already in circulation. It would not be practical, while minting new rupees, to call in old rupees and remint them, a process which would take years, given the large total circulation. More importantly, any step that meant more rupee circulation would be 'disastrous' for Indian prices.

As regards the mechanics of the alteration of the exchange value of the rupee from 1s 8d to 2s, an increase of 20 per cent, Keynes did not 'have any very decided opinion as to whether it should be done at one blow or gradually by steps'. In the latter event, 'the Government of

India should even be prepared to sell forward drafts at the new rate . . . put on offer drafts at different rates for a certain period of time, and ration them out.' Keynes was careful to add that it 'would be easier for practical bankers, particularly the exchange bankers, to say whether that would be more disturbing to trade than a sudden change'. However, Keynes also did not wish to appear to exaggerate the importance of the speed and mechanics of the exchange-rate adjustment of the rupee. 'These sort of changes are apt to go through very easily, more easily than people expect.' His object was to 'harmonize Indian and world prices by so fixing the rupee that world prices can be what they are now and increase still further without too great a movement on the part of Indian prices. . . . My only reservation is that I should like to examine the Indian index number of a more recent date than I have examined it at present. . . . I want a rupee which keeps prices in India as stable as possible' (ibid., p. 298).

Keynes also said that he would welcome further absorption by India of the gold dishoarded by Europe as contributing to global stability. India, according to him, was 'one of the few countries which will be in a position to afford gold and also willing to take it'. This affords a good historical example of the role of India in the global adjustment process. Keynes conceded that particular groups like exporters would lose as a result of a high-value rupee but the export trade was a very small part of the total production of the country. As against this, a high rupee would enable 'the ryot [Indian farmer] to clothe himself more cheaply, and the great mass of foodstuffs that are sold in India itself would be prevented from soaring upwards in sympathy with the comparatively small margin which is exported' (ibid., p. 289). This was the classic wage-goods argument in favour of a high exchange value of the rupee. Even with regard to exports, Keynes noted that there were redeeming factors, notably, India's monopoly of jute and its commanding position in rice and cotton textiles, which meant that export prices would not be affected whatever the exchange value of the rupee. Keynes agreed that Indian tea exports might suffer a little from the competition of Sumatra and Java in the event that the Government of the Dutch East Indies also chose to fix their exchange rate so as to stimulate their exports. The exporting interests might lose only temporarily the excess profits they might make with a lower rupee and higher prices but would gain more in the long run from the stability of prices in India and from satisfactory conditions of labour. Thus, on the whole, the burden of

Keynes's testimony was the overriding importance of insulating the Indian economy from the high world prices and preventing a further rise of Indian prices through the instrumentality of a high value for the rupee. His theme song was: 'I should always be influenced in a period of any rapid changes in world prices by the importance of maintaining prices in India as stable as possible, and I should try to adapt my currency arrangements to achieve that end from time to time' (reply to Sir Christopher Needham, ibid., p. 293).

The Babington Smith Committee, which reported in February 1920, fixed the rupee at 2s and its ratio to the gold sovereign at ten, and recommended the support of the new exchange value if necessary by the sale of Reverse Council bills. The Report also recommended, as Keynes had favoured, the repeal of the wartime Gold Import Act (which gave the Government the first claim on all imported gold) after the new ratio had been established. But the Committee recommended, against Keynes's stated views, a fixed minimum percentage of 40 per cent of the gross circulation as the statutory minimum of the metallic part of the reserve, 'an arrangement which all experience proves to be vicious in that not a single further note can be cashed without a change in the law once the cash has reached the minimum percentage. . . . A possible variant is to prescribe that no more notes shall be issued when the cash reserve has fallen below a certain percentage. This would not interfere with the encashment of notes already in circulation' (Keynes's letter of 27 December 1919 to Frank Lucas, Financial Secretary to the India Office, ibid., p. 301). However, the Report, while adhering to the 40 per cent statutory minimum, added that it would be 'desirable to keep a substantial margin of cash above the minimum, especially at the start of the busy season'. The Indian Paper Currency Amendment Act of 1 October 1920 specified that after the cash reserve had become established 'at an amount not less than 50 per cent of the circulation, the issue of any new notes raising the total circulation to more than twice the amount of the cash in reserve was prohibited'.

Keynes had, in the course of his testimony, stated: 'There is no subject on which it is more dangerous to prophesy than prices, but I see no likelihood of a sensible amelioration within five years' (reply to Sir Christopher Needham, p. 293). In perverse substantiation of Keynes's hesitations to forecast price trends, world prices dropped sharply in 1920 and the flow of gold into India had begun to be reversed. The rupee exchange rate was supported by sale of Reverse Council Bills by the Secretary of State for India by disinvesting the sterling securities in the paper currency reserve. The latter was facilitated by temporary legislation which permitted reduction in the reserve without a corresponding reduction of the currency with all its concomitant consequences. But the Government was unable to maintain the rupee rate at 2s and the exchange dropped to 1s in 1921, and rose back to 1s 4d in 1924, and 1s 6d in 1925.

ROYAL COMMISSION (HILTON YOUNG) ON INDIAN CURRENCY AND FINANCE, 1926

Once again, Keynes appeared as a witness on 22 March 1926 before the next Commission on Indian Currency with The Right Hon. Edward Hilton Young as Chairman and the following members, of whom three were Indians: Sir Rajinderanath Mookerjee and Sir Purshotamdas Thakurdas (prominent businessmen from, respectively, Calcutta and Bombay), Professor J. C. Coyajee, a prominent economist, and a pupil of Marshall at Cambridge. The English members were Sir Northcote Hastings Yeeles Warren; Sir Reginald Mant; Sir Henry Strakosch; Sir Alexander Robertson Murray; and Mr William Edward Preston. But on this occasion Keynes's oral testimony was preceded by a most cogent written memorandum which saw no advantages in a gold currency over a gold exchange standard except the political advantage of placating Indian opinion and which argued that the stability of internal prices in India was much more important than stability of foreign exchanges. 'Moreover, the gold exchange standard, whilst open to most of the objections against a pure gold standard, does at any rate secure most of the advantages, such as they are, as economically as possible without a waste of resources; the Royal Commission would do well to do nothing whatever . . . the present situation in India is the best possible . . . there is . . . reasonable stability of the exchanges, and India maintains her freedom in the event of future happenings rendering any alternative course more desirable' (ibid., p. 491) (CW, XV, p. 479). Keynes also based this judgement on the view that 'currency history of India for the last 15 years or so is more favourable than that of any other country in the world' (ibid., p. 493). Keynes thought that the only solid argument in favour of a gold currency was the likelihood of bringing gold out of hoards but, equally, it might have the opposite effect 'in that gold would be a little easier to obtain then otherwise'. By far the most important point made by Keynes in his evidence was: 'The notion that gold standards work by themselves without interference by the authorities is a myth' (CW, XV, p. 492). An element of discretionary control was not only unavoidable but even desirable and in the Indian system it was provided by the policy of the Secretary of State in buying and selling Council bills, and by the ability and willingness of the banking authorities in increasing or diminishing the rate of discount and basis of credit. Furthermore, Keynes reaffirmed what he had advocated before the Chamberlain Commission; namely, the establishment of a state (central) bank for India for better control of Indian currency and credit, including the assumption of the paper currency reserve.

Keynes, however, was more concerned about centralisation than unification *per se* and did not see any great advantage in the unification of the paper currency and gold reserve which were held for separate purposes, viz., to meet the internal and external drain, respectively. In his replies to Sir Purshotamdas Thakurdas (Question 13002) Keynes reaffirmed that 'he would not have her [India] allow the question of the rate of exchange to overbear every other object, but . . . she should maintain the liberty to have a different exchange from the present one if the maintenance of the present exchange would cause internal prices either to rise or fall to a marked extent' (CW XIX, Part II, p. 496). The sterling exchange should be regulated so that the cultivator would continue to get more or less a steady and constant return in rupees, with recourse to devices like export duties in boom times.

Keynes was also pleased to note the steady popularisation of paper currency in India. He thought that 'Indian opinion has a feeling that gold currency is, so to speak, the smartest sort of currency; it is the most chic thing and that India is, by some malicious contrivance, being deprived of this outfit.' In reply to a question from Sir Purshotamdas Thakurdas (13042) Keynes said: 'I have read a great many pamphlets and memoranda and books on this matter, and that is the impression which that reading makes on me' (CW, XIX, p. 502). Evidently, Keynes had kept up his old India Office habits of reading Indian newspapers and literature. But he recognised India had a legitimate and substantial interest in the stability of silver given its importance as a store of value in the economy. On the other hand, he cautioned against regarding the demand for silver as so inveterate that no matter how far silver falls the more it will be bought. He refuted the hoary maxim that 'people are conservative in matters of money' and remarked how it was 'most astonishing to see, the way in which the public will rapidly adapt themselves to a new situation in currency matters'. He cited the experience of Egypt which was always represented as the one country which would never handle anything but hard metal; in fact 'there was no country in which paper currency was introduced more easily during the war period than Egypt' (ibid., p. 489).

Keynes estimated that the gold required to introduce a gold currency in India would be roughly three times the value realised for her silver. This he thought, was 'a foolish and dangerous proposition to spend some £67 million in destroying the purchasing power of the favourite store of value of the mass of the population' (ibid., p. 490).

The Hilton Young Commission's report submitted in July 1926 recommended: an exchange rate of 1s 6d for the rupee on the grounds that prices in India had adjusted substantially in relation to world prices; the creation of a gold bullion standard wherein gold would not circulate as currency, but the currency authority would be under an obligation to buy and sell gold without limit in quantities of not less than 400 fine ounces at rates determined with reference to a fixed gold parity of the rupee; amalgamation of the paper currency and the gold standard reserves; and the creation of a central bank. There was, predictably, a strong minute of dissent by Sir Purshotamdas Thakurdas, one of the two Indian members of the Commission, which, among others, advocated a ratio of 1s 4d against what was regarded as the artificial appreciation of the rupee to 1s 6d. The Government of India accepted the Commission's recommendations, and the Currency Act of March 1927 established what may be described as a gold-bullion-cum-sterling currency. Keynes, understandably peeved by all this, wrote in high dudgeon to C. H. Kisch of the India Office: 'the Commission . . . have introduced into their recommendations an unnecessary amount of make-believe. The gold bullion business is mostly make-believe. So is the attempt to hand over the central bank to the control of private individuals. At least if the latter is not make-believe it is undesirable and dangerous' (letter of 22 December 1926, *Keynes Papers*, King's College).

But it was the recommendation of a 1s 6d ratio for the rupee as against the 1s 4d ratio which excited Indian public opinion more than the question of the currency standard and led to the historic ratio controversy in the following period (1927–39). The 1s 6d rate appeared viable, at least for the first three years, because of a substantial favourable balance of trade, but thereafter the steep fall in the prices of India's agricultural exports following the onset of the world economic depression in 1930 put a severe strain on the foreign exchanges. Following the British government's decision to abandon the gold standard, the rupee was officially linked to sterling as from 24 September 1931. The unchanged rupee–sterling ratio implied a depreciation of the rupee, too, in terms of gold and, consequently, a rise in the price of gold in terms of rupees. The price of gold in the Bombay market rose from around Rs 21–4 per tola (= 11.6638g) in August 1931 to Rs 36–12 in April 1935. But on the basis of the exchange rate of the rupee being around 1s 6d, the price of gold in India was consistently lower than the price abroad, which therefore made it profitable to export gold. This consequently led to massive exports of gold, which in the ten years ended March 1941, amounted to 43 million ounces valued at Rs 3750 million, or an average price of Rs 3–12 per tola. The real nature of these gold exports, which marked a dramatic reversal of India's historic role as a perennial sink for precious metals from the West, was hotly disputed. Keynes called this a 'great and extraordinary event in the monetary history of the world' noting that 'the discount of sterling in terms of gold . . . had almost solved the financial problem of the Government [of India]', by means of 'the export of gold previously hoarded'.[16] The higher value of India's exports in terms of depreciated sterling made it so much easier to meet the Government's sterling obligations. Keynes added that India by exporting gold (L 80 million) had 'rehabilitated her finances and purchasing power' and 'is politically easier in her mind'.[17] The official view was that, allowing for a certain proportion of distress sales, the bulk represented profit realisations on an asset hoarded for capital appreciation. Indian opinion, however, was inclined to regard them as mostly distress sales, whose proceeds should have been absorbed by government to augment the country's metallic reserves. Keynes's assessment of Indian gold exports in the early thirties is well conveyed in the following letter to Malcolm Darling, ICS:

> I was vaguely aware that the selling of gold had started on a moderate scale before we went off gold. But it was surely on an altogether different scale from September onwards. The large scale shipments synchronised very closely. Do you believe that India's exports of gold would have reached anything approximating 50 million sterling if the rupee had remained at its old parity with the metal? I agree, however, that probably in speaking of the phenomenon one ought to describe it as a combination of the premium on

gold and impecuniosity of the producers. (*Malcolm Darling Papers*, Box XIVA, Centre of South Asian Studies, Cambridge)

Privately, Keynes saw no objection to a tax on export of gold and believed that if Sir George Schuster (Finance Member) had anticipated the volume of gold export 'he would perhaps have imposed one'. However, the export was so valuable to Government that 'he probably did not wish to do anything to discourage'.[18] Conceding Keynes's argument, Indian gold would have remained in private hoards if the old parity had been maintained. But then, Keynes never at any time really addressed the question of how to mobilise the massive private hoards of precious metals in India.

Keynes was as 'surprised at the weakness of the Rupee [c 1927]' as Sir Basil Blackett, the Finance Member of the Viceroy's Executive Council, but was more inclined to attribute it not so much to the factors affecting the visible balance of trade, such as the low price of jute exports, and the importation of cotton from America, to the capital movements and speculation against the rupee in the period of uncertainty regarding the ratio.[19]

Although Keynes was not directly involved with Indian matters in the thirties, his counsel was eagerly sought by high-ranking officials of the Government of India, like Sir George Schuster, the Finance Member of the Viceroy's Executive Council, in the context of 'the Indian demand for the return to 1s 4d ratio' which 'had passed far beyond the Bombay agitators and went right through the country with the strength of a religious belief'.[20] Schuster was under constant pressure from the India Office to enforce a tough financial policy, including raising the Bank Rate to high levels, but he resisted this pressure because he thought that 'the methods proposed would be ineffective in the conditions of the Indian money market and would merely increase hostility to British policy'. (Schuster, ibid., p. 100). Schuster, in addition to seeking the advice of Sir Otto Niemeyer, who had moved from the Treasury to the Bank of England as Chief Adviser to the Governor, and Sir Henry Strakosch of the Secretary of State for India Council, was 'constantly in touch with Keynes and had his unqualified support in his controversy with the India office about monetary policy' (Schuster, ibid., p. 125). But Keynes's general support for the Indian viewpoint on the rupee ratio, although never made public, is evident from the following communication to the author from Mr. L. K. Jha, a distinguished Indian civil servant and ex-Governor of the Reserve Bank of India:

I was trying to locate in my old papers copies of letters I had exchanged with Keynes on the subject of the par value of the Indian rupee to which you refer as the King Charles's head of Indian economic thinking. Unfortunately, I have not been successful in finding the papers which are nearly half a century old. . . . Therefore, what follows is based mainly on memory . . . soon after I returned to India as a member of the ICS, an article appeared in the *Economic Journal* saying in the light of the experience of the 30s, the judgement to maintain the rupee/sterling ratio at 1 shilling 6 pence had been proved to be sound. The article had been written by Thomas [an Indian economist], who was Economic Adviser to the Government of India. Though I myself was serving as a Sub Divisional Officer in Bihar, I wrote a rejoinder to that article arguing that the trend in commodity prices and India's foreign trade vindicated the stand of people like Sir Purushottam Das Thakurdas, who . . . wanted the ratio to be 1 shilling 4 pence. At that time, Keynes was the editor of the *Economic Journal*. Imagine my thrill at getting a letter from Keynes himself saying that he wants to publish my article not as a rejoinder to Thomas, because it would then mean his giving further chance to Thomas to defend his thesis, but rather as an original piece. He thought that the points I had made had greater validity than those which Thomas had advanced. . . . I had said that since I was a civil servant and advancing a view point which was contrary to the official government view on the subject, the article should be published without my name. Keynes pointed out that the *Economic Journal* never carried an article without revealing the writer's identity. So, he asked me to get the permission of the authorities to get the article published over my signature. When I asked the Chief Secretary of the Bihar Government for the requisite permission, he pointed out that only a few days before, the Viceroy addressing the annual meeting of the Associated Chambers of Commerce in Calcutta, had spoken of the wisdom of preserving the exchange rate at 1 shilling 6 pence and indicated that no change was under contemplation. The Chief Secretary took the view that in the circumstances, I had better not seek formal approval to the publication of the article since permission was bound to be refused. That is where the matter rested. The only point of relevance . . . which comes out . . . was that perhaps Keynes was sympathetic to the India view-point regarding the par value of the rupee.

Interestingly, this interpretation by Jha is also confirmed by Malcolm Darling, who has recounted that Keynes was 'inclined to think that a $\frac{1}{4}$ penny rupee would suit India better at the same time he did not hold this view sufficiently strongly to think it worthwhile to state it. The maintenance of the rupee $\frac{1}{6}$ was, he thought, due as much to the high moral attitude of the Governor of the Bank of England as to anything else. The latter saw in depreciation a repudiation of contract which to him was immoral. He [Keynes] did not think that the ratio had been affected in any other way by international finance.'[21]

This was perhaps the very last occasion on which Keynes touched upon the question of the exchange rate of the rupee. In retrospect, it is significant that Keynes attached far less importance to the historic rupee ratio controversy, if at all, than he did to what he thought was the more basic issue of the appropriate monetary standard for India. This reflected his deep-seated conviction that given the nature and size of the Indian economy with its low ratio of foreign trade and payments to GNP, to use a latter-day terminology, and its semi-monopolistic position in many export items like jute, tea, textiles, and so on, the exchange rate of the rupee was economically not as significant a policy variable as ensuring a fair rate of return for primary producers in India, although the two were not unconnected. Keynes was more concerned about the real income and protection of the real value of savings of the Indian *ryot* (farmer) than the profits of exporters.

ROLE OF GOLD IN THE INDIAN ECONOMY

In examining the merits and feasibility of gold exchange standard for India, Keynes was naturally led on to analysing the overall role of gold, both as bullion and sovereigns, in the Indian economy. From time immemorial India has been regarded as the sink of the precious metals, to use the oft-quoted phrase of Stanley Jevons, and its economic history affords the classic example of the continual large-scale competition for gold and silver between the rival claims of hoarding, circulation, the mint, the melting-pot and exports. Keynes's analysis of gold distinguished throughout between the effects of gold-hoarding on India's internal economy and its impact on the world economy. Although Keynes reverted off and on to the theme of the role of gold in India, his earliest analyses of this problem are of interest as also being the most systematic, and merit close examination.[22]

Although Keynes was fully mindful of the role of silver as a store of value and medium of exchange in the rupee coinage and as ornaments and jewellery, he was more concerned with gold in view of its greater importance as a monetary metal in India and as a store of value in the context of the discussions of gold currency and the gold standard. There was also the consideration that 'the taste of India for gold, as against silver has been very considerably developed during the last ten years' [1903–13] (CW, Vol. I, p. 53). As always, Keynes sought a reasonably secure statistical and data base for his analysis; and his acute observations on the role of gold in the Indian economy are based on a very diligent sifting and evaluation of official statistics relating to gold in the annual reports of the comptroller general of paper currency for 1910–11 (written by R.W. Gillam) and for 1911–12 (by D. M. F. Gauntlett). (See Table 4.2).

Keynes remarked that the annual net addition to the stock of gold in India (that is, imports and production less exports) as given in the first column, usually neglected the steady leakage of gold from India across the land frontiers, particularly as India was the main source of supply of gold for Central Asia. Given the distribution of the addition to gold stock, between sovereigns and gold bars, and making allowance for the increase or decrease of sovereigns in the paper currency and the government treasuries, Keynes estimated the net annual additions to sovereigns in the hands of the public (column 5) but added that as to 'the uses to which the public put the sovereigns our information is exceedingly vague and unprecise' (ibid., p. 53). It was therefore, according to him, difficult to say what part of this total was used for 'hoarding, for ornamentation, for melting and what part was therefore left truly to serve as currency' (ibid., p. 54). This in many respects was the crux of the question: to determine the true monetary demand for sovereigns. It was estimated that about a million 'shield' sovereigns were imported annually. These were in great demand as ornaments and were usually quoted at a premium, and a considerable number of sovereigns were also melted every year to be used as bullion because for certain purposes the sovereign was cheaper and more convenient than the same quantity of gold. For instance, if a jeweller wanted only a small quantity of gold, a full-weight sovereign met his purpose very well with its known exact weight, fineness, and value, and easy availability whereas the smaller

Table 4.2 Net Additions to Gold Stock in India 1901–13

	(1) = (2) + (3) *Net addition to stock of gold: imports-exports and production*	(2) *Net addition to gold in paper currency reserve and treasuries*[1]	(3) = (4) + (5) *Net addition to stock of gold in hands of public*	(4) *Net addition to bullion in hands of public*	(5) *Net addition to sovereigns in hands of public*
			In thousands of pounds		
1901–2	3 223	−5	3 228	2 261	967
1902–3	7 882	2 870	5 012	2 814	2 198
1903–4	8 963	944	8 019	4 741	3 278
1904–5	8 841	38	8 803	5 866	2 937
1905–6	2 698	−6 840	9 538	5 806	3 732
1906–7	12 061	−193	12 254	7 098	5 156
1907–8	13 677	−993	14 670	7 243	7 427
1908–9	5 022	−2 843	7 865	4 422	3 443
1909–10	16 620	6 347	10 273	7 407	2 866
1910–11	18 153	71	18 082	9 991	8 091
1911–12	27 345	9 347	17 998	9 117	8 881
1912–13[2]	24 551	4 231	20 320	9 320	11 000

Source: Reports of Comptroller General of Currency, India, reprinted in *Collected Writings*, Vol. I, p. 54.

[1] Since 1908 the whole of this has been held in sovereigns.

[2] Estimate.

gold bars manufactured in England were sold in 5-and-10-ounce bars. Thus for many non-currency purposes sovereigns were as good as other forms of bullion, and, consequently for these purposes the Indian treasury served as the bullion dealers' cheapest source of supply when the exchange was relatively low[23] (ibid., p. 69). Generally it would seem, judging by the negligible receipts of sovereigns at post offices and railways (see Table 4.3), the most common and profitable employment of the sovereigns was as bullion. The use of sovereigns as currency was chiefly confined to the United Provinces, the Punjab, Madras, and Bombay, whereas it was negligible in Assam, Bengal, Burma and the Central Provinces. To advocates of more gold coins for India, Keynes's reply was that it would be extravagant and wasteful to have gold coins as the actual media of circulation through devices such as minting of distinctively Indian

Table 4.3 Receipts of sovereigns at post offices and railways (*in thousands of pounds*)

	Post offices	*Railways*
1906–7 (2nd half-year)	553	468
1907–8	1 358	1 045
1908–9	1 001	710
1909–10	265	134
1910–11	638	597
1911–12	1 363	1 222

Source: Reports of the Comptroller General of Paper Currency, cited by Keynes, *Collected Writings*, Vol. 1, p. 52.

sovereigns of 10 rupees denomination at Bombay and then forcing them into circulation even to the extent of refusing to issue more rupees on demand. This would only serve to diminish not increase the stability of the currency system as a whole. Keynes made some unusually perceptive but candid observations on the undesirability of a gold mint in Bombay to issue a distinctively Indian 10-rupee gold coin (12s 4d).[24]

Keynes also referred to the heavy potential loss and expense of a gold currency for India by having to forgo the profits of increased use of paper currency, rupee coins and the interest on the invested portion of paper currency reserve. During the period 1900–12 the Government had accumulated about £21 million from the profits of the rupee coinage and the interest on the invested portion of the paper currency was running at about £300 000 annually. The annual income from the interest on the resources released by the use of cheaper forms of currency amounted to about £1 million, which could be expected to increase steadily in the future with the increasing use of notes.

Keynes also pointed out that the greater infusion of more gold into the circulation would not necessarily reduce the amount of reserves which ought in prudence to be kept because in times of crisis there was a greater probability that the bankers and the public would keep as much of their surplus currency balances as possible in the form of gold and it would be in large part the surplus currency and not gold that would be paid into the government treasuries. Thus, if it became necessary to contract currency, the authorities would be in a worse position unless the larger part of 'what was withdrawn came from the gold portion of the circulation and not from the rupee or paper portion' (ibid., p. 64). This was not 'an expectation upon which it would be prudent to act' (p. 64).

Furthermore, from the point of view of the country as a whole, it was more efficient and economical to centralise gold reserves in the hands of the authorities than to have a larger amount of gold coins in circulation in the hands of the public. There was therefore a strong macroeconomic argument in favour of centralisation of gold reserves in India on the basis of the argument, first presented, as Keynes was never tired of reminding, by Lord Goschen. Such centralisation would also be helpful from the point of view of maintaining stability in a country like India with its pronounced variations, seasonal, cyclical, and annual, of currency circulation.[25]

The greater part of the Indian currency circulation, argued Keynes, must continue to consist of rupees for reasons of convenience, economy, elasticity and stability. For large payments the sovereign was a rival to the note but 'for small payments which in India make in the aggregate an enormous total, the sovereign can no more supplement the rupee than it can supplement the shilling in England' (ibid, p. 66). More importantly, in a country where cheques were not likely for many years to be used to a dominating extent, the only feasible means of ensuring the required degree of seasonal elasticity was the currency.

Keynes also identified a minor indirect but undesirable effect of the contemporary arrangements insofar as it allowed Indian bullion dealers in the summer months to obtain their gold 'at the government's cost slightly cheaper than they otherwise could' (ibid., p. 69). He noted that the small English-manufactured gold bars, so popular with Indian purchasers of bullion, were worth more than an equivalent weight of sovereigns and they were consequently imported throughout the year. In the summer the bullion dealers always drew their supplies from the Treasury, so long as the Treasury was willing to supply them. Whenever, therefore, gold was available to the public in India, the Government stood to lose during the summer whatever the amount the bullion dealers required. 'On every sovereign thus drawn out, the Government loses about $1\frac{1}{2}$d. For the gold could have been kept in England by selling bills at a rate more advantageous than the par of exchange by about this amount. The annual amount which is drawn out by bullion dealers when gold is available all the year round is probably not less than £2 000 000' (p. 69).

Keynes repeatedly stressed that India 'already wastes far too high a proportion of her resources in the needless accumulation of the precious metals' and 'the government ought not to encourage in the slightest degree this ingrained fondness for handling hard gold. By elimination of both precious metals, to the utmost extent that public opinion will permit, from amongst the hoards and the circulation of the country, they ought to counteract an uncivilised and wasteful habit' (p. 70). It will be noted that Keynes, although mindful of the economic waste of the hoarding of precious metals, duly qualified his economic analysis by the need to respect the limits of Indian public opinion. This may perhaps explain partly why Keynes did not address the problems of mobilisation of gold hoards. However, he was equally perceptive in recognising that 'India's love of the precious metals, though it has been to her own economic development, has flourished in the past to the great advantage of western nations' (p. 70) by absorbing their surplus and insulating Europe from the more violent disturbances to her price level. Interestingly, Keynes envisioned futuristic scenarios involving a reversal of roles. If India disgorged even a part of her hoards of gold at a time of substantial new production 'she may involve the world, nevertheless, in a very great inflation of world prices. If, however, India is thus to turn the tables in the West, she must not delay too long. The time may not be far distant when Europe, having projected her mechanism of exchange on the basis of a gold standard, will find it possible to regulate her standard of value on a more rational and stable basis. It is not likely that we shall leave permanently the most intimate adjustment of our economic organisation at the mercy of a lucky prospector, a new chemical process, or a change of ideas in Asia.' Although the monetary standards of the world are no longer at the mercy of the vicissitudes of the gold mining industry, there has been still no change of ideas on gold in Asia. The barbarous relic of gold-hoarding still exercises its sway despite the accepted use and value of gold as an international reserve asset.

PROBLEMS OF MONEY SUPPLY: THE INDIAN MONETARY SYSTEM

Keynes's concerns with Indian monetary problems did not end with questions relating to the monetary standard or the appropriate rupee ratio. They extended to the other minutiae of the monetary system, particularly rupee coinage, the development of the paper currency, and the important policy issue of ensuring the necessary degree of seasonal elasticity in the currency, an important consideration in a economy susceptible to climatic and other variations of economic activity. He regarded the Indian monetary system as complex, yet 'an exceedingly coherent one', but its very complexity and coherence required the 'constant attention of anyone who would criticise the parts' (ibid., p. 181). But Keynes, who never lost his sense of proportion and perspective, was also quick to note that this was not 'a peculiarity of Indian finance' but 'the characteristic of all monetary problems' which also gives rise to the difficulty of the subject (p. 182). Consequently, Keynes was led on to analyse and prescribe for the monetary problems of India in terms of the interdependent policy criteria of stability, and confidence, economy, convenience and elasticity.

Keynes thought that the rupee ('virtually a note printed on silver'), although convenient for small payments, was extravagant because 'when rupees are issued, the government instead of being able to place to reserve the whole nominal value of the coin' was 'able to return only the difference between the nominal value and the cost of the silver'. He estimated the average rate of profit on coinage of rupees from 1910–May 1912 at about the 42 per cent of the nominal value. Keynes argued that notes, being cheaper than rupee coin, and being better suited to ensure adequate elasticity in the seasonal supply of currency, it was important to popularise notes to the utmost extent possible, particularly for large payments.

Keynes, in keeping with his characteristic approach of 'analyse, quantify, and prescribe' always first attempted to estimate the orders of magnitude of the relevant variables before making any policy recommendation. It was his typical stance of judicious rather than casual empiricism. In order to estimate the demand for reserves necessary to support the currency, Keynes was led to estimate the existing volume of currency which 'sets or suggests, a limit to the maximum amount which can possibly be spared from active circulation'. Keynes's concern was to estimate the total currency in the hands of the public (that is, of rupee coins or notes, or the whole circulation not in the hands of the government, but including that in the hands of the banks). Strictly, Keynes should have excluded the balances with the banks since they include the cash base for multiple creation of credit, and their lumping with the balances of the non-bank public amounted to double counting. But in extenuation it could be argued that Keynes's concern was not so much with the classic problem of money supply with the public but of estimating the total circulation of notes and coins and the requisite amount of reserves to sustain them. Keynes's estimates of the total currency at the end of each financial year (31 March) are a brilliant demonstration of statistical skills in synthesising and improving upon existing official estimates of currency circulation derived from the annual rupee census (operative since 1875) and the reports of two comptrollers of the currency department (Mr Harrison and Mr Adie) as well as those of an independent statistician (Mr Atkinson). These are discussed in detail in *Indian Currency and Finance* (op. cit., pp. 105–10). The annual census of rupees was based on examination of a bag of Rs 2000 in each government treasury. The census data enabled F. C. Harrison's application of Professor Stanley Jevons's method based on the assumptions that the proportions of coins issued at different dates found in the given samples correspond to their proportions in the circulation at large; that the proportions of rupees of each date in the bag examined in government treasuries are a fair sample of the proportions still in circulation. Keynes was also quick to notice the probable sampling errors due to the likelihood of the coins returned to the treasuries being a sample rather of the 'floating surplus of coinage with a relatively high velocity of circulation, than of the total stock which includes semi-hoards passing from hand to hand comparatively seldom' (p. 106). Insofar as these samples contained an undue proportion of recently-issued coins, any estimates of the total circulation based on them were more likely to 'fall short of the truth than exceed it'. There were also the administrative lapses of not examining samples conscientiously. ('A tendency was noticed for the returns of one year to resemble those of the previous year more closely than they should, and not infrequently would be attributed to a year in which it is known that more were minted'; ibid., p. 107). Atkinson's calculations (*Statistical Journal*, March 1897 and March 1903) excluded rupees in hoards, currency reserves and government balances. Assuming a base public circulation of 120 cores of rupees in 1900 (excluding rupees in the currency reserves and government balances), which was near to Harrison's estimate, Keynes worked out the annual (financial year April 1–March 31) estimates of currency for the period 1900 to 1912.

Having made the estimates Keynes was equally scrupulous in stressing their limitations, notably that they made no allowance for wastage of rupees through loss and other causes and, more importantly, for the steady and sizeable drain of rupees across the land frontiers of India which was not adequately accounted for in the trade returns. The unrecorded statistics of India's overland trade showed a large annual balance against India which Keynes suspected was probably financed by an unrecorded export of gold, silver, bullion, and rupees. The official statistics of the export of treasure, Keynes also noted, did not tally with the known fact of the circulation of rupees beyond the Indian frontiers. Keynes placed the total wastage of rupees from circulation for the period 1900–1912 at Rs 41 lakhs and the total public rupee and note circulation together at not more than Rs 250 crores.

The question which then engaged Keynes was: How much of this could possibly be spared from circulation? He estimated that the government was not likely to be called on to redeem more than a quarter of the total circulation (notes and rupee coins) – that is, about Rs 60 crores (£40 million). He was firmly of the view that it 'would be extravagant to maintain a reserve adequate for all conceivable emergencies' since it would always be open to the Secretary of State for India to borrow through issue of India bills. Keynes's argument was that any conceivable rate of interest on government borrowing would be much less than the expense of maintaining an uneconomically large reserve against unlikely emergencies. He cited that the Government of India had in fact contemplated the possibility of borrowing in 1899, if necessary, to maintain the currency reserve (dispatch of 24 August 1913, p. 13, cited by Keynes, CW, I, p. 111). He added that 'few countries have so good a market for their loans at a foreign centre as India' (CW, I, p. 120).

More importantly, Keynes was firmly of the view that India's reserves policy should not be geared exclusively to the requirements of the domestic currency circulation. While conceding that the proportion of reserves ought to grow, *pari passu* with the note and rupee circulation, it would be extravagant to hold much more than £40 million of total reserves considering that the option of external borrowing was always available to make up for any shortfall in reserves. Keynes was emphatic that for a country such as India, 'where all available resources are required for capital expansion', it was 'not sound or humane policy to burden the present as much for the sake of the future' and it was 'nearly as important to avoid extravagance in the reserve policy as to avoid parsimony' (CW, I, p. 120). However, he added the sagacious caveat that India's foreign reserves should be allowed to reach some such figure as £40 million by the 'natural processes of growth, before sums are diverted from them to other purposes'. He was clearly averse to any mechanistic approach to reserve management and appreciated the spontaneity and inevitability of gradualness no less than the merits of judicious and purposive management. Altogether Keynes gave a cogent rationale for an optimal reserves management policy for a poor developing country like India, which was far in advance of historical or contemporary discussions of the issue. Keynes recognised that the size of India's reserves must be comfortably large, firstly, to cope with climatic fluctuations in her trade and prosperity; secondly, because a large amount of short-term foreign capital is held in India against which India does not hold any appreciable amount of easily realisable international securities.

Keynes was very critical of the illogical fragmentation of the Government of India's reserves into several segments, which was an outcome of purely historical origins. The sterling reserves were divided into (a) gold (currency reserve in India and London); (b) money at short notice (gold standard reserves and cash balances in London); (c) sterling securities (in currency reserve and gold standard reserve). Keynes did not see any economic advantages in keeping gold in India which involved a direct monetary loss through the costs of originally shipping the gold to India and of later shipping it back to London if required to support the exchange. Keynes regarded it as a manifestation of misplaced economic nationalism and primitive prejudice which was not necessarily peculiar to India. Gold reserves were meant to be used for the discharge of pressing obligations. Their location was less important than the assurance that they were readily available for international commitments. But he realised that Indian public opinion, however ill-founded, viewed with suspicion the holding of the bulk of India's gold reserve in London and also the costs of keeping gold in India was not great in relation to its perceived advantages. It might, he thought, even be worth the expense to 'avoid the currency system falling under a suspicion' (ibid, p. 123). He suggested as a possible satisfactory compromise to hold the gold in the gold standard reserve as 'earmarked' at the Bank of England and to retain the gold in the currency reserve in India.

Keynes was wholly supportive of Indian criticism of the policy of holding large cash balances in London and lending them out in the London market. He favoured the use of surplus funds in the paper currency reserve to provide elasticity in the busy season supply of currency in India through advances (in note or rupees) at a fairly high rate of interest for periods not exceeding three months so that the government regained possession of their funds and reduced the advances to nil in each stock season. However, Keynes rightly pointed out that the Indian money market could not expect very much assistance from the government cash balances and should therefore rely more on the paper currency reserves for the requisite elasticity in the money supply in the busy season which would also take into account the seasonality of government revenue collections.

The most serious defect of the Indian currency system, according to Keynes, was its absolute internal inelasticity since there was no method by which currency could be expanded by some domestic credit mechanism to meet the regular recurrent seasonal demand for credit, like credit creation by banks in cheque-using countries or by central bank discount of domestic bills of exchange. The only way to expand currency was through import of sovereigns or purchase of Council bills in London which also explained the exceptionally high rates of discount in India during the busy season.

Keynes was equally concerned to reform and rationalise the paper currency system in India which comprised seven 'currency circles' (offices of issue) corresponding roughly to the principal provinces of India: Calcutta (Bengal and Assam); Cawnpore (the United Provinces); Lahore (the Punjab and North-West Frontier Province); Madras (the Madras Presidency and Coorg); Bombay (Bombay and the Central Provinces); Karachi (Sind); and Rangoon (Burma). He noted that successive changes consolidated in the Act of 1910, particularly the universalisation of high denomination notes (Rs 50 and Rs 100), had rendered the old system of circles virtually inoperative and irrelevant. Consequently, he favoured the abolition of the 'circles of issue' in name and effect, as these did not serve any useful purpose and only hindered public acceptance of universal legal tender character of all paper currency throughout the country. Somewhat perversely, along with the universalisation of higher denomination notes, the Government had stopped the receipt of such notes in circles other than the circle of issue in payments to the government, railways, post and telegraph offices. Just as coinage was based on a unified system, so also the paper currency merited a unitary system of issue and redemption as a necessary step in the development of India as a single currency area and the promotion of the use of paper currency.

Keynes was also severely critical of the needlessly restrictive manner of keeping the reserves against the rupee note issue in blind imitation of the rules governing the Bank of England's note issue, whereby apart from the portion which is permanently invested, the balance was required to be kept in gold and silver. Instead, Keynes suggested that the note-issuing banks of Europe afforded a better model than the Bank of England. Accordingly, he proposed to prescribe by law the holding of a certain proportion of the reserve against the note issue (say one-third or a proper proportion depending upon the policy in regard to the gold standard reserve) in gold and silver, with a further amount held, as at present, permanently in Government of India securities (CW, I, p. 135). He thought that the government should permit itself much greater latitude to lend out the balance on suitable security either in London or India for periods not exceeding three months to cope with busy-season demands.

Keynes's overall assessment of the Indian monetary system was that on the whole it met the requirements of stability and economy, but that it suffered from fragmentation of reserves and the lack of adequate elasticity in the seasonal supply of currency. All this pointed to the creation of a central bank in India. As he put it, 'the objections to the existing arrangements largely arise, therefore, out of the absence of a state bank! India ought to have a state bank, associated in a greater or less degree with the government' (CW, I, p. 41). The latter qualification is particularly noteworthy, as will be shown in the subsequent chapters, in as much as Keynes was consistent in his advocacy of a government-owned central bank for India.

Notes

1. For elaboration of this line of thought, see A. G. Chandavarkar, 'Money and Credit, 1858–1947', *The Cambridge Economic History of India*, Vol. 2: *c.*1757–*c.*1970, Chapter IX, (ed.) Dharma Kumar (Cambridge University Press, 1983), pp. 762–63.
2. 'Recent Economic Events in India' (*Economic Journal*, March 1909) reprinted in *The Collected Writings of John Maynard Keynes*, Vol. XI, *Economic Articles and Correspondence*, (ed.) Donald Moggridge (Macmillan, London, 1983), p. 1.
3. Review of M. de P. Webb, *The Rupee Problem, A Plea for A Definite Currency Policy for India* (Karachi, 1910). (From *Economic Journal*, September 1910), reprinted in *Collected Writings*, Vol. XI, pp. 23–4.
4. Review of G. Findlay Shirras, *Indian Finance and Banking*, Third

impression (Macmillan, London 1920) in *Economic Journal*, September 1920, in *Collected Writings*, Vol. XI, pp. 40–42.

5. *Economic Journal*, March 1923, Vol. XI, pp. 42–4.
6. *The Collected Writings of John Maynard Keynes*, Vol. XV, Activities 1906–14, India and Cambridge, (ed.) Elizabeth Johnson (Macmillan, London, 1971), p. 38.
7. F. A. Hayek, 'The London School of Economics, 1895–1945', *Economica*, New Series, Vol. XIII, No. 49, February 1946, p. 17.
8. *The Collected Writings of John Maynard Keynes*, Vol. I, *Indian* Currency and Finance (Macmillan, London 1971) [first edition 1913], p. 23.
9. *Collected Writings*, Vol. XV, p. 88.
10. *The Collected Writings of John Maynard Keynes*, Vol. I, Indian Currency and Finance, op. cit.
11. 'These are points which Mr. Keynes may have omitted for purposes of compression; but they deserve notice in some future edition.' H. S. Foxwell in his review of *Indian Currency and Finance* (1913) in *Economic Journal*, Vol. XXXVI . . ., No. 92 . . ., December 1913 p. 564.
12. Arthur Smithies, 'Keynes Revisited'. *Quarterly Journal of Economics*, Vol. LXXXVI, August 1972, No. 3, p. 465.
13. 'Yes, I think it is . . . the true explanation has never been put before the public. What has been put before the public is rather the view that this Indian branch is a bulwark against hasty coinage, which does not very much commend itself to my mind. I think that what I regard as the true view is quite comprehensible, but I should agree that though comprehensible it is perhaps not easily comprehensible' (Abrahams, *Collected Writings*, Vol. XV, p. 105).
14. Minutes of Evidence taken before the (Babington Smith) Committee on Indian Exchange and Currency, Vol. II (Cmd 528, 1920), pp. 166–75, cited in *Collected Writings*, Vol. XV, pp. 273–98.
15. If under ordinary conditions it was announced that for a certain period 'the Government of India would give 15 rupees for a sovereign and that thereafter they would give 10 or 12, you could make that announcement with out much risk of being swamped by gold if the bazaar price was above 15; but once I came down to my definite level as between rupees and sovereigns I should then face the gold market so as to bring the bazaar price for gold down to parity.' *Collected Writings*, XV, p. 284.
16. *The Collected Writings of John Maynard Keynes*, Vol. XXI, Activities, 1931–1939, World Crises and Policies in Britain and America (ed.) Donald Moggridge (Macmillan, London, 1982.), p. 56.
17. Ibid., p. 142.
18. Memo of talk with Keynes. By M. L. Darling, 8 February 1934 (*M. L. Darling Papers*, Box I 21–46, South African Centre, Cambridge).
19. 'I should be inclined to suspect invisible forces in the way of movement of capital. India has been borrowing abroad practically nothing, whether through the Government or otherwise, for some considerable time. The effects of capital transactions are always delayed. Have you worked on how much comparative difference the cessation of foreign borrowing may make? I suppose also there was a good deal of speculation against the Rupee during the period of doubt as to the ratio. Presumably funds

remitted abroad at that time have not yet come again.' Keynes's letter of 17 May 1927 to Sir Basil Blackett, *Keynes Papers*, King's College.

20. Statement by Sir Malcolm Hailey ICS, cited by Sir George Schuster in his autobiography *Private Work and Public Causes, A Personal Record 1881–1978* (Cowbridge D. Brown and Sons, Glamorgan, Wales, 1979), p. 109.
21. Malcolm Darling Papers, Box I 21–46, op. cit.
22. See Chapter 4 on 'The Present Position of Gold in India and Proposals for a Gold Currency', (*Indian Currency and Finance*, in *Collected Writings*, Vol. I, pp. 45–71) and Keynes's memoranda on 'Gold in Internal Circulation', and 'Gold Currency' for the Chamberlain Commission (*Collected Writings*, Vol. XV, pp. 225–36).
23. *Collected Writings*, Vol. I, p. 69.
24. 'The establishment of a mint, however, would flatter at small expense an ignorant vanity. The government by granting it in response to popular appeal (though I doubt whether, in fact, there is any such appeal) would have a pleasant feeling of being democratic on an occasion when to yield involves no more evil than any other expenditure on a piece of fairly cheap ostentation. . . . It is very difficult to prophesy with regard to the popularity of a new coin. (I have, however, seen no evidence, which suggests that half-sovereigns are especially popular on account of their lower denomination) . . . it is generally a bad thing to introduce a new coin and add to the confusion of currencies. For purposes of export, at times of depression, the 10-rupee piece would be worth less than two-thirds of a sovereign. The sovereign, moreover, is fast becoming the international gold coin par excellence far beyond the bounds of the British Empire . . . to force a coin on a people is not always the best way to popularise it. Keynes (*Collected Writings*, Vol. I, p. 62).
25. 'If only one quarter or one-fifth of the circulation consists of gold, I do not think that a government can rely on getting more than a *fraction* of this, when it becomes necessary to contract the circulation by one-sixth or one-seventh; whereas if the gold is in the government's reserves, the *whole* of it is available.' Ibid., p. 65.

5 Creating a Central Bank for India

'Central banks . . . must be quick to adapt their methods to suit the changing economic structure . . . they must be perspicacious and versatile.' *R.S. Sayers (1948)*

'where banking habits touch only a minor part of the economy, the contribution that a central bank can make to development is more important than what it can do in the way of stabilization'. *Ursula Hicks (1962)*

RATIONALE OF CENTRAL BANKING

Keynes's pioneering contributions to the theory and organisation of central banking were made in the course of the prolonged discussions of the case for establishing a central bank for India. They are all the more remarkable considering his total lack of practical exposure to central banking, which unlike any other branch of macroeconomics, requires a uniquely complex amalgam of institutional as well as theoretical knowledge. Keynes had no formal connections with any central bank, except for his short and rather nominal stint as a Director of the Bank of England during the last five years of his life (1941–6). The nearest he came to any assignment as adviser to any central bank was in 1920 when he was approached by General Smuts to visit South Africa for two months to assist in formulating monetary policy and drafting legislation for a central bank. Keynes could not accept the invitation due to other commitments. Instead, he recommended Henry Strakosch who, together with Arthur Gillet, later drafted the legislation to establish a central bank for South Africa.[1] Again in 1920 Keynes was requested by Smuts to serve on a selection committee with Strakosch, to choose a Governor for the new South African Reserve Bank. Keynes, while agreeing to serve, wrote later to Smuts that 'it is a difficult post to fill, and well qualified candidates are scarce; but we met yesterday and there are good prospects, I think, of a strong appointment (CW, XVII, pp. 200–201). Eventually, W. H. Clegg (a Bank of England official born in Bloemfontein,

South Africa) was appointed to the post. The South African episode is instructive as the only recorded instance of Keynes being approached to formally advise on the creation of a central bank.

Keynes thought and wrote extensively on central banking in his *Indian Currency and Finance* and later in the course of his work as a member and/or as an expert witness for successive Indian Currency Commissions and committees (1913–26), the Macmillan Committee in England (1929–31) and in the second volume of his *Treatise on Money* (*The Applied Theory of Money*, 1930) which contains the first systematic analytic and comparative discussion of central banking.

Keynes's involvement in central banking matters derived from his strong interest, as an essentially policy-orientated monetary economist, in the development of an appropriate institutional framework for the effective and efficient operation of the monetary system in India, notably to ensure the elasticity of the note circulation in the busy season in India, the centralised management of the foreign reserves, and the development of a widely ramified commercial banking system and the popularisation of cheque payments. Keynes rightly perceived that it was not meaningful to make monetary policy prescriptions without a clear prior formulation of the institutional framework of central banking and of the transmission mechanism of monetary and credit policy. The scope and limitations of the instruments of central banks are determined by institutions and the nature of the transmission mechanism. However, in assessing Keynes's contributions to the development of central banking in India it should also be borne in mind that India has had a long history of several abortive attempts to set up a state banking institution with some elements of a central bank, although that term was not specifically used. The earliest recorded scheme to establish an institution in India with some characteristics of a central bank was the Plan for a General Bank in Bengal and Bihar (at that time the main British territories in India) prepared by Warren Hastings (Governor – later Governor-General – of Bengal) in January 1773 and placed before the Board of Revenue. This Bank, which was set up in April 1773, proved to be a very short-lived project. Between this and Keynes's initial ideas on central banking in India there were a number of infructuous schemes.[2]

Keynes's ideas on central banking in India are spread over the various sections on the case for the establishment of a central bank for India in his *Indian Currency and Finance* (pp. 41–2, 114, and 164–8); his comments on Lionel Abrahams's memorandum as well as his own memorandum, in collaboration with Sir Ernest Cable, on 'Proposals for the Establishment of a State Bank in India' for the Chamberlain Commission (1913); his evidence before the Hilton Young Commission (1926); and his correspondence with Sir Basil Blackett, the Finance Member of the Government of India (1927–33).

Long before the universal acceptance of the case for establishing central banks in 1920 when the Brussels Conference had recommended that 'in countries where there is no central bank, one should be established',[3] Keynes had presented the most detailed operational blueprint for establishing a central bank in India, even though it was still a British dependency. This latter aspect is particularly noteworthy considering that half-a-century later the question was still under discussion. 'Whether a central bank should be established in every independent political unit is very much an open question.'[4] Keynes delinked the economic rationale for creating a central bank from the political status of India and made a cogent case for creating a central bank, emphasising both its regulatory and developmental role and functions in Indian conditions. He specially noted that successive proposals for a state bank in India were so often 'smothered in the magnificent and empty maxims of political wisdom' and also that 'the two classical pronouncements on the fundamental problems of Indian finance, which have stood the test of time – Mr Dickson's, in 1867, on the question of a central bank, and Mr A. M. Lindsay's, in 1878 and subsequently, on the regulation of a gold standard' – both came 'from secretaries of the Bank of Bengal, not from high officials of State.'[5]

Although the issue of establishing a central bank for India did not figure in the terms of reference of the Royal (Chamberlain) Commission on Indian Finance and Currency (1913), the Commissioners recognised that it was impossible to ignore it inasmuch as the State Bank question was unavoidable in any discussion of the management of the note issue, the proper size of Government balances or the Government's remittance business. But there was no general agreement either among the commissioners or witnesses on the definition and scope of a state bank. Accordingly, Lionel Abrahams (Financial Secretary, India Office and later Under-Secretary of State for India), who was called upon to assist the Commission, prepared a Memorandum on Proposals for the Establishment of a State Bank for India.

Keynes noted that the contemporary (c. 1913) arguments in favour of a state bank for India were far stronger than in 1867 or even in 1898. He initially argued the case for a state bank on the grounds that the divorce between the responsibility for the note issue and that for banking generally was a source of weakness leading to the keeping of two distinct reserves, the Government's and the bankers', with no clearly defined relation between them, so that the reserves of the latter would be insufficient without the assumption of responsibility by the Government. The multiple reserve system in theory was inadequate and unreliable and led to a lack of elasticity in the note issue in the busy season. Also the absence of a state bank made it difficult for the Government to centralise and use its cash balances to the maximum advantage. It could not prudently place all of its free reserves in a private institution and deprive itself of a source of continuous financial advice and experience.[6] Keynes also noted that while the average Indian bank rate was not 'at all unduly high for a country in India's stage of economic and financial deployment' it was the 'high maximum rate almost invariably reached [during the busy season] which calls for inquiry.'[7] Keynes therefore also envisaged the role of a central bank as a source of alleviating seasonal shrinking of funds.

BLUEPRINTS FOR A CENTRAL BANK

Evidently, there was considerable excitement among informed Indian circles following reports of Keynes's projected State Bank of India.[8] This was formulated in Keynes's 'Memorandum on Proposals for the Establishment of a State Bank in India' (6 October 1913) to the Royal (Chamberlain) Commission on Indian Currency and Finance.[9] It explicitly rejected the model of the Bank of England as unsuited to Indian conditions and evolved a model adapted from the German Reichsbank but somewhat more akin to the Federal Reserve which was then being established in the United States. Even earlier Keynes had exhorted 'the framers of the new bank's constitution' to 'put far from their minds all thoughts of the Bank of England. It is in the state banks of Europe, especially in that of Germany, or in those perhaps of Holland or Russia, that the proper model is to be found' (*Indian Currency and Finance*, p. 168). Keynes's memorandum covered the Bank's constitution, capitalisation, division of profits, management of a flexible proportional reserve note issue, Government balances, public debt, and centralisation of reserves. Keynes proposed that the bank could be constituted by the amalgamation of the capital and reserves of the Presidency Banks of Bombay, Bengal, and Madras. This points to Keynes's preference for an incremental approach to institution-building rather than setting up a wholly new institution. Interestingly – considering his subsequent change of views on this issue – he considered that Government subscription to the capital was not necessary as it would complicate rather than simplify the relations between the Government and its shareholders. The management of the bank was to be vested in a Central Board consisting of the Governor (Chairman) to be appointed by the Monarch on the recommendation of the Secretary of State, the Deputy Governor, a representative of the Government, and three or more assessors (with no right to vote) to be appointed by the Viceroy of India. The assessors were to be the Managers, or their deputies, of the Presidency Head Offices or of other Head Offices. The Presidency Boards were to consist of the Manager (as Chairman with a casting vote), Deputy Managers, a representative of the Local (i.e. Provincial) Government and three or four non-official members. He conceived that the Secretary of State would be behind the Bank but his authority would only come into play on important changes of policy and on amendments of clauses in the Bank Act. He would delegate responsibility to a far greater extent than heretofore in the daily conduct of financial business, in respect of which the executive officers would be free from the administrative interference of Government and from excessive pressure of shareholders. This meant that the broad strategic aspects would be the charge of the Secretary of State and the tactical aspects would be vested in the executive officers. The finely tuned distribution of authority and functions, and the blending of official and non-official elements, the interplay of checks and balances, all attest to the political acumen and organisational flair of Keynes. Significantly, he never at any point invoked the trite colonialist litany of insufficiency of banking talent in India or the unwillingness of the right type of expatriate banker to serve in India.

Altogether, the memorandum shows several novel features of Keynes's thinking on central banking in India. First, there is the emphasis on professional expertise and management insulated from political interference and on discretionary monetary management as opposed to fixed rules, an aspect eminently in consonance with the modern concepts of central banking.[10] Secondly, Keynes was a pioneer in stressing the primacy of the promotional and developmental role of a central bank in a developing country like India, which is particularly noteworthy since the rationale of central banking has been argued almost exclusively in terms of its conventional functions of note issue, government's banker, lender of last resort, and controller of credit. That the emphasis in the early days of central banking must be on the development of a banking system may be regarded as both logical and historically valid insofar as the question of regulating and controlling credit arises only after there is an adequately developed banking system. Consequently 'the central bank must be venturesome in the kind of business it is willing to handle, even at the cost of making some mistakes. It must be not only central but also, and very actively, a bank.'[11] This is a succinct latter-day presentation of the appropriate agenda for a new central bank in an underdeveloped country, which is well anticipated by Keynes's writings and attitudes. Keynes envisaged that the proposed central bank would address such problems as 'the absence of a final banking reserve in India and the question of giving Presidency Bank access to London, the extension of cooperative credit in India, the improvement of banking facilities and the encouragement of sound banking in that country.'[12] Keynes stated that it should be the declared policy of the Central Board of the proposed State Bank of India (c. 1913) to open branches as rapidly as possible at most places where there is a district treasury. This 'would gradually bring sound banking facilities to many parts of India, where they are now almost entirely wanting, both directly and by supplying a basis, in reliance on which private and cooperative banking could be built up.'[13] Keynes was, however, careful to add that the opening of new branches should not jeopardise the State Bank's profitability.[14] He was equally conscious of the legitimate interests of shareholders, and consequently his proposals aimed at a virtually guaranteed dividend because he felt that such 'a generous treatment is both just and politic' and 'an attempt ought to be made to meet any of their reasonable demands.'[15] Keynes was also innovative in advocating the introduction of appropriate rediscount facilities by the State Bank (to 'aid the eventual development of Indian banking on the most desirable lines which European experience has evolved') and for the State Bank to do rediscounting to the maximum extent possible. Thus the State Bank proposed by Keynes was intended to combine central and commercial banking functions, but he deprecated any notion of direct competition by the State Bank with exchange banks in attracting deposits in London or entering into the regular business of trade remittances. It is a revealing commentary on the time-lag between ideas and implementation in India's monetary history that it was not until the 1950s that the Reserve Bank of India established a Department of Banking

Development and it was not until the sixties and seventies that the nationalised State Bank of India (the former Imperial Bank) and the commercial banks embarked on a planned programme of branch expansion in the rural and semi-urban areas!

Subsequently, Keynes in his evidence to the Royal Commission (Hilton Young) on Indian Currency and Finance (1926) reiterated the views that he had expressed before the Chamberlain Commission (1913) on the establishment of a central bank for India. Although some progress had been made in that direction since then Keynes thought that the 'biggest thing not done is the handing over of the paper currency to the bank' (CW, XIX, p. 494). Keynes disagreed with other witnesses who thought that the time was not yet ripe for establishing a central bank merely because India's banking organisation was rather limited. On the contrary, in responding to a question from Sir Henry Strakosch, he argued that a central bank would be very helpful in expanding commercial banking.[16] Curiously, Keynes, in responding to a related question from Sir Rajendranath Mookerjee, one of the two Indian members, did not see the relevance of the development of the commercial banking habit (drawing of cheques, and so on) to the efficacy of the management of paper currency and of central banking techniques such as the operation of the discount rate policy. This seemed to contradict Keynes's standing argument for the creation of a central bank willing and able to discount approved internal bills of exchange in order to provide the necessary elasticity of note circulation in the busy season.

Keynes was severely critical of the recommendations of the Hilton Young Commission on gold bullion and the 'attempt to hand over the central bank to the control of private individuals' [shareholders] as being, if not make-believe, both 'undesirable and dangerous' in Indian conditions 'where the Government has necessarily the whole responsibility.'[17] In the circumstances prevailing in India, Keynes maintained that while the central bank should be given a 'high degree of independence from the Secretariat of Finance and from the Bureaucracy' it must in effect be a 'Government concern, certainly subject in the last resort to the instructions of the Viceroy-in-Council'. The Commission, according to Keynes, confused the desirability of separating the Central Bank from the Secretariat of Finance and from the 'daily control of the Bureaucracy' with handing it over to private shareholders. Keynes made these valid points too late and in private at that. It is interesting to contrast Keynes's advocacy of a Government-owned central bank in India in 1926 with his solicitude for due protection of shareholder's rights in his earlier scheme of a State bank in 1913. This, however, would not appear wholly contradictory if viewed in the light of Keynes's consistent advocacy, in the course of his work on Indian currency issues, of the need to protect the basic interests of the mass on the Indian people – the *ryots* – which he thought, like many a British official in India, to be safer in the hands of an alien bureaucracy than with a Board of directors representing predominantly landlord and business shareholders.[18] This stance of paternalism was of course strongly characteristic of the more constructive and meliorist British Indian officials like Malcolm Darling and F. L. Brayne, both well-known for their work on rural reconstruction in the Punjab. But then Keynes was also emphatic that even a privately-owned central bank like the Bank of England (which it was in his lifetime) 'should feel quite free not to be influenced in the slightest degree by the necessity of earning a given income',[19] in discharging its obligations of efficient conduct of monetary policy. While Keynes recognised that the Bank of England valued its independence and its freedom from any political pressure, he stressed that this 'does not depend on the fact that they have private shareholders'.

Keynes was equally cognisant of the prudential role of a central bank and the case for regulation of commercial banks in India with 'enormous nominal capital and high sounding titles', many of whom suffered from serious problems like gaps between nominal and paid-up capital, inadequate cash balances, mismanagement, and, more seriously, the conduct of non-banking business ('coach building and medical attendance'). He was concerned that although the 'growth of banking habits in India' was of utmost importance to the country's economic development, 'a startling series of failures will do much to retard it'.[20] Keynes, for all his innovativeness in central banking doctrine, was surprisingly conventional on a major policy issue – the disposal of central bank and currency seigniorage profits. His earliest pronouncement on this subject, in the Indian context, bears this out: 'With regard to the growth of the gold standard reserve through the profits of coinage, the Government has announced that they will divert half of the future profits to capital expenditure on railways. But it is to be hoped that this decision will be reconsidered before the time comes.'[21] In his subsequent comments on Lionel Abrahams's State Bank Memorandum (1913), Keynes argued that it would not be easy to determine the net profits of the note issue and thought that the shareholders should have the profit up to a certain percentage, with the surplus to be divided between them and the Government, subject to decennial revision.[22] There was no change in Keynes's position in later years. His scheme for a State bank, prepared for the Chamberlain Commission on Indian Currency (1913), provided for a division of the annual net profits of the bank, after due allowances for depreciation, preference dividends (if any), and so on, to shareholders, reserves and government.[23] The scheme for all its meticulous attention to the disposal of central bank profits, did not provide for any productive use of the profits of currency issue such as investment in industry and railways for which there was a substantial and continuing need in India. As Abrahams was quick to point out to Keynes: 'What is the good of an economical currency if the fruits of economy are to be put in a sarcophagus? The economic error of India tends to be to hoard wealth instead of using it. It would be a calamity if the Government falls a victim to this error in its own action' (ibid., p. 215). For once, Keynes the innovative economist was wholly on the side of the angels whereas a bureaucrat like Abrahams was cast as a heterodox maverick! Perhaps all this also reflects Keynes's habitual neglect of the real sector of the economy. But a latter-day Keynes might equally well have wondered if the use of Reserve Bank of India's profits even as seed capital for development finance institutions, and its liberal rediscount and refinancing facilities, was not as inflationary as the automatic transfer of all its residual central bank profits to the Government of India. Such potent engines of inflation might well have prompted Keynes to recommend judicious periodic sterilisation of the Reserve Bank of India's profits and a critical scrutiny of its burgeoning rediscount facilities. All this only prompts the thought that even Keynes was no exception to the rule that the generation and disposal of central bank profits has hardly evoked much serious analytic debate among either economists or even central bankers.[24]

Following his evidence to the Hilton Young Commission, Keynes had just one more final occasion to revert to problems of central banking in India in the course of a private communication to Sir Basil Blackett, Financial Member of the Viceroy's Executive Council (1927–33) who had proposed 'to make membership of the Reserve Bank of India system a privilege which would be sought for by the banks in India'. This was supposed to take the form of 'putting a few banks . . . into a schedule instead of having a comprehensive definition of "bank" and banker' and giving them an interest in the profits of the Reserve Bank so that the membership of the Reserve Bank system would be 'a real privilege' instead of being 'universally regarded as an oppressive bit of compulsion to make them keep a proportion of their reserves with the Reserve Bank, in return for which they say they get no privileges worth speaking of. . . .'[25] Keynes, in responding to Blackett, said that he 'had seen a little of the controversy about the compulsory proportion which the bankers are to keep in future with the Reserve Bank' which suggests that he maintained his interest in Indian monetary affairs. Keynes was generally supportive of Blackett's scheme, on its merits 'as well as on the analogy of practice elsewhere (Britain and USA)' but was utterly opposed to giving the scheduled banks an interest in the profits of the Reserve Bank of India, or even to giving them anything like an adequate rate of interest on their compulsory reserves with the Reserve Bank. His reasoning was as follows: 'The creation of credit by the member banks of a system is only practicable with safety to themselves if the Reserve Bank is sufficiently strong to be able to support the exchanges and the whole financial system in time of trouble. This entails the Reserve Bank in keeping assets, either idle or earning a low rate of interest. This sacrifice of interest is made in the interest of the banking system as a whole. Clearly, therefore it is fair that the member banks should contribute to this by having a certain quantity of balances with the Reserve Bank also yielding no interest.'[26] Keynes also cited the practice in Great Britain where the joint stock banks, even in the absence of any legal requirement, maintained normally reserves of about 11.5 per cent, of which probably half was kept with the Bank of England. Similarly, the member banks of the Federal Reserve System in the USA were compelled to keep non-interest-bearing deposits with the Reserve Banks which worked out on balance at about 10 per cent of their deposits. Keynes also noted that the proportion of compulsory reserves proposed by Basil Blackett was not higher than for the member banks in the USA. He hoped that eventually all joint-stock banks in India would become part of the Reserve Bank system. All this was an elegant presentation of the rationale of maintaining low or non-interest-bearing commercial bank reserves with the Reserve Bank in keeping with its role as a lender of last resort and controller of the financial system. It also, concurrently, argued the case for eventual universality of the membership of the Reserve Bank system.

There were prolonged discussions preceding the Reserve Bank of India Act of 1935 and when the last of the successive Bills was in process the Secretary of State for India appointed a Departmental

Committee to study and review the Bill. At the suggestion of Montagu Norman, Governor of the Bank of England, Harvey (the Deputy Governor) and W. H. Clegg (Executive Director of the Bank of England and former Governor of the South African Reserve Bank, 1920–31) were included in this Committee. Keynes with his knowledge and lifelong interest in Indian monetary affairs and cogent advocacy of a central bank for India might have been a natural choice for such a Committee. Ironically, while South Africa, a country on the fringes of his life and work, and one in which he had never shown much interest and of which he had no expert knowledge, had invited Keynes at a much younger age to be a technical adviser on central banking, the British authorities ostentatiously overlooked Keynes in the preliminaries leading to the creation of the Reserve Bank of India. It could of course be argued that as much as Keynes's expertise, it was Smuts's high regard for him and their strong personal rapport developed during the Peace Conference at Versailles (1919) which were jointly responsible for the South African invitation. But then Montagu Norman, too, never lacked in appreciation of Keynes's economic acumen, as is evident from the enthusiastic letters he wrote to Keynes around the time of the preparations for the Reserve Bank of India Bill.[27] Perhaps, more plausibly, Keynes, as a consistent critic and gadfly of the Bank of England's policies, had talked and written himself out of court with the British establishment. This possibly explains why the wondrous wartime alliance of Montagu Norman and Keynes, based among others, on the commonality of attitudes on exchange control between Keynes and the Bank of England, would have been 'unthinkable 10 or 15 years earlier'.[28] Possibly in other respects too Keynes was still regarded as much too controversial a figure in British financial circles for him to be entrusted with the establishment of a central bank for a British dependency like India. For instance, the suggestion attributed to Keynes, that Graham Towers, who had been Governor of the Bank of Canada for eight years, could be a possible successor to Montagu Norman, as Governor of the Bank of England, was ruled out by the Court of the Bank of England on the grounds that he was too 'Keynesian' – no longer a term of abuse, but enough to send shivers down Threadneedle Street spines – and the idea was quietly dropped in favour of Lord Catto, who 'could be regarded as within the traditions' and 'a wise trusted adviser at both ends of the Strand'.[29] However, it still remains a matter for conjecture whether it was such considerations that ruled out the nomination of Keynes to the select committee on the Reserve

Bank of India bill, or was it an apprehension of his well-known doctrinal position that the Bank of England was an unsuitable model for a country like India? Yet whatever the reasons, it is one of the more abiding ironies of Indian economic history that Keynes was never called upon to advise on the establishment of the Reserve Bank of India (1935) which, in the event, turned out to be a spitting image of the Bank of England down to the organisational chart, almost in wilful contradiction of Keynes's magisterial exhortation to the architects of India's state bank 'to put far from their minds all thoughts of the Bank of England'.

Notes

1. R. W. K. Parsons, 'Keynes and South Africa', *The South African Journal of Economics*, Vol. 51, No. 3, September 1983, p. 421.
2. See S. L. N. Simha, 'Genesis of Central Banking in India', Chapter 1 in *History of the Reserve Bank of India*, 1935–51 (Reserve Bank of India, Bombay, 1970).
3. R. S. Sayers, 'Are Central Banks Universally Necessary?' *Central Banking after Bagehot* (Oxford University Press, 1957), p. 110.
4. Sayers, ibid., p. 108.
5. *Collected Writings of John Maynard Keynes*, Vol. I, 'Indian Currency and Finance', (Macmillan, London, 1971), p. 168.
6. Ibid., pp. 166–8.
7. Ibid., p. 173.
8. A leading Indian businessman, B. S. Wacha, wrote in response to Keynes's letter of 4 September 1913, '. . . delighted to note you are devising a scheme for a State Bank which will make any banking mouth water . . . anything coming from you will be most interesting and readable it will raise deep thought and reflexion.' From 51 Apollo Street, Bombay, September 25, 1913, *Keynes Papers*, IB/1 King's College.
9. *The Collected Writings of John Maynard Keynes*, Vol. XV, Activities 1906–14, India and Cambridge (ed.) Elizabeth Johnson (Macmillan, London, 1971), pp. 151–219.
10. Sayers, 'The Theoretical Basis of Central Banking' in *Central Banking after Bagehot*, op. cit., p. 1.
11. R. S. Sayers, 'Central Banking in Underdeveloped Countries', op. cit., p. 115.
12. *Collected Writings*, Vol. XV, p. 149.
13. Ibid., p. 193.
14. Ibid., p. 171.
15. Ibid., p. 270.
16. '(Sir Henry Strakosch) would you not rather say that a central bank would be helpful in expanding the commercial banking organization? Yes, I should (Keynes).' *The Collected Writings of John Maynard*

Keynes, Vol. XIX, Activities 1822–29, The Return to Gold and Industrial Policy, Part II, (ed.) Donald Moggridge (Macmillan, London, 1981), p. 524.

17. Keynes to C. H. Kisch, of the India Office, dated 22 December 1926, *Keynes Papers*, King's College.
18. '. . . the results were quite other than its promoters intended, for the Central Board [of the Reserve Bank of India] was, under the bank's charter, to be mainly elected by the shareholders, and within four years it came to be dominated by those Hindu big business men who were more than sensitive to suggestions from the Congress caucus, and some of whom had contributed largely to its funds. This might have had serious consequences. That it did not was due very largely to the skill and tact of Sir James Taylor, who was Governor for most of the time I was in India. . . .I wanted to give my policy a tilt in the direction of benefiting the peasant as against the previously over-favoured townsman.' Sir James Grigg (Finance Member, Government of India, 1935–9), *Prejudice and Judgement*, Jonathan Cape, London, 1956, p. 290.
19. *Collected Writings of John Maynard Keynes*, Activities 1929–31: Rethinking Employment and Unemployment, edited by Donald Moggridge (Macmillan, London, 1981), Vol. XX, p. 244.
20. *The Collected Writings of John Maynard Keynes*, Vol. I, 'Indian Currency and Finance' (Macmillan, London, 1971), p. 159.
21. 'Recent Developments of the Indian Currency Question', *Collected Writings* Vol. XV, p. 275.
22. Ibid., p. 136.
23. Ibid., p. 170.
24. Even the standard work of M. H. de Kock (a Governor of the South African Reserve Bank) on *Central Banking*, Fourth Edition (St Martin's Press, New York, 1974), has only a very brief descriptive subsection on 'Distribution of Profits', pp. 307–9.
25. Sir Basil Blackett, Simla, 28 April 1927, to Keynes, *Keynes Papers*, King's College.
26. Keynes to Sir Basil Blackett, 17 May 1927, *Keynes Papers*, King's College.
27. From Montagu Norman to Keynes (18 January 1932): 'your article "An End of 'Reparations'", of which you were so kind as to send me an advance copy, seems to me to express many truths succinctly and with conviction, I hope it has been widely read'. The second letter (Thorpe Lodge, Campden Hill, W8. 13 September 1932) said 'I approve your letter in this week's *New Statesman* – whole heartedly. I have lately written the same thing in a lumbering fashion for it is too seldom realised abroad and indeed at home.' *Keynes Papers*, King's College.
28. R. S. Sayers, *Bank of England, 1891–1944*, Vol. 2 (Cambridge University Press, 1976), p. 591.
29. Sayers, ibid., p. 654.

6 To Bretton Woods and Savannah: The Longest Journey

'In the matter of . . . India's rights . . . Keynes rendered valuable assistance and guidance.' *Sir Chintaman Deshmukh*

INDIAN ECONOMIC ISSUES IN THE THIRTIES

The conclusion of Keynes's evidence to the Hilton Young Commission on Indian Currency (1926) marked a temporary suspension of his formal links with India which had been forged over the preceding decades of his work on Indian monetary issues. The subsequent period until the outbreak of the Second World War was comparatively quiescent and uneventful in terms of Keynes's association with India which was limited to sporadic contacts with a select few personalities like Sir Basil Blackett and Sir George Schuster, both Finance Members of the Government of India, and Malcolm Darling of the Indian Civil Service or occasional correspondence with former pupils like B. P. Adarkar and L. K. Jha. Superficially, India would seem to have virtually faded from Keynes's economic consciousness during the thirties, judging from the absence of any public pronouncements on Indian economic affairs and as confirmed by the recollections of some of his closest pupils and associates at Cambridge during the thirties. Thus Polly Hill recalls: 'from 1933, when I got to know him well, I do not remember JMK ever referring to India. And am I not right in thinking that he had few Indian friends in Cambridge in the 1930s?' (letter to the author 1 May 1987). These recollections find an uncanny echo in other communications. According to David Bensusan-Butt (Keynes's pupil at King's College (1932–6), 'I do not remember him [Keynes] talking about India whether in lectures, supervisions, or at the Monday night club I faithfully attended for four years' (letter to the author 5 May 1987). Likewise, Hans Singer, who did his doctorate at Cambridge during the thirties under Keynes, also does not recall any references to India by Keynes in his lectures or in the Political Economy Club discussions (interview given to the author in

Washington, DC). Sir Alec Cairncross, a prominent member of the Political Economy Club in the mid-thirties wrote as follows:

> Keynes did not, so far as I know, take any Indians for supervision in my time (he was only in Cambridge for the weekend plus Monday). In the years I heard him lecture I recall no reference to India . . . when [V.K.R.V.] Rao gave a paper to Keynes's Club Keynes introduced him as a future Finance member [of the Government of India] . . . But I have no recollection of what Keynes *said* on India, not even in his summing-up after Rao's paper, on any occasion when I heard him speak. (Letter to the author, 26 July 1987)

Mr L. K. Jha (ex-Governor, Reserve Bank of India, who was also a member of the Political Economy Club) also confirmed to the author that his 'conversations [as an undergraduate] with Keynes rarely touched upon the Indian situation'. Possibly the only occasion when the Political Economy Club came nearest to an Indian topic was in the mid-thirties in a paper on the East India Company in the eighteenth century which managed to attract just three students – the person who wrote the paper, Bob Bryce and Lorie Tarshis.[1]

The fact that Indian matters did not engage Keynes's attention during the thirties is not surprising considering that there were no pressing issues of Indian economic policy – at least from Keynes's point of view. This, in keeping with his characteristic intellectual stance, also meant a suspension of interest for Keynes who never had any purely academic interest in Indian economic affairs. Moreover, this was also a period of intense intellectual ferment and preoccupation for Keynes's transition from the *Treatise* to the *General Theory*. Nevertheless, the thirties were not without significance in terms of Keynes's interest in Indian economic affairs, particularly after the publication of his celebrated essay on 'The Means to Prosperity', which used the multiplier concept of Richard Kahn to formulate a world economic recovery programme based on cheap and abundant bank credit and large-scale Governmental loan expenditure. Keynes was concerned to demonstrate that governments should stop 'thinking of a loan as a liability and more as a link in the transformation of the country's surplus resources, which will otherwise be wasted, into useful capital assets. . . . It should not be difficult to perceive that 100,000 houses are a national asset and 1 million unemployed a national liability. Yet if we are to raise world prices, which is our theme, loan expenditure must spread its beneficent influence round the world.' For this purpose, Keynes advocated the creation of an international authority to provide 'not a permanent addition to the world's monetary supply, but as a balancing factor to be released when prices are abnormally low as at present and to be withdrawn again if prices were to be rising too much'.[2] (This notion of injection and withdrawal of money may well have been the embryonic concept of deferred compulsory savings in *How to Pay for the War*.) The international note issue was designed to free the hands of central banks to promote loan expenditure and restore employment. The authority would issue gold notes (with face value expressed in terms of the gold content of the US dollar) to a maximum of $5000 million obtainable by the participating countries against an equal face value of the gold bonds of their countries, up to a maximum quota for each country (shades of the IMF!) to be based on an agreed formula (such as the amount of gold held in reserves at some recent normal date, for instance, end of 1928) provided that no individual quota should exceed $450 million. Under this plan, seven countries would qualify for the maximum of $450 million each (Great Britain, United States, France, Germany, Spain, Argentina, and Japan) with others ranging from Italy (266) to Estonia (2). It is particularly noteworthy that Keynes's scheme provided India, although a dependency, with a quota of 124 which was lower than those for Holland (175), Brazil (149), and Belgium (126) but higher than for Canada (114), Australia (108), South Africa (39), and New Zealand (35). At the same time, Keynes welcomed any increase in the output of gold or 'a reduction in India's sterile hoards' (ibid., p. 353) which would increase the quantity of reserve money. However, in another context he also noted that while 'the West as well as the East, has learnt to hoard gold' the 'motives of the United States are not those of India' (ibid., p. 175). But then in the case of India the massive gold exports of the thirties, which so rejoiced Keynes, did not add to the reserve base of the Indian banking system given the low level of financial intermediation.

A more critical stumbling block to any major change in Indian economic policies was the hostility to Keynesian ideas in the India Office, a solid bastion of the Treasury View of balanced budgets and tight money as well evidenced by the recollections of Sir George Schuster, who was the Finance Member, Government of India (1929–33) and a close friend of Keynes. Schuster, one of the most innovative of the Government of India's Finance Members, resisted the pressure from the India Office to enforce a tight financial policy by raising the bank rate to high levels because he 'thought that the methods proposed would be ineffective in the conditions of the Indian money market and would merely increase Indian hostility to British policy'.[3] He was at this time 'constantly in personal contact with Keynes and had his unqualified support in [his] controversy with the India office about monetary policy' and even 'claimed some success' for his policies.[4] But Schuster's successor as Finance Member of the Government of India (1934–9), P. J. (later Sir James) Grigg, was an unreconstructed Gladstonian, who thought 'Keynesian ideas' as either 'silly or vicious' despite the advocacy of capital expenditure by eminent financiers like Cecil Kisch and Henry Strakosch. Grigg 'proposed to revert to virtue' and to damn 'all capital projects unless they were likely to be more or less directly productive'.[5] He then went on to denounce Schuster for having incited his colleagues to put forward projects such as roads in the Tirah (North-West Frontier) and for launching 'a grandiose economic programme – mostly eye-wash by the way – on the day he left'. Grigg refused to sign the dispatch on the ground that it was nothing but the first step in an unbalancing of he Budget, and objected strongly to the 'Keynesian arguments' used to justify the proposed expenditures on civil aviation.[6] Grigg's own achievement was to have presented five successive balanced budgets which were all rejected by the Indian Legislative Assembly and had to be certified by the Viceroy.[7] Grigg thus brought to nought the modest 'Keynesian' programmes of public capital expenditure proposed by Schuster. Even otherwise the intellectual climate in India was inhospitable to formal economics, let alone Keynesian ideas. Thus Otto Niemeyer, Keynes's civil service contemporary, and then an Adviser to the Bank of England, wrote to Grigg expressing strong opposition to a proposal of the Government of India to recruit candidates with a good economics background to staff key positions in the Finance and Commerce Department of the Government of India. Niemeyer remarked, in a barely veiled sarcastic reference to Keynes, that civil service candidates 'could learn finance in India much better than they can through King's College, Cambridge'.[8] Contemporary British officials in India went even further in regarding a Cambridge economics education as 'dangerous'.[9] Such sentiments were doubtless congenial to Grigg, who later went on to appoint, in the teeth of Indian opposition, an avowedly laissez-faire British economist, T. E. (later Sir Theodore) Gregory (Ernest Cassel Professor of Economics, with special reference to Banking and Currency, University of London), as Economic Adviser to the Government of India (1938–46). Grigg jistified his choice of Gregory not for any ideological reasons but solely on the ground that there were no suitable Indian economists whom he regarded at best as 'school masters'.[10] Evidently some of the leading contemporary Indian economists, incidentally, among Keynes's best pupils – B. P. Adarkar and V. K. R. V. Rao (among academics) and J. V. Joshi, S. Bhootalingam and L. K. Jha (among civil servants), were out of the reckoning for Grigg. Strangely, the Gregory episode does not figure in Grigg's autobiography. However, the general hostility to Keynesian ideas in the thirties in a political dependency like India is hardly to be wondered at, considering that even in metropolitan Britain the conversion of the Government to Keynesian doctrine was not complete until 1944 with the adoption of the White paper on Employment Policy. Budget deficits in Britain during the thirties, as established by modern research, were a result of the expenditures on rearmament rather than of any reasoned acceptance by the British Government of Keynesian principles, as Keynes himself recognised.[11] Keynes's argument was far more basic. He rightly contended: 'If we can cure unemployment for the purpose of armament, we can cure it for the productive purpose of peace.' (BBC talk, printed in the *Listener*, 1 June 1939). But then India lacked the requisite fiscal autonomy to enable Keynes's star Indian pupils serving in the administration to apply Keynesian policies, even if they were so minded, in a manner that was possible for Keynes's Canadian and Australian pupils. In Canada, Robert Bryce, a pupil of Keynes who held a succession of senior posts leading to Deputy Minister of Finance, used the framework of the *General Theory* for policy analysis. His 'first ideas appeared in the Canadian budgets of 1939, both the peace budget and the war budget in September'. Since then, according to Bryce, although 'Keynes's thought has not gone on uninterruptedly in Ottawa since that time, it has become accepted as a routine part of the analysis and work'.[12] It could justifiably be argued that Canada was perhaps the first country to implement consciously Keynesian economic policies. Similarly, in Australia the adoption of the 1941 budget was based on an assessment supported by an exchange between Keynes and Professor L. F. Giblin (who was at King's in the early thirties).[13] Keynesian policies may not have been implemented in depression India, but there is, however, a most interesting unpublished record of Keynes's views on Indian economic policy in the thirties in Malcolm Darling's memo of a talk with Keynes who made the following points (ibid., pp. 1–2).

On the question of overall policy, Keynes 'saw future salvation [of India] not in restricting private enterprise . . . but in bringing it under socialized control through the State'. He thought that 'the civil service should be reorganized to handle this control effectively . . . (e.g., currency, finance, and banking)'. Clearly, Keynes envisioned a macro– rather than a microeconomic role for the Indian Civil service. Hence his supposition that for the most part private enterprise would 'be unconscious of it'. Keynes's innovative suggestion for the economic reorientation of the Indian Civil Service – The Retort Courteous to Niemeyer's snide reference to Keynes and King's College! – went beyond the concept of the Finance and Commerce Pool of the Service. Its full fruition, as with Keynes's design for a central bank for India, had to await the creation of the Indian Economic Service after independence. As regards fiscal policy, Keynes lamented that 'financiers are dominated by Gladstonian finance and by what they learned 40 years ago . . . the old economics had successfully taught . . . there was something immoral in borrowing for a purpose which was not directly remunerative'. On the contrary 'by judicious spending, the State could play the part of investing the savings of the country and doing it in a way that the wealth of the country would be increased . . . that existing taxes would be more remunerative'. Keynes favoured two budgets in India, ordinary for administrative expenditures and the other for capital works. In the past India had financed a large amount of capital works from [tax] revenue which Keynes thought 'was unsound'. He advocated borrowing for productive projects, even if they were not directly productive, as for instance, cooperatives, but education 'was more doubtful' since 'it would depend upon the nature of education'. Keynes was supportive of Darling's proposal for Government borrowing to develop cooperatives and to raise a 25-year £100 million loan for rural reconstruction. Keynes's reference to government borrowing for 'cooperatives' is unclear. In any event this would have contravened the spirit of self-reliance which is the basis of cooperation. More interesting was his notion of borrowing for education presumably for vocational education, which is suggestive of his conviction of its development role.

As regards the projected schemes of rural debt reconciliation in India, Keynes 'did not see how debts could be cut down by a stroke of the pen' and approvingly cited President Roosevelt's programme 'to offer all mortgagees state bonds for the value of their debts up to 60 per cent (or thereabouts) of the present value of the mortgaged property, in return for which the mortgagee was required to forgo all claims on the balance. If he refused the offer, he was left to recover what he could from the debts through the courts'. Interestingly, Keynes favoured 'reviving usury laws which were operative through the Western world till about a 100 years ago.' Responding to Darling's doubts about the difficulties of enforcing them, Keynes said 'that was largely a matter of sufficiently drastic penalties for their breach'. Keynes plainly overestimated the deterrent effects of legal penalties on usurers. He added that 'it would be very useful for the new Government in India to have reconstruction schemes to play with and quoted an Indian of his acquaintance (Dr V. K. R. V. Rao) as saying that this was essential if they were to avoid unpopularity with the masses!' Keynes therefore 'thought the political reasons for such a scheme should be pushed' (*Darling Papers*, ibid, pp. 1–2).

Keynes had also an interesting exchange of views with two Indian economists on an article, 'The Economic Basis of Islamic Tithe' by Jatindra Mohan Datta (*Economic Journal*, June 1939) which was criticised by Mr Ataullah of the Muslim University, Aligarh, India on the grounds that Datta's authorities were 'secondary'. Keynes, in addition to seeking Datta's reactions (letter dated 1 September 1939) wrote back to Mr Ataullah as follows: 'I confess his [Datta's] authorities look to me to be secondary in character and might easily be wrong. But at present you have given no authority at all. So perhaps the next move is with you' (4 January 1940, *Keynes Papers*, King's College). This little episode, apart from its Indian and Islamic interest, is demonstrative of Keynes's scrupulousness as an editor of an academic periodical.

THE WAR YEARS

Keynes as one of the two wartime (1939–45) advisers to the British Chancellor of the Exchequer (the other was Lord Catto) 'had special authority in discussion of Indian financial questions and both took a prominent part in advising Ministers on this matter throughout the war.'[14] The various Keynes-inspired proposals for immobilising Indian and other sterling balances, such as writing off as a contribution to war finance comparable to Lend-lease, or funding at low or high rates of interest for gradual release over fifty years, did not come to fruition. However, this wartime stance did not inhibit Keynes from taking a more constructive and helpful attitude towards the same issue in the postwar period. Surprisingly, the innovative proposal for war-time gold sales in India and the Middle East as an anti-inflationary measure did not originate with Keynes but with R. A. Harri, Chief Economic Adviser, General Headquarters, Middle East, and was passed on by R. F. Kahn to Keynes.[15]

Towards the end of 1943 Keynes had an interesting correspondence with an Indian economist, A. K. Datta, on international monetary reform and its impact on developing countries, arising from two articles on this subject by Datta in the *Eastern Economist* of New Delhi (20 August and 1 October 1943). Keynes wrote to Datta as follows:

> Thank you very much for sending me [your] two very interesting and excellently written articles for the *Eastern Economist* [New Delhi, 'British and U.S. Currency Plans', 9 July 1943 and 'Lord Keynes and Equilibrium', 1 October 1943]. It is not the purpose of the Currency Schemes to deal with different rates of capital expansion causing some countries to be long-term borrowers from the rest of the world and others to be long-term lenders. When you say that 'neither the Keynes Plan nor the White Plan touches this' you are entirely right. They do not pretend to and in the Keynes Plan at any rate this is clearly stated. To deal with that problem requires another type of institution. White's Reconstruction Bank tries to fill that bill. . . . The Currency Plan aims at providing reserves to tide over short-term fluctuations and an orderly method for altering exchange rates when necessary, and for ensuring multilateral clearing of current trade transactions. No currency plan can properly attempt to do more than this. But they are important objects, and India has, surely, as much to gain from this as any other country. Moreover, it is also a way of beginning to learn the technique of international co-operation in the economic field. (30 December 1943 – *Keynes Papers*, King's College)

Keynes also forwarded Datta's articles to Lord Catto, Governor of the Bank of England ('You may like to glance at this. Mr. Datta's articles are really very good. The *Eastern Economist* seems to me to be a higher grade product than appreciated.') who responded suitably ('very interesting').

BRETTON WOODS AND SAVANNAH

Keynes's last official involvement with Indian matters was during the Bretton Woods Monetary Conference (1944) as the leader of the

British Delegation and later at the Inaugural Meeting of the International Monetary Fund and World Bank at Savannah (March 1946). On both these occasions, he came into close contact with the Indian delegations.

The Indian delegation at Bretton Woods was an admirable blend of economical and financial expertise and acumen, official and non-official as well as British and Indian elements. The leader of the delegation, Sir Jeremy Raisman, was the Finance Member of the Viceroy's Executive Council. He was ably assisted by Sir Chintaman Deshmukh, a distinguished member of the Indian Civil Service, and the first Indian Governor of the Reserve Bank, who played a leading role in the deliberations in championing the cause of the less developed countries in general and of India in particular.[16] Sir Chintaman was nominated Chairman of Committee 4 of Commission II which was concerned with the form and status of the Bank for Reconstruction and Development (later the World Bank). The other British Indian delegate was Sir Theodore Gregory, Economic Adviser to the Government of India. Sir Chintaman and Sir Theodore attended meetings of Committees 3 and 4 of Commission I which were concerned with organisation and management, and form and status, respectively, of the Fund. The two non-official Indian delegates, Sir Shanmukham Chetty (1892–1953; Minister of Finance, India 1947–8) and Ardeshir D. Shroff (1899–1965; Director, Tata Sons Ltd, Bombay) had a more or less similar background and experience in private business and finance, including the shared distinction of having been rejected, although for very different reasons, for the post of the first Indian Deputy Governor of the Reserve Bank of India. Curiously, both seem to have aroused the animosity of Sir James Grigg, who was then the Finance Member of the Viceroy's Executive Council.[17] In the event both, having missed an official vocation, flourished in the private sector. Chetty was duly knighted later by the British Government despite his 'unsoundness' on the twin litmus tests – the tariff and rupee ratio issues, and Shroff's being out of court with Sir James Grigg proved no bar to his membership of the Indian delegation to the Bretton Woods conference. The appointment of two such articulate non-officials as members of a British Indian delegation in the pre-independence days to so important a conference as Bretton Woods was not uncharacteristic of the consummate British diplomacy which quite often expressed itself in the appointment of Indian officials, even those critical of British rule, to sensitive positions. A classic example was Sir Benegal Rama Rau (contemporary of Keynes at King's) of the Indian Civil Service who 'made no concealment of the fact that – though a devoted Government servant – he nevertheless felt sympathy with the general aims of the Indian nationalist movement'. Some of his senior British colleagues, 'noticing his abilities, his tact, and his political leanings, were responsible for his being chosen as Secretary to the Indian Delegation [to the Round Table Conference] in London, from 1931 to 1934'.[18] In the same vein one could also argue that the nomination of Chetty and Shroff, as two committed and able non-official Indians, showed a discerning concern on the part of the British authorities for India's national interests on the eve of independence. Dr B. K. Madan (then Director of Research, Reserve Bank of India and later an Executive Director of the International Monetary Fund) was the Secretary of the Delegation, and Sir David Meek, Indian Trade Commissioner in London was associated as Adviser. The Indian delegation at Bretton Woods was small (5) in comparison with other delegations like China (9), the United Kingdom (7) and the United States (12). Sir Chintaman D. Deshmukh felt subsequently that the Indian delegation could have been larger considering not only the size and importance of the country but also to cope with the problem of numerous committees often sitting at the same time. Nonetheless, the Indian delegation, although small, was also 'a hand-picked and a high-powered one' and played a far more influential role than was warranted by its size or its political status, representing as it did the only non-self-governing country participating in the conference. The principal issues that concerned the Indian delegation at Bretton Woods were: the extension of the purposes of the Fund to include economic development and the equitable settlement of the abnormal indebtedness arising out of the Second World War (the sterling balances problem); securing a satisfactory quota for India; and a permanent seat (an appointed as opposed to an elected seat) on the Executive Board of the Fund (and the Bank).

The Indian delegation proposed two major amendments to Article I (ii) on Purposes of the Fund. The first amendment called the Fund 'to assist in the fuller utilization of the resources of economically underdeveloped countries',[19] and the second for the settlement of 'abnormal indebtness arising out of the war',[20] The first amendment was supported by Ecuador but was opposed by the United Kingdom and South Africa mainly because the development of underdeveloped countries was regarded more properly as a matter for the Bank rather than for the Fund. To counter this criticism India proposed a revision of Article I (ii) which called for 'the development of the resources and productive power of all member countries with due regard to the needs of economically backward countries.'[21] The Indian delegation (Sir Shanmukham Chetty) stated that though an increase in the volume of exports and imports was an important aspect of balanced growth, the economically backward countries attached 'great importance also to the balanced character and composition of international trade' since 'a predominant flow of raw material and foodstuffs in one direction and a flow of highly manufactured goods in the other direction is not a really balanced international trade. . . . It is only by greater attention to the industrial needs of countries like India that you achieve a real and rational balance.' For this reason the Indian delegation wanted specific mention of 'the needs of economically backward countries, in the description of objectives of economic policy, which the Fund cannot directly assist but may indirectly facilitate'.[22] This, however, encountered similar criticisms, and eventually Commission I agreed to the present wording of Article I (ii) of the Fund 'to facilitate the expansion and balanced growth of international trade, and to contribute thereby to the promotion and maintenance of high levels of employment and real income and to the development of the productive resources of *all members* as primary objectives of economic policy' (emphasis provided).

Keynes did not take any position on these proposals of the Indian delegation although he was in close contact with them. For instance, Sir Chintaman Deshmukh was present, along with Sir Jeremy Raisman and Sir Theodore Gregory, at the second informal meeting with Dominion and Indian representatives which was held in Keynes's room, Atlantic City, on Sunday, 25 June 1944. This meeting was convened to enable Keynes to report on his discussions with Dr White, the US delegate, which, however, did not cover the broad objectives of the Fund.[23] Keynes's silence on this proposal of the Indian delegation could more properly be interpreted as an implicit acknowledgement that the developmental role properly belonged to the proposed Bank for Reconstruction and Development (IBRD). Keynes was the Chairman of the Second Commission on the Bank but according to Sir Chintaman Deshmukh he could not see much of Keynes at this point because of Keynes's indisposition.[24] Interestingly, Deshmukh in commenting to Sir James Taylor (his predecessor as Governor of the Reserve Bank of India) on an earlier draft of Keynes's Bank Scheme, remarked that 'it might prove inflationary' to which Sir James concurred heartily: 'I agree with you about Keynes –

a monetary quack preferring a monetary paradox of the worst inflationary type for what is fundamentally an international political problem'.[25] Sir James's rather brusque dismissal of Keynes was perhaps nothing more than a typical bureaucratic reaction to an academic's nostrums.

India as the largest holder of wartime sterling balances, also proposed an amendment, calling for the settlement of 'abnormal indebtedness arising out of the war' which was supported by Egypt (the second largest holder of sterling balances). In an eloquent but well reasoned statement, Mr Shroff fully appreciated the 'unfortunate loss of valuable foreign investments by the United Kingdom' and its inability to meet the capital requirements of India 'for a fairly long period'. He added that India 'never intended the International Monetary Fund . . . to take over straight away in one lump sum the entire accumulated credit balances during the war'. Rather it 'sought multilateral convertibility for a reasonable portion of these accumulated balances'. Shroff compared India's position to 'a man with a million dollar balance in the bank but not sufficient cash to pay his taxi fare.'[26] Both the Indian and Egyptian delegations invoked the strains of war economics on their countries but the proposal was rejected by all the other delegations including the British, on the ground that the problem of war balances was too large for the Fund to tackle with its available resources. In attempting to counter this argument the Indian delegation submitted a revised amendment as follows:

> To facilitate the multilateral settlement of a reasonable portion of the foreign credit balances accumulated amongst the member countries during the war so as to promote the purposes referred to in subdivision 2, without placing undue strain on the resources of the Fund.[27]

This too was opposed and rejected by the UK, the US, and French delegations. Keynes, on behalf of the UK delegation at the meeting of Commission I, made a most statesmanlike presentaion of the case for the UK as 'the only country here represented which has incurred large-scale war debts to her Allies and associates also here present, these alternative amendments must be assumed, as Mr Shroff had indeed made clear, to relate primarily to her' (CW, XXVI, p. 86). Equally, Keynes recognised that India, alone of the wartime group of sterling holders (Egypt, Palestine, and Iraq) had borne a heavy share of war expenditures (CW, XXIV, p. 286). The UK also held the bulk of the currency reserves of India. Keynes, while pointing out that there was 'inevitably no equality of financial sacrifice' during the Second World War, expressed 'Britain's gratitude to those Allies, particularly our Indian friends who put their resources at our disposal without stint and themselves suffered from privation as a result. Our effort would have been gravely, perhaps critically, embarrassed if they had held back from helping us so wholeheartedly and on so great a scale. We appreciate the moderate, friendly and realistic statement of the problem which Mr. Shroff has put before you today.' [A characteristic 'amend honourable' by Keynes who had by then overcome his earlier aversion for Shroff.] 'Nevertheless, the settlement of these debts must be in our clear and settled judgement, a matter between those directly concerned. When the end is reached . . . we shall take it up without any delay, to settle honorably what was honorably and generously given. . . . We concur entirely in the view which has first been expressed by the American Delegation that the Fund is not intended to deal directly with war indebtedness . . . this amendment could be of no practical effect, and is therefore better discarded if misunderstanding is to be avoided about the role which the Fund can expect to play' (ibid, p. 86). Thus Keynes, while conceding the merits of India's case, and not seeking any special treatment for the UK, wanted to treat the sterling balances as a bilateral issue beyond the terms of reference of the Fund. The rejection of the Indian proposal on the settlement of the wartime balances occasioned considerable disappointment in India and there was later even a demand in India for the recall of the Indian Delegation. Keynes's statement, however, certainly helped to allay Indian concerns on the sterling balances which related basically to the measures and modalities necessary to enable India 'to receive the payment that Britain might be in a position to make from time to time in the form of goods . . . the objective being the establishment of a suitable surplus of imports from the U.K. over exports representing the repayment of our sterling balances'.[28]

The specific concern of the Indian delegation in this context was the convertibility of sterling. Mr Shroff therefore sought an interpretation from the UK delegation as to how the provision in Article VIII Section 2(a) would 'affect foreign trade transactions between member countries who are ordinarily accustomed to carry on their foreign trade in terms of sterling . . .'. To this the UK delegation (Dennis Robertson) clarified their understanding that only sterling currently acquired as the result of current transactions 'would be really convertible either into rupees or into any other currency'.[29] There was, of course, Keynes's celebrated exchange with Dennis Robertson on the latter's 'Note on the International Monetary Fund (An Essay in Rabbinics)' specifically on the precise meaning of 'convertibility' of India's sterling balances (that is, in the 'Bretton Woods Pickwickian Sense') and 'convertibility into dollars' (CW, XXVI, pp. 121–2). Keynes was, however, emphatic that no assurances be given 'to the Indians, or to the Egyptians, or to anyone else, on unrestricted convertibility into dollars quite outside the ambit of IMF'. But equally, in a different context, Keynes affirmed, in reiteration of his opposition to 'all horse-trading', that it would be out of the question to suggest to India that the price of a further advance towards complete self-government should be a concession by the new Indian Administration in the matter of the UK wartime debt to India.[30]

But by far the most arduous task of the Indian delegation was to ensure a satisfactory quota for India in the Fund and also a permanent seat on the Executive Board of the Fund (and the Bank). Both the India Office and the Government of India were unhappy that India's initial (provisional) quota (suggested by the US delegation in January 1944) was too low ($300 million) as against China ($600 million). The Government of India contended that India 'should receive a quota at least as large as that assigned to China' on both technical and political considerations and that Indian public opinion was likely to be extremely sensitive on size of the quota and that any attempt to put India below China . . . would gravely imperil acceptability of the scheme'.[31] It was at this juncture that Keynes played a decisive role in supporting India's case. He shrewdly sensed that 'India is much more concerned with equality or near equality with China than with the absolute amount, though they would like something extra' adding that he was going to see Harry Dexter White, the US delegate, privately to put up to him a solution to 'satisfy India and help Australia a little'. However, Keynes felt that if Australia was 'still dissatisfied . . . she must fight her own battles' and expressed his concern to 'avoid horse-dealing arguments about this in public'.[32] In a subsequent letter (4 July 1944) to Lord Catto, Governor of the Bank of England, Keynes said, 'I have persuaded him [White] to make a sufficient concession to India to keep them moderately satisfied and enough for Australia to meet their deserts, though not their demands' (CW, XXVI, p. 79). Clearly, Keynes felt a special concern for India on the quota issue and his support was critical in persuading the US delegation to fix India's quota at $400 million (out of the aggregate final quotas of $8800 million for all the 44 countries represented at the conference) on 'due recognition of India's economic significance'. Even so the Indian delegation was dissatisfied, as noted by Sir Jeremy Raisman, not so much with the absolute size of the quota but about 'her relative position among the countries that form the general set-up of the Fund' since it was not only a question of the quota but 'the arrangements relating to the management of the Fund'.[33] Governor Deshmukh too echoed the same sentiment when he said that 'having regard to the size, significance, and any other economic criteria, . . . India was entitled to take a continuous and active part in the deliberations of the Managing Committee (of the Fund).[34] This was a critical moment, as reported by Deshmukh.

> Sir Jeremy announced to the rest of the delegation one morning that there was a danger of India's quota being fixed so low as to imperil the chance of her representation on the governing bodies of the Fund and the Bank even by an elected Executive Director of her own. On this I said, that in that case, the Indian delegation must withdraw, and I was wholeheartedly supported by Chetty and Shroff. Raisman lost poise for a moment and said this was another manifestation of the unfortunate Indian tendency to non-cooperate. Half an hour afterwards, he came to me and said that he had thought over the matter and was convinced that withdrawal was the only honourable course to take, should there be no improvement in the proposed quota for India. As a result of his resolute attitude and supported, I am happy to record, by the United Kingdom delegation, India ultimately succeeded in securing her proper quota, which, as events have transpired, secured her a place among the permanent members of the Executive Board for over twenty-five years.[35]

The reference to the support of the United Kingdom delegation for India was clearly to Keynes. Following the Joint Committee of Experts' stand that 'the Executive Committee (of the Fund) shall consist of at least nine members, including the representatives of the five countries with the largest quotas' the Indian delegation tried unsuccessfully to increase the number of appointed directors from five to six. Eventually, due to the fortuitous circumstance that the USSR decided not to join the Fund, India automatically became one of the five countries entitled to appoint an Executive Director; that is, without having to go through the formality of election. This, however, in turn posed the problem raised by the Indian delegation (Sir Ramaswami Mudaliar) at the Inaugural Meeting of the Fund and Bank at Savannah, Georgia, on 13 March 1946 regarding the position of India as a country which now was an appointed member on the strength of its quota but 'which may find itself elbowed out . . . when a country with a higher subscription and therefore entitled to an appointed member enters the Fund' prior to the second election of the Executive Directors (Fund Document 12). Keynes supported the proposal of the Indian delegation that this particular matter should be referred to an Ad Hoc Committee of which Keynes was the Chairman. This Committee proposed that there shall be one additional Executive Director who shall hold office until the second election if at any time before the second election both of the following conditions exist.

(1) There have been admitted to membership the Governments of one or more countries not listed in Schedule A; and
(2) The members not entitled to appoint Executive Directors, whose votes are not included in those entitled to be cast by Executive Directors holding office at the time the additional director is elected, have votes totalling 4,000.

This report and resolution was approved and adopted by the Board of Governors at the fifth session, 15 March 1946 (*Selected Documents*, Board of Governors, Inaugural Meeting, Savannah, Georgia, 8–18 March 1946, International Monetary Fund, Washington, DC, April 1946, p. 39). Deshmukh publicly acknowledged the valuable assistance and guidance rendered by Keynes 'in the matter of interpreting India's rights to representation on the [Fund-Bank] Board of Directors.'[36] Keynes also expressed his wholehearted support for the provision in the Fund's Articles, sponsored by the Indian delegation, that 'in appointing the staff the Managing Director shall, subject to the paramount importance of securing the "highest standards of efficiency and technical competence", pay due regard to the importance of recruiting personnel on as wide a geographical basis as possible' (Article XII, 4(d)). Incidentally, the Indian delegation, along with France, initially supported Keynes's (unsuccessful) proposal to locate the Fund in New York rather than in metropolitan Washington.[37] Keynes remarked that the UK Government considered the choice of Washington as the location of the Fund to be 'a grave error.' Later, India, together with France and Canada, withdrew their objections to the Washington location in order to make the Report unanimous. It is noteworthy, as remarked by Sir Chintaman Deshmukh, that the fact that India 'on the threshold of national independence, could and did take an independent line on such questions was warmly appreciated, particularly by Lord Keynes.'[38] During a memorable meeting with Keynes, Dr Madan (secretary of the Indian delegation) asked him 'regarding his view of the duration of the [post-war] transitional period' . . . 'not less than five years' was the instant and prophetic reply.[39]

All these significant episodes attest to the close contacts and rapport between Keynes and the Indian delegation during the Bretton Woods and Savannah conferences. What, in turn, was Keynes's own assessment of his special relationship with the Indian delegation? Keynes found Deshmukh, as told to him earlier by Raisman, to be 'loyal' and 'a good civil servant'. Ironically, the reputedly political and ambitious Chetty, as he was described by James Grigg, was regarded by Keynes as 'very amenable and sensible' (CW, XXVI, p. 79). Shroff, the highly articulate maverick of the Indian delegation, was initially not a great favourite with Keynes. ('Shroff is clearly, as Raisman says, a snake in the grass, trying to catch us out and filled with suppressed malice.') It is easy to sense that Shroff, a seasoned polemicist, was trying to catch the British delegation out on – convertibility of sterling balances but hard to fathom Keynes's reference to the springs and objects of his 'suppressed malice'. However, such acerbic comments have also to be viewed in the customary ambience of the cut-and-thrust of international negotiations on sensitive issues, where it is not always sweetness and light. But, as noted earlier, Keynes, with his ingrained sense of fairness, did later revise his opinion of Shroff. Keynes, the accomplished polemicist, must have found Shroff a sporting and worthy exponent of his own *métier*. Keynes never elaborated on why Sir Theodore Gregory declared 'that he is fed to the teeth with the prevailing Indian attitude on everything, and his only idea is to escape as soon as he can do so without disloyalty to Raisman'. Keynes seemed to echo these sentiments rather uncritically, when he said: 'Raisman, I fancy, feels much the same; so do we all. If only some heavenly power would apply almighty shears and cut the painter. However, I do think we shall succeed in preventing them from making any extra trouble here or in India in connection with the monetary plan as such.' These are rather intriguing reactions considering that Sir Jeremy Raisman's espousal of the Indian case, despite some initial wavering, earned high praise from no less a person that Sir Chintaman

Deshmukh. Sir Jeremy was the last of a certain distinctive breed of British officials of the Government of India, like Sir George Schuster, who felt and acted as 'a responsible member of the Government of India and not in any sense a Whitehall civil servant' who in the event of a conflict 'between British and Indian interests' would 'fight for the latter'.[40] In assessing the relationship of Keynes with the Indian delegation it is only fair to recognise that both Sir Jeremy Raisman and Sir Theodore Gregory seem, most commendably, to have put themselves under a self-denying ordinance during the most sensitive stages of the conference, and did not at any point attempt to exploit their status or eminence to upstage or pressurise the Indian members of the delegation. This was particularly remarkable in respect of Gregory who had known Keynes closely as a member of the Macmillan Committee in Britain. In sum, Keynes emerged as a most persuasive and singleminded advocate of India's interests at the formulation and inauguration of the International Monetary Fund. What made Keynes espouse India's case? He sensed perceptively India's economic significance and potential importance in Fund-Bank membership. More than that, it reflected his characteristic concern for the underprivileged. Equally, as an eminent economist he was struck by the highly competent and persuasive presentation of India's case notably by Sir Chintaman Deshmukh and Shroff, ably assisted by the meticulous staff work of Dr Madan. Doubtless, the patrician *gravitas* and versatility of Sir Chintaman (brilliant civil servant, prizewinning botanist at Cambridge, and Sanskrit poet) must have also struck a responsive chord in Keynes the Renaissance man, who at the end of the farewell banquet remarked, prophetically, to Sir Chintaman: 'I hope you will have great influence for good in your country.'[41] Towards the end Keynes singled out the Indian delegation for a glowing tribute ('The excellence and closeness of our relations with the Indian Delegation deserves special comment. Sir Chintaman Deshmukh handled his case with high dignity, ability, and reasonableness: we always supported him on his interests and he always supported us on ours', CW, XXVI, p. 231). No other delegation evoked such spontaneous and sincere appreciation from Keynes. There was not the slightest element of patronage in all this since neither Keynes nor the Indian delegates suppressed any legitimate differences of opinion for the sake of a mindless political consensus. Keynes's tribute to the Indian delegation, the only one representing a political dependency at Bretton Woods, was, if anything, a graceful and merited recognition of the intellectual and personal credentials of a distinguished delegation. Keynes did not live to see the operations of the International Monetary Fund but he would have been highly gratified that the US idea of a full-time Executive Director devoting his whole attention to Fund affairs was, reportedly, fulfilled most completely by J. V. Joshi, one of his most brilliant pupils at King's and the first Indian Executive Director.[42]

Notes

1. Lorie Tarshis in Symposium on 'Keynes as Seen by his Students in the Thirties' in *Keynes, Cambridge and the General Theory*, (ed.) Don Patinkin and J. Clark Leith, (Macmillan, London, 1977), pp. 48–9.
2. The *Collected Writings of John Maynard Keynes*, Vol. IX, Essays in Persuasion (Macmillan, London, 1972), pp. 354–55, 358.
3. Sir George Schuster, *Private Work and Public Causes, A Personal Record*, 1881–1978 (Cowbridge, D. Brown and Sons, Glamorgan, Wales, 1979), p. 100.
4. Schuster, ibid, p. 125.
5. Grigg to Sir Findlater Stewart (India Office), from Simla, 16 June 1934 (No. 2/20/3(a)) *Grigg Collection*, Churchill College, Cambridge.
6. Grigg to Findlater Stewart (India Office), from Simla, 14 May 1934, p. 2, 2/20/1(a) *Grigg Collection*, Churchill College, Cambridge.
7. Sir James Grigg, in his autobiography *Prejudice and Judgement* (Jonathan Cape, London, 1956), p. 297.
8. Otto Niemeyer (Bank of England) to Grigg, letter dated 17 July 1936, p. 2, 3/4/25(b) *Grigg Collection*, Churchill College, Cambridge.
9. '. . . Sir Eric Coates, who as Finance Secretary along with the Auditor-General, the Commerce Secretary and the Chairman, Central Board of Revenue, had the responsibility of selecting officers for the [Finance-Commerce] Pool, had reservations about taking me on the ground that I had studied Economics in Cambridge and might have imbibed dangerous theoretical ideas which might prevent me from learning from experience' L. K. Jha (Indian Civil Service) *Mr Red Tape* (Allied Publishers, New Delhi, 1987) p. 141.
10. As remarked by Grigg during the discussion in the Indian Central Legislative Assembly on the appointment of Gregory. Cited by D. H. Butani, 'The Quality and Perspective of Indian Economic Thought', *Indian Journal of Economics*, January 1942, Conference Number 86, Vol. XXII, Part III, p. 280.
11. Roger Middleton, *Towards the Managed Economy: Keynes, the Treasury, and the Fiscal Policy Debate of the 1930's* (Methuen, London, 1985).
12. 'Keynes as Seen by His Students in the 1930s' in *Keynes, Cambridge and the General Theory*, edited by Don Patinkin and J. Clark Leith, op. cit., p. 43. Unfortunately, this symposium did not have any contribution from Dr. V.K.R.V. Rao (Gonville and Caius College), who did pioneering work on India's national income at Cambridge and was regarded by Keynes as his best Indian pupil, as noted by Malcolm Darling, Memo of

Talk with Keynes, 8 February 1934, *Darling Papers*, Box I21–46. *South Asia Centre*, Cambridge.

13. H. C. Coombs (ex-Governor, Reserve Bank of Australia), *Trial Balance* (Macmillan Co. of Australia, Melbourne, 1981), p. 11.
14. R. S. Sayers, *Financial Policy 1939–1945* (Her Majesty's Stationery Office, London, 1956), p. 260, footnote 2.
15. D. E. Moggridge, 'Economic Policy in the Second World War', in Milo Keynes (ed.), *Essays*, op. cit., p. 199.
16. Sir Chintaman Dwarkanath Deshmukh (1896–1982); Secretary, Reserve Bank of India (1939–41); Deputy Governor (1941–43); Governor, Reserve Bank of India (1943–49); Finance Minister, Government of India (1952–56).
17. Sir James Grigg to Sir Findlater Stewart (India Office), 'I don't care for Chetty and I don't want him as Deputy Governor of the Reserve Bank because he is too ambitious and political – and moreover he is unsound both on the rupee ratio and on protection.' (Letter from Simla, 23 July 1934, 2/20/60/c, in the *Grigg Collection*, Churchill College, Cambridge). Grigg turned down Shroff for the Deputy Governorship ('a perfectly frightful man and an intimate crony of [Sir Osborne] Smith's . . .' [the first Governor of the Reserve Bank of India, and a pet aversion of Grigg!]. Letter to Sir Findlater Stewart dated 27 July 1936, 3/4/27(a)). Grigg was also prejudiced by Otto Niemeyer's assessment of Shroff ('All brains and no character, I guess', 31 July 1936, 3/4/32(6), 63 *Grigg Collection*).
18. *Annual Report of the Council, King's College*, November 1971, p. 47. This anonymous obituary was written by Ian Stephens, former editor of the *Statesman*, Calcutta, and a Fellow of King's College.
19. Document F. 1. Alternative C. *Proceedings and Documents of United Nations Monetary and Finance Conference,* Bretton Woods, New Hampshire, July 1–22, 1944, Vol. I, p. 23.
20. Alternative G. *Proceedings*, ibid, p. 24.
21. Alternative I (Document 162), *Proceedings*, Vol. I, p. 184.
22. Document 383, *Proceedings*, Vol. II, pp. 1180–81.
23. The *Collected Writings of John Maynard Keynes*, Vol. XXVI, 'Activities 1941–1946: Shaping the Post-war World Bretton Woods and Reparations, (ed.) Donald Moggridge (Macmillan, London, 1980), p. 56.
24. C. D. Deshmukh, *The Course of My Life*, (Orient Longman, New Delhi, 1974), p. 120.
25. Deshmukh, ibid, p. 127.
26. *Proceedings and Documents of the United Nations Monetary and Financial Conference,* Bretton Woods, New Hampshire, July 1–22, 1944 (United State Government Printing Office, Washington, 1948), Vol. II, Department of State, Publication 2866, pp. 1171–1173.
27. Alternative K, *Proceedings*, p. 278.
28. Address of Sir C. D. Deshmukh to the Bombay Rotary Club, cited in Simha, 'Genesis', op. cit., p. 429.
29. Joseph Gold, 'The Multilateral System of Payments: Keynes, Convertibility and the International Monetary Fund, Articles of Agreement'. (International Monetary Fund, Washington DC., August 1981), p. 15.

30. *The Collected Writings of John Maynard Keynes,* Vol. XXIV, 'Activities 1944–46, The Transition to Peace,' (ed.) Donald Moggridge, (Macmillan, London, 1979), pp. 490–491.
31. Simha, 'Genesis', op. cit., p. 431.
32. Keynes's letter dated 30 June 1944 to Sir Richard Hopkins, Permanent Secretary to the British Treasury in CW, XXVI, p. 79.
33. Simha, 'Genesis', op. cit., p. 433.
34. Ibid., p. 433.
35. C. D. Deshmukh, *The Course of My Life* (Orient Longman, New Delhi, 1974), p. 128.
36. C. D. Deshmukh, *Central Banking in Retrospect*, op. cit., p. 20.
37. 'He [Keynes] was particularly pleased at my support to his plea that the Bank's [and the Fund's] headquarters should be established in New York (away from U.S.A. official influence in Washington and in close touch with Wall Street). I cited the example of the Reserve Bank of India, which I said was happy to be in Bombay (with a winter camp office in Calcutta) and not in Delhi, the official metropolis.' Deshmukh, *The Course of My Life*, op. cit., p. 14.
38. Simha, 'Genesis', op. cit., p. 596.
39. Dr B. K. Madan, 'Echoes of Bretton Woods', *Finance and Development*, June 1969, Vol. 2, 1969, p. 33.
40. Sir George Schuster, *Private Work*, op. cit., p. 90.
41. C. D. Deshmukh, *The Course of my Life*, op. cit., p. 140.
42. J. Keith Horsefield, *Annals of the Fund*, International Monetary Fund, Washington, DC, 1969, p. 132. Joshi's Memorandum on the *Problem of India's Sterling Balances* (The Times of India Press, Bombay, 1949) also served as an invaluable position paper for Indian negotiators on this thorny postwar issue.

7 Keynes Economicus: The Indian Conjuncture

'He was essentially a monetary economist; his writings are an intellectual counterpart to the monetary revolution of our time.' *Sir John Hicks*

'Keynes was an economic adviser first and foremost.' *Lord Kaldor*

THE TWO KEYNESES

Keynes's Indian Connection explains and typifies some of the most characteristic features of the mind-set and general intellectual stance of 'Keynes Economicus' as the quintessential applied monetary economist who was first and foremost a policy adviser for whom economic analysis was basically a tool for addressing pressing issues of public policy. But any appraisal of the interface between Keynes and India has to take account of the critical distinction between the economics of Keynes in relation to India and the influence of Keynesian economics on Indian economic thought and policy, as well as the two distinct facets of Keynes's writings, activities and even persona, namely, the Classical and Institutionalist Keynes of the India Office, Indian Currency and Finance and the Indian Currency Commission and the Revolutionary Keynes of the *General Theory* and after. Such a functional dichotomy seems more relevant and meaningful at least for this study than Hans Singer's chronological divide of Keynes I (before Bretton Woods) and Keynes II (after Bretton Woods).[1] According to Singer Keynes I in this *General Theory* actually deals with the 'Special Case' of Great Britain and the hypotheses he formulates are obviously far from representing the reality of developing countries. It is in Keynes II that Singer thinks it possible to find a broad conceptual view relevant to the problems of developing countries. Therefore, in his scheme of thought the relevance of Keynes I is to a considerable degree a function of the recognition and acceptance of Keynes II.

THE CLASSICAL AND INSTITUTIONAL KEYNES

Keynes's early involvement in Indian economic affairs affords valuable insights into how and why he was led on to applied and institutional monetary economics and to very specific policy issues like reforming the Indian currency system or establishing a central bank for India. Consequently he was never interested in the grand themes of class conflict or the economics of exploitative imperialism in India or in historical topics like the monetisation of the Indian economy. In fact he was inclined to be rather dismissive of the whole 'drain' controversy as a 'widely held' but mistaken view 'now repudiated by an increasing number of [Indian] economists of the younger school'. (*Economic Journal*, 1911, p. 429) After his India Office service and his early Cambridge years Keynes never evinced any interest in non-monetary themes as he did during those few years when he addressed a wide range of topics like the condition-of-the people problem, British investments in India, the salt tax, and free trade. Even in regard to the nature and magnitude of British investment in India, it is interesting to note that although the controversy centred on India it was not in fact related to Indian problems and policies but to the much wider issue raised by tariff reformers that free trade policies had stimulated an excessive outflow of British capital overseas thereby depriving the British economy of much-needed capital. This early and consistent preoccupation with monetary matters in the Indian context might even have induced just the kind of *déformation professionale* in Keynes which prompted a perceptive observer to remark that he 'cannot help thinking that he [Keynes] looks at large political problems too much from the aspect of currency and exchange'.[2] In regard to Indian economic policy Keynes's failing was not so much the monetary angle on Indian political problems which did not concern him as the excessive concentration on monetary problems amounting to a virtual exclusion of basic non-monetary issues. Thus, Keynes was sceptical of India's industrialisation, and argued with almost Physiocratic fervour that 'her future prosperity is to be sought almost entirely in the application of more skill and knowledge, and especially of more capital, to the methods of agriculture'.[3] In the same vein, almost like a romantic pastoralist, he did not find 'it easy to believe that India will find in mills and factories the non-economic goods, which make up along with wealth the dignity of a nation'.[4] Keynes was even critical of a British economist,

Sir Theodore Morison, whom he thought, argued 'too lightly from the past to the future and from the West to the East, without a full consideration of the deep underlying factors, upon which the most advantageous direction depends of the resources of a nation'. Keynes's evaluation of Indian industrialisation was based on a peculiarly static view of comparative costs and an implicit denial of externalities which also made him strangely impervious to the infant-industry argument even when he became a 'reluctant protectionist' as Kaldor described him. This remained a perennial blind spot in his mind-set. Perhaps this stance was also a reflection of Keynes's lack of 'interest in technology for its own sake . . . in how industrial processes worked, or in the scientific development of new techniques'[5] and his lack of familiarity with and his neglect of non-monetary factors in the economic process. One has only to contrast the perceptive analysis of financial markets and the behaviour of investors in the *General Theory* based on his own practical experience with the total omission in all his works of any significant examination of the structure and processes of production and the behaviour of the firm or the farm, except for his sporadic forays into problems of internationally-traded commodities. In point of fact Keynes did have a strong interest in agriculture and pig-farming which never found public expression outside King's College estates and his Sussex farms. He even wrote nostalgically of Silvio Gessels's idyllic retirement in Switzerland where he was 'able to devote the last two decades of his life to the most delightful occupations open to those who do not have to earn their living, authorship and experimental farming'[6] – an exquisite testament of a cultivated rentier! Keynes's lone excursus into the economics of agriculture was 'a thoughtful paper' on the pricing of pigs given to Galbraith on his first meeting with him at the US Office of Price Administration in the early days of the Second World War. This paper is 'one of the few documents missing from his collected papers'.[7] Keynes's conventional antipathy to Indian industrialisation may have also persisted partly because of his lack of familiarity with the more sophisticated Indian critique of British policies in India, except for specific criticisms of Indian monetary policy by analysts like Gokhale, to whom Keynes often paid handsome tributes. Paradoxically, while Keynes was fully conversant with the sentiments of Indian political nationalism, particularly from his diligent readings of the Indian press, he did not make a comparable effort to understand the rationale of Indian economic nationalism as expressed in the analyses and views of the most notable contemporary Indian economists on the more significant economic issues like Dadabhai Naoroji (on Indian poverty and the economic 'drain'), R. C Dutt (famines and land revenue), M. G. Ranade (the analytic foundations of Indian national economics), K. T. Telang (protection of Indian industry), G. V. Joshi, and G. Subramaniya Iyer (economic aspects of British rule in India). Keynes's tendency to neglect historical or contemporary scholarship in economics was thus manifested early in his writings on India, which perhaps partly reflects the fact that he was in a unique sense an auto-didact in economics, although not quite in the manner of Ricardo or Kalecki, with limited exposure to formal instruction and scholarship in economics. The solitary exception to this trait of Keynes is the meticulous scholarly apparatus of his *Treatise on Probability*, where perhaps its origins as a fellowship dissertation dictated the format. While Keynes may have been remiss in overlooking the developmental angles of Indian industrialisation and economic policy, he always remained acutely sensitive to the welfare aspects. Thus on the overall objective of Indian economic policy he was consistently unequivocal in according primacy to the stability of internal prices as against the level or stability of the rate of exchange, and he was always more concerned about the interests of the Indian peasant as against those of the urban or exporter classes. In his classic evidence to the Indian Exchange and Currency Committee, 1919 (Babington Smith) Keynes argued for a high rupee as 'enabling the "ryot" (Indian farmer) to clothe and feed himself "cheaply"' (CW, XV, p. 289).

In contrast to his total neglect of the non-monetary aspects of Indian economic policy, Keynes found himself wholly in his intellectual element in the analysis of Indian monetary economics. In fact the Indian nexus played a crucial role in the making of Keynes the monetary economist. *Indian Currency and Finance* was his first publication and an acclaimed classic of monetary literature on a highly complex subject which established his public reputation as a professional economist of the highest rank. 'It has a permanent niche in the history of thought on central banking but it will chiefly be remembered for its place in the history of the gold exchange standard.'[8] India was the first country to adopt it. To this one should add an equally important contribution of the book, namely, its distinctive place in the evolution of Keynes's own monetary thought. Keynes's vivid appreciation of the bearing of Indian monetary management not only upon prices, exports, and imports but also on output and employment was 'something new', and if one adds 'the theoretical implications of the English experience in the 20s to the theory of Indian Currency and Finance' one gets 'the substance of the Keynesian ideas of 1930s'.[9] The theoretical advantages of the gold exchange standard were of course first enunciated by Ricardo but Keynes's exposition, although not as original as one might suppose, is not only the 'best English work on the gold exchange standard'[10] but has also fulfilled the prophecy that it 'is likely long to remain the standard work on its subject'.[11] It was also the first complete and systematic account of the history and operations of the highly complex Indian monetary and banking system, except for Keynes's regrettable failure to follow Marshall's hints to examine two characteristic features of the Indian monetary system – the role and operation of 'native financiers' and the extent of 'native hoarding'.[12] Apart from the masterly analysis of the role of seasonality in the movements of monetary aggregates in India and of capital between India and England, it is also notable for its pioneering formulation of the economic rationale of foreign exchange reserves as primarily a means of external payment which should not be sterilised unproductively as backing for domestic legal tender currency or wasted in public internal circulation. Keynes's *Indian Currency and Finance* has also been described as his only major work in what would now be called 'development economics'.[13] This is a curiously far-fetched and totally misleading claim. Although it certainly ranks as a major work on a developing country, it does not deal with either the determinants, problems, or policies of economic development in India. This work, like almost all of Keynes's major contributions, in fact abstracts from the real sector, but in one respect it makes, together with his memorandum to the Chamberlain Commission, a major, albeit indirect, contribution to development economics which, however, is nowhere mentioned by Harry Johnson. Keynes was the first economist to present the economic rationale for a central bank as a developmental agency to promote financial intermediation and finance economic development in an emergent economy, instead of being merely a controller of the monetary system as in developed economies like England.[14] Apart from its substance, *Indian Currency and Finance* is even more notable as a singularly cogent and elegant synthesis of history, statistics, institutional economics, macro- and micro-analysis, and policy. It occupies a distinctive niche in Keynes's writings, for he never again wrote a book with this unique combination of qualities. It was his solitary excursus in a rare and difficult genre and could justifiably be ranked as one of his most influential and seminal works alongside *The Economic Consequences of the Peace* and *The General Theory*. It was the Indian conjuncture which enabled him to write an enduring if sadly neglected classic of economic literature, which escaped the notice of even four Nobel Laureates in economics (Hicks, Hayek, Friedman, and Samuelson) in their centennial appraisals of Keynes.[15]

Keynes's work on Indian monetary issues is also notable for an early demonstration of his distinctive but little-known flair and talents as an institutional architect. Keynes's blueprint for the State Bank of India which covered meticulous details relating to the Board of Directors, operational management and the disposition of profits, is a striking refutation of the observation that Keynes, 'in devising all of his schemes, did not give much thought to the technical details of organization and management of institutions'.[16] It is also often overlooked that one of Keynes's most enduring institutional contributions to Indian economic policy was his energetic and innovative role in giving the right technocratic and scientific orientation to the newly-created Directorate of Statistics in the Government of India which eventually helped to give India an economic data-base far superior to that of most developing countries and even comparable to those of the developed countries . One can only regret that Keynes's imaginative scheme for an economic orientation of the Indian Civil Service in the thirties was smothered by the animus and prejudices of Sir James Grigg and Sir Otto Niemeyer.

THE REVOLUTIONARY KEYNES

The impact of the Keynesian paradigm (General Theory) on Indian economic thought and policy are also of singular interest because at 'least in the theoretical literature [on developing countries] there has been little discussion of the applicability of Keynes outside India'.[17] In fact, India and Indian economists have been the earliest and most fertile breeding- and testing-grounds for the relevance and applicability of Keynesian economics, conceptual as well as practical, to developing countries, as will be evident from the following review, which, although not a state-of-the-art survey of the Indian critique of Keynesian economics,[18] does subtantiate that the primary intellectual fall-out of the Keynesian Revolution in the developing world was in fact on India and Indian economists. One can discern the genesis of the Indian critique of the Keynesian paradigm as far back as 1947–8 in the pioneering dissertation of K. N. Raj at the London School of Economics.[19] This theme was followed by two doctoral dissertations at the University School of Economics Bombay by R. M. Honavar ('Theory of Employment', 1949) and D. R. Khatkhate ('Monetary Policy and Economic Development of Underdeveloped Countries', 1952). Interestingly, the very first academic symposium of its kind on Keynesian economics in relation to the underdeveloped countries was also held in India during the December 1953 session of the Indian Economic Conference in Jaipur.

The relevance of the *General Theory* itself to the Indian Economy is best assessed in terms of its main concept and building blocks, notably employment, the multiplier, liquidity preference, and the growth models derived from it. The Indian critique of the Keynesian paradigm has broadly taken the form of a detailed examination of the scope and limitations of the concept of full employment; the dampening of the multiplier due to institutional and behavioural factors; and liquidity-preference as a constraint on growth and development. Since Keynes defined full employment as the absence of involuntary unemployment at a given level of capital, knowledge and skill in free enterprise market economies based on wage labour, the main problem for developing countries must be conceived of in terms of development, to higher levels of development and employment. It is also too often overlooked that the concept and measurement of disguised unemployment, so widely discussed in the Indian context, and which is based on the assumption of a zero or even negative marginal productivity of labour in agriculture, does not derive from the Keynesian paradigm. It is also totally different from the concept originally formulated by Joan Robinson as the shift of labour during mass cyclical unemployment from high to low productivity occupations.[20] The implicit difference between the money and social (alternative opportunity) cost of labour has also been used as a basis for policy proposals in India and other developing economies without adequate recognition of the limitations of the savings and investment potential of disguised unemployment. Surprisingly, the extensive discussion of the problem of choice of techniques of production in India shows no awareness of Keynes as the originator of the concept of 'technological unemployment . . . due to . . . economising the use of labor outrunning the pace at which we can find new uses for labor'.[21]

The dampening of the multiplier in an underdeveloped economy like India is explicable in terms of time-lags, leakage (because of high marginal propensity to import, hoarding of gold and currency, and so on), inelasticities of agricultural output, marketed surplus, working capital, predominance of household enterprises and family farms, and various supply-side constraints. Therefore the difference between the operation of the multiplier (and the accelerator) in a developed economy and a backward economy consists in the manner rather than the substance of its operation.[22] While Indian economists have no doubt made a signal contribution to the conceptual exegesis of the multiplier, there has been no matching effort at its empirical substantiation in Indian conditions. Keynes himself thought it 'most important . . . to investigate statistically the order of magnitude of the multiplier, and to discover the relative importance of the various facts which are theoretically possible'.[23]

The single most influential post-Keynesian paradigm in India has been the Harrod–Domar equation based on Harrod's extension of the Keynesian model for the explanation of short-run unemployment in a market economy into a model of self-sustaining economic growth in such an economy.[24] The Harrod–Domar equation states, briefly, that the growth of fixed investment will generate just sufficient increased sales and profits to validate the investment involved in increasing the stock of capital if G (rate of growth) is equal to S (proportion of savings at full employment-of-capital output) divided by R (normal ratio of capital stock to output). This equation provides a framework for planned growth insofar as the feasible rate of growth depends on the proportion of total output that the planners can extract as saving, and the amount of additional output that can be obtained per unit of investment by the planner's choice of projects (the capital–output ratio). This model has been the basis of successive Indian Five Year Plans albeit in a somewhat uncritical fashion, principally because of a failure to integrate investment in human capital, and an implicit exaggeration of the role of fixed and physical investment. The high-grade intellectual effort expended by Indian economists on issues like capital–output ratios and choice of techniques has not been even remotely matched by research and policy analysis of the economics of education and the return to human capital in India. Does this in any sense suggest Keynes's neglect of the importance of human capital in development? Admittedly, Keynes did not, either in his writings or his public utterances, refer to the role of investment in human capital, which in any case is very much of a latter-day intellectual construct developed largely by Chicago economists. Yet it was Keynes who in the thirties, writing to Malcolm Darling, sought to justify government borrowing in India for education of the right variety. Almost a decade later Keynes, in one of his rare unpublished pronouncements, stressed the role of human capital as a key factor in development, as is vividly brought out in the following communication to the author by I. G. Patel.

> Another occasion which brought out Keynes's farsightedness . . . was his speech before the Marshall Society where he narrated that before leaving Washington, D. C. he had been invited to speak at the Federal Reserve. Because of his failing health he had requested that only the economists of the Federal Reserve should be invited. But when he went to the Federal Reserve, he found more than a hundred persons present and was told on enquiring that they were all working as economists at the Federal Reserve. At this point, Kaldor and Mrs. Robinson, in particular, laughed rather loudly to indicate their amusement that more than a hundred persons claimed to be economists at the Federal Reserve. This was, of course, precisely what Keynes was leading them to and he came down on them rather sharply: 'Don't laugh. That is precisely the trouble with us. We think we have done our duty when we have produced a few great economists – a few Nobel Laureates – in one generation. The Americans believe in producing hundreds and thousands of competent technicians or professionals as their first priority. In the ultimate analysis, economic prosperity depends not on how brilliant a few people are but on how large a scale you are able to produce competent people in all walks of life.' Everyone was duly chastised; and no sounder statement on the economics of development has since been made.

Keynes's message was unequivocal. The key to development lies in the creation of a society based on mass competence rather than on elitism as so well exemplified by the economic history of the USA. Interestingly, this theme of Keynes harks back to a much earlier statement (1930) casting economists in a modest role when he proclaimed, 'if economists could manage to get themselves thought of as humble, competent people, on a level with dentists that would be splendid'.[25] These sentiments seem singularly apposite for India, which although it boasts of the third largest trained scientific and industrial manpower in the world still tends to be ruled by an elitist view of the technocrat and the scientist in an ascriptive rather than a performance or productivity-oriented society – a syndrome once graphically described by Thomas Balogh as 'Oxbridge Rampant'.

One of the strange quirks of intellectual history in India, however, is the striking contrast between the prolific and sophisticated Indian critique of the concepts of Keynesian economics, such as full employment, the multiplier, investment-finance, and the pervasive intellectual hegemony of the Harrod-Domar model on the one hand, and the virtual neglect, on the other hand, of precisely those elements of the *General Theory* which are of direct relevance to an underdeveloped agrarian economy like India, notably the role of the high liquidity premium on land as well as money and precious metals as barriers in retarding investment in newly-produced capital assets.[26] Keynes argued that the high liquidity premium on land (which like money has low elasticities of production and substitution) in 'certain historic environments' leads to high interest rates on mortgages 'often exceeding the probable net yield from cultivating the land, and has been a familiar feature of many agricultural economies' (ibid, p. 241). This is an apt description of the Indian rural economy. Likewise, Keynes cites Indian economic history as 'an example of a country impoverished by a preference for liquidity amounting to so strong a passion that even an enormous and chronic influx of the previous metals has been insufficient to bring down the rate of interest to a level which was compatible with the growth of real wealth'. (ibid, p. 337). Keynes was, however, careful to qualify that there is no absolute standard of liquidity which is more a matter of scale varying with carrying costs and yield of use. Consequently 'the conception of what contributes to "liquidity" is a partly vague one, changing from time to time and depending on social practices and institutions' (ibid, p. 240).

Keynes thus made liquidity preference a major causal factor in the retardation of investment in an underdeveloped economy but his analysis of gold-hoarding has to be substantially qualified in respect of India.[27] Furthermore, the actual extent of misdirection of resources in gold-hoarding is much less than commonly supposed and even where there is such misdirection its mechanics are also different from those postulated in the Keynesian framework. Gold-hoarding in India is more akin to a non-monetary phenomenon notwithstanding some formal similarities between money and gold, such as their liquidity and non-interest-yielding character. It is actuated by a combination of three conceptually distinct motives, namely, precautionary purposes, the psychic income accruing from jewellery and ornaments, and expectation of capital appreciation. Corresponding to these motives, gold can be viewed as a liquid asset, a store of value, as a durable consumer good (not mentioned by Keynes) and as a hedge. The bulk of gold stocks in India is in the form of jewellery and ornaments, unlike in countries like France where gold is held in the form of bullion or coins. To the extent that gold in India is hoarded for its use-value and esteem-value, its stocks are insensitive to changes in the rate of interest and monetary conditions. Historically, the import of gold into India has not been monetised because its virtually once-for-all absorption (the perennial sink theory) into ornamental hoards has acted as a permanent leakage from the monetary stream. Similarly, gold ornaments play a negligible role as bank collateral. On the other hand, gold has arguably played the vital role of an incentive good for the primary producer in India and to that extent it may even have been instrumental in maintaining an adequate export surplus. Of course, since hoarded gold also represents potential foreign exchange which can be mobilised for productive investment, it imposes considerable social opportunity costs on a country like India which has been subject to periodic foreign exchange constraints. Studies of savings in India show that the proportion of gold in household savings has averaged around 3.6 per cent and 0.2 per cent of actual income, which should also qualify the traditional notion of the secular 'thesaurisation' of the Indian economy. All these nuances are missing from Keynes's analysis of liquidity preference.

Keynes's analysis of liquidity preference as a social phenomenon and of the rate of interest as 'a highly conventional phenomenon' (ibid, p. 203) are, however, both highly relevant for Indian conditions, where institutional and social factors seem more influential than behavioural factors as determinants of interest rates. Thus, interest rates in India could conceptually be regarded as an aggregate of a behavioural factor, namely, the liquidity premium (that is, the pure Keynesian rate of interest); and institutional factors reflecting the risk premium (that is, the risk of default); transactions and information costs; and market imperfections because of oligopolistic merchant-money lenders who also function as oligopolistic buyers of rural produce. The aggregate of the risk premium, the costs of administration and the market imperfections is more important than liquidity premium – the main element of the Keynesian analysis – in determining the overall height of interest rates in India. But even more than liquidity preference and its implications for the rate of interest, it is the availability of credit which is perhaps more significant in Indian conditions. Because of market imperfections the clearing mechanism operates not so much through price movements (rate of interest) as quantity adjustments (that is, because there is always a 'fringe of unsatisfied borrowers who are not considered to have first claims on a bank's funds, but to whom the bank would be quite ready to lend if it was to find itself in a position to lend more': Keynes, *Treatise*, 1971, pp. 326–7). This notion, which is the genesis of the concept of credit rationing, is more relevant to Indian conditions than the *General Theory*'s apparatus. In fact, the importance of usurious non-institutional finance in India suggests that credit rationing is an even more influential factor than the rate of interest in the credit market. But the role of credit rationing in the transmission mechanism in India has hardly evoked any analytic discussion or empirical investigation by Indian economists.

Despite the impressive Indian critique of Keynesian economics it is easy to overlook that Keynes himself intended the *General Theory* to be primarily a 'theory of employment and output as a whole' and that much of it is 'illustrated and expounded mainly with reference to the conditions existing in the Anglo-Saxon countries'.[28] The few sections in the *General Theory* which have some relevant implications for development problems and policies of an economy like India's relate essentially to constraints on investment and development, notably the twin liquidity traps of premia on land and the precious metals, and not to the determinants of development. There is, in fact, no systematic discussion of the basic determinants of economic development in any of Keynes's Collected Writings, although there are numerous scattered insights. The nearest he came to this subject was in his essay on 'Economic Possibilities for Our Grandchildren', which lists the basic determinants of the pace at which we can reach our destination of economic bliss: (a) 'our power to control population' [Keynes the neo-Malthusian], (b) 'our determination to avoid wars and civil dissensions' [Keynes the Pacifist], (c) 'our willingness to entrust to science the direction of those matters which are properly the concern of science' [Keynes the Technocrat], and (d) 'the rate of accumulation as fixed by the margin between our production and our consumption'; of which the last will easily look after itself, given the first three[29] [Keynes, the Classical Economist]. The last condition, which makes prior saving a determinant of investment, was superseded by the later formulation in the *General Theory* of the equality of savings and investment and its corollary that since investment creates its own saving the latter is not in effect a constraint on development – a doctrine which has provided the theoretical rationale for deficit financing of development plans in India. This approach to deficit financing overlooks that it is the resources constraint rather than deficiency of demand which explains mass structural unemployment, underemployment, and excess capacity (due to market imperfections) in an economy like India.

Keynes was never directly concerned with economic development, and the most influential paradigms of modern development economics do not owe any intellectual debt to Keynes. Among these one could list concepts like cumulative causation, backwash, and spread effects (Gunnar Myrdal), two-gap models (Chenery et al.); dependency, centre and periphery (Raul Prebisch and the structuralists); immiserising growth (Bhagwati); balanced growth, forward and backward linkages (Hirschman); big push (Rosenstein-Rodan); take-off (Rostow); human capital (Schultz); dual economy (Boecke); unlimited labour (Arthur Lewis); choice of techniques (Bhatt and Amartya Sen); vent for surplus (Myint); and investible surpluses (Dobb and Nurkse). It is hardly surprising that an authoritative survey of the state of development economics does not contain a single reference to Keynes.[30] It is therefore far-fetched to talk of the Keynesian Theory of Development.[31] A fairer assessment would be that although Keynes himself was not directly concerned with economic development, 'the claim of development economics to stand as a separate body of economic analysis and policy derived intellectual legitimacy and nurture from the prior success and parallel features of the Keynesian revolution.'[32]

In conclusion, one is constrained to say with some regret that Indian economists, like their German counterparts, have yet to fulfil the hope expressed by Keynes: 'And if I can contribute some stray morsels towards the preparation by German economists of a full repast of theory to meet specifically German conditions, I shall be content.'[33] Keynes, true to his spirit and approach of always treating economics as a technique of analysis and not as a body of settled conclusions, had hoped that the *General Theory* would act as a catalyst for path-breaking country-specific applications. In the event, Indian economists have provided an impressive extension of the building-blocks of the *General Theory* to a developing country, but the complete edifice is still to emerge from the drawing boards.

Notes

1. Hans Singer, 'The Relevance of Keynes For Developing Countries', *Estudos De Economia*, Vol. IV, No. 4, July – September 1984.
2. Earl of Crawford and Balcarres, 'A Private View by a Cabinet Minister, 1919,' in Milo Keynes (ed.), *Essays*, op. cit., pp. 24–5.
3. *Collected Writings*, Vol. XI, pp. 28–9.
4. Ibid., p. 29.
5. Austin Robinson in Milo Keynes (ed.), *Essays*, op. cit., p. 22.
6. *The Collected Writings of John Maynard Keynes*, Vol. VII, *The General Theory of Employment, Interest and Money* (1936) (Macmillan, London, 1973), p. 354.
7. John Kenneth Galbraith, in 'John Maynard Keynes' (1984), a review of the Collected Writings of John Maynard Keynes originally published in the *New York Review of Books*, 22 November 1984, and reprinted in *A View from the Stands*, (Houghton Mifflin, Boston, 1986), pp. 315–16.
8. Sayers, *The Young Keynes*, op. cit., p. 593.
9. J. A. Schumpeter, 'John Maynard Keynes, 1883–1946', *American Economic Review*, Vol. XXXVI, No. 4, September 1946, p. 499.
10. J. A. Schumpeter, ibid., p. 265.
11. H. S. Foxwell, 'Review of Indian Currency and Finance', *Economic Journal*, December 1913, p. 561.
12. Possibly the solitary note of discord in the chorus of acclaim is the singularly inept and dismissive comments of John Kenneth Galbraith: 'he [Keynes] became concerned with the *trivial* intricacies of currency and banking in India [Keynes himself found the Indian financial system "exceedingly difficult to understand!"] On this he wrote a monograph, Indian Currency and Finance . . . Any scholar of *moderate capacity* could have learned all that there was useful to know about the subject in around three months, perhaps less . . .' (emphasis provided). 'John Maynard Keynes' in *New York Review of Books*, 22 November 1984, reprinted in his collected essays *A View from the Stands* (Houghton Mifflin Company, 1986), p. 315.
13. Harry G. Johnson, 'Keynes and Development' in *The Shadow of Keynes*, (ed.) Elizabeth Johnson and Harry Johnson (Basil Blackwell, Oxford , 1978), p. 227.
14. For details, see Anand G. Chandavarkar, 'Keynes and Central Banking', *Indian Economic Review*, Vol. XX, No. 2.
15. See *The Economist* (London, 4, 11, 18, and 25 June 1983).
16. Donald Moggridge, 'Keynes and the International Monetary System 1909–46' In Jon S. Cohen and G. C. Harcourt (eds) *International Monetary Problems and Supply-Side Economics* (Essays in Honour of Lorie Tarshis), (St Martin's Press, New York, 1986), p. 77.
17. H. W. Singer, 'Relevance', op. cit., p. 433.
18. Among the more notable contributions are: J. J. Anjaria, 'The Limitations of Full Employment', *Papers in Economics* (Silver Jubilee Memorial Volume), (ed.) C. N. Vakil, University of Bombay, 1947, pp. 9–17; R. M. Honavar, 'Generation of Secondary Income in an Undeveloped Economy', *Economic Weekly*, 26 January 1952, pp. 82–5; V. K. R.

Rao, 'Investment Income and the Multiplier in an Undeveloped Economy', *Indian Economic Review*, February 1952; 'Full Employment and Economic Development', *Indian Economic Review*, August 1952; D. R. Khatkhate, 'The Multiplier Process in Developing Economies' and K. S. Gill, 'Keynesian Economics and Underdeveloped Countries', *Indian Economic Journal*, Vol. II, No. 2, October 1954; Ashok Mathur, 'On "Throwing the Baby Away with the Bath Water"' (An Essay in 'Defence of Keynesianism in Relation to the Underdeveloped Countries,' *Indian Economic Journal*, Vol. XII, No. 4, April – June 1965; A. K. Dasgupta, 'Keynesian Economics and Underdeveloped Countries', *Economic Weekly*, January 1954, 'Keynesian Economics and Underdeveloped Countries Again', *Economic and Political Weekly*, Vol. XXVII, No. 38, 19 September 1987, pp. 1601–6, and ibid, No. 47, 21 November 1987, pp. 2019–20.

19. See K. N. Raj, *The Monetary Policy of the Reserve Bank of India* (A Study of Central Banking in an Underdeveloped Economy), (National Information and Publications, Bombay, 1948), particularly Chapter II, 'Monetary Theory in Relation to Backward Economies'.
20. 'Disguised unemployment as I conceived it, had nothing to do with the question of surplus labour in what is nowadays called an underdeveloped economy. At that time [ca. 1937], there were no ex-colonial nations clamouring for "development".' Joan V. Robinson, 'Disguised Unemployment', *Collected Economic Papers*, Vol. 4 (Basil Blackwell, Oxford, 1973), p. 175.
21. *The Collected Writings of John Maynard Keynes*, Essays in Persuasion, 'Economic Possibilities for Our Grandchildren', Vol. IX (1931) (Macmillan, London, 1972), p. 325.
22. These aspects have been analysed by Honavar, V. K. R. V. Rao, and Khatkhate in the cited references.
23. *The Collected Writings of John Maynard Keynes*, The General Theory and After, Part II: Defence and Development, Vol. XIV (Macmillan, London, 1973), p. 299.
24. Appropriately it was left to an Indian pupil of Schumpeter, V. V. Bhatt, to trace the genesis of the Harrod-Domar model to Keynes's Galton lecture on 'Some Economic Consequences of a Developing Population' (1937). See V. V. Bhatt, *Employment and Capital Formation in Underdeveloped Economies* (Orient Longman, Bombay, 1960), who states that 'Keynes's arithmetic example contains in embryonic form all the essentials of the Harrod-Domar formula', (p. 74). This book, based on the author's doctoral dissertation at Harvard (1951–2), is also notable for being the first to suggest the application of input–output techniques for development planning (pp. 82–3) and to initiate the extended debate on choice of techniques of production (p. 76).
25. *The Collected Writings of John Maynard Keynes*, Vol. IX, Essays in Persuasion (1931) (Macmillan, London, 1972), p. 332. In a similar vein Keynes wrote to W. S. Salant (27 July 1941): 'I have been greatly struck during my visit by the quality of the younger economists and civil servants in the [US] Administration . . . we have a few good people in London but nothing like the *numbers* which you can produce here'

(emphasis provided). *The Collected Writings of John Maynard Keynes*, Vol. XXIII, Activities, 1940–43, External War Finance, (ed.) Donald Moggridge (Macmillan, London, 1979), p. 193.

26. *The General Theory*, pp. 241 and 337. One of the very few exceptions is K. N. Raj, 'Keynesian Economics and Agrarian Economies' in *Reflections on Economic Developments and Social Change*, Essays in Honour of Professor V. K. R. V. Rao, (ed.) C. H. Hanumantha Rao and P. C. Joshi (Allied Publishers, New Delhi, 1979).
27. See A. G. Chandavarkar, 'The Nature and Effects of Gold Hoarding in Underdeveloped Economies', *The Oxford Economic Papers*, Vol. 13, No. 2, June 1961, pp. 137–48.
28. *The General Theory*, Vol. VII, Preface to the German edition, p. xxvi.
29. *Collected Writings*, Vol. IX, ibid., p. 331.
30. Jagdish N. Bhagwati, 'Development Economics: What Have We Learned?', *Asian Development Review*, Vol. 2, No. 1, 1984, pp. 23–8.
31. Kenneth K. Kurihara, *The Keynesian Theory of Development* (Columbia University Press, New York, 1959).
32. Albert O. Hirschman, 'The Rise and Decline of Development Economics', *Essays in Trespassing,* (Cambridge University Press, 1981), p. 7.
33. Keynes, ibid, p. xxvi.

8 Keynes: The Guru

'He was not merely a very great man, he was a very good man also.' *James Meade*

'he was magnificently generous . . . to his country . . . to servants and dependents, particularly to his less fortunate friends . . . his supreme virtue was his deeply affectionate nature.' *Clive Bell*

INDIANS AT CAMBRIDGE: THE MILIEU

Keynes's Indian connections were much more than purely intellectual and academic. In fact, the human facets of Keynes's personality as a teacher and mentor are perhaps nowhere better exemplified than by his sustained interest in and constructive empathy for Indian students, who at least in his lifetime were the largest single foreign national group in *statu pupillari* at Cambridge. Keynes had varied contacts with Indian students, academic and social, at Cambridge as an undergraduate and Fellow of King's, as President of the Cambridge Union, as Secretary of the Cambridge University Free Trade Association, as a frequent guest speaker at the Cambridge Majlis (the Indian students' society), as founder of the Political Economy Club, and as University lecturer in economics. His service at India Office had served as an invaluable introduction not only to Indian economic affairs but also to the strength and sensitivities of Indian nationalism during the eventful period following the High Noon of Empire (1905–10) which witnessed the upsurge of Indian nationalism following Curzon's partition of Bengal (1905) and the rise of the Swadeshi (Buy Indian) movement.

It is revealing that Keynes even in his undergraduate days had a reputation as a 'well-wisher of India' and figured prominently in the debates and the social activities of the Indian Majlis. On 28 February 1904 he spoke as the proposer on 'That in spite of appearances to the contrary politics may still be considered the profession of a gentleman' with Mr Ismail Khan (Jesus) as the Host and on 27 November 1904 he was the third speaker on 'That this House deplores the growth of business instincts' with C. R. Reddy (St John's) as the Host. Keynes was also the guest of honour at the Annual Dinner of the Indian Majlis (2 March 1906 at the Lion Hotel and on 25 February 1911 at the Bull Hotel).

Keynes's closest friend during his undergraduate days was C. R. (later Sir) Reddy, who after a First in the Historical Tripos, had a distinguished career in India as a Professor of History in Mysore state, as Vice-Chancellor of the Andhra and Mysore Universities, and also as a noted literary critic of the Telegu language. Reddy, as President of the Cambridge Majlis, had a particularly close rapport with Keynes and often relied upon Keynes for friendly advice. In organising a function of the Cambridge University Liberal Club on 1 November 1904 in the rooms of H. Rackham at Christ's College which was to be addressed by the Hon. G. K. Gokhale, CIE Member of the Viceroy's Legislative Council ('On Some Problems of Indian Politics'), Reddy deferred willingly to Keynes's advice to have a private meeting, instead of a public lecture, and wrote to him as follows:

> I have undertaken to make the necessary arrangements trusting in the cordial atmosphere of the well-wishers of India, whose number cannot, I think be complete unless it includes you and your father. (Letter from Reddy, 15 October 1904 from Tibberton Court, Gloucester, *Keynes Papers*, King's College)

During Keynes's presidency of the Cambridge Union (1905), Reddy was elected the Secretary of the Union, an event which evoked the following eulogistic comment from the organ of undergraduate opinion:

> We deserve to congratulate the new officers, and particularly Mr. Reddy the new Secretary. He has thoroughly deserved his new position by the consistent ability displayed in his speeches. (*Granta*, 16 March 1905, p. 263)

It is particularly symptomatic of Keynes's support for Indian political aspirations that despite his earlier advice to Reddy to arrange a private meeting to be addressed by Gokhale he supported Gokhale's resolution at a subsequent meeting of the Cambridge Union (November 1905): 'that the House would welcome the introduction in India of government on more popular lines'. The resolution was carried by 161 to 62 votes. Keynes was highly appreciative of Gokhale's speech and remarked that 'he has feeling but feeling guided and controlled by thought, and there is nothing in him which reminds us of the usual type of political agitators'.[1]

The focal point of social and political activity for Indian undergraduates was the Majlis, which had also its counterpart at Oxford. The

Cambridge Majlis was founded (c. 1890) largely on the initiative of Aurobindo Ghose of King's who, after a Double First in Classics, took to revolutionary politics for the freedom of India and ended as a philosopher-mystic of world renown. The Majlis was an active political forum for Indian students and a nursery of Indian nationalism, a sentiment shared by most Indian undergraduates.[2] It was customary for leading Indian politicians of different persuasions, like Bepin Chandra Pal, Lala Lajpat Rai, both leaders of the Extremist Group of Indian nationalism, as well as moderates like Gokhale to address the Majlis during their visits to England. The Majlis met for a weekly debate, most often on a political subject concerning India. Its procedures and style of debate were modelled on the Cambridge University Union, but some Indians, like Jawaharlal Nehru, did not like this formalism and felt that matter and content merited more attention than form. Although the bulk of Indian undergraduates were from traditionally loyalist families, who could scarcely contemplate challenging British rule in India, virtually every Indian student joined the Majlis at Oxford and Cambridge despite emphatic parental warnings.[3] Nehru joined the Majlis despite his father's disapproval but spoke rarely, although he attended many of its meetings.[4] The only record of a speech by Nehru was at the festival marking the end of Ramadan, the Muslim month of fasting.[5] The reputation of the Oxford Majlis (c. 1914–16) as an extremist body where 'one heard the most blood-curdling speeches . . . often highly seditious, calling for the establishment of freedom . . . for India' fitted the Cambridge Indian Majlis no less.[6] There was no contradiction between the nationalist fervour of Indian undergraduates and their subsequent entry into the Indian Civil Service, or similar Government employment.[7] Even the most radical contemporary Indian politicians like Tilak, Jinnah, and Vallabhbhai Patel were known to have advised Indian students to stick to their studies as eventually the country would need the services of trained as well as patriotic Indian officials. The classic example of this is the advice by Jinnah, the founder of Pakistan, to Subhas Chandra Bose (the Cambridge graduate who later became the President of the Indian National Congress) not to resign from the Indian Civil Service – which in the event he did – because if 'people like Subhas left the service the future of the country would be dark; since we would not have patriotic men serving the country'.[8] In any event the understandable transformation of yesteryear's revolutionaries becoming the establishmentarians of today is a much too common phenomenon in all societies to merit any kind of moral censure. There is perhaps even a natural life-cycle of ideology in the lives of all politically conscious individuals – revolutionary in youth, liberal in middle age and conservative in old age. It is against this background that one has to view the problems of Indian students at Cambridge in Keynes's early days as a don.

INDIAN STUDENTS AT CAMBRIDGE: KEYNES TO THE DEFENCE

Keynes's first year as a don at King's College, after leaving the India Office, saw him involved once again in Indian matters in a most unexpected manner. It was as though the fates had ordained that it was too soon for him to sever links with Indian affairs. Keynes felt called upon to take up the cause of Indian students at Cambridge who were the subject of a singularly scurrilous yet patronising anonymous article in the *Cambridge Review* of 13 May 1909.[9] Its strident tone is evident from the following extract:

> The present stamp of Hindu undergraduate is not so good as his forebears: he is often morally, socially, and intellectually inferior . . . the greater number . . . are not prepared nor fitted intellectually for the University course. . . . Selection is important, but mistakes may sometimes be made. Absolute restriction as to numbers is a further safeguard . . . if the Indian undergraduates are allowed to congregate at two or three colleges or hostels, the tendency is naturally for them to make their own exclusive society; they keep to themselves, the difficulty of their mixing with the British undergraduate is made more difficult, and the opportunity of their gaining in 'character' is lost. Not only so: there is political danger. . . . If they have returned [to their country] embittered against the British government in India, many of them with one sole object, to help in expelling the British administration, what is the outlook for India but what Lord Morley [the Secretary of State for India and subsequently the co-architect of the Morley Minto Reforms in India (1909) said, 'Anarchy and bloody carnage?' The University cannot calmly disregard an open intention to destroy a part of the British Empire, or to those who hold those views hospitably open her doors and grant degrees, and call herself their dear Mother![10]

The article asked whether the establishment in London of an Information Bureau and Advisory Committee to help Indian students in England and the colleges to which they applied 'would have any effect upon the problems concerning the Indian students at Cambridge'. The main thrust of the article was to restrict the number of Indian students at Cambridge, to seek their dispersal over a larger number of colleges, and, above all, to interdict political activism among them. It argued the case for 'concerted action on the part of the colleges so as to make their residence here [Cambridge] a benefit and not a bane to all concerned'. It patronisingly invoked the 'sacred duty of hospitality to lead the white man to make allowances', and to understand the ordeal for an Indian of dining in Hall on 'those hunks of mutton and beef, beef and mutton'. It recognised, in a more judicial vein, that 'race antipathy is an existing fact, which we cannot ignore though we may deplore' but which 'in some cases is as strongly felt by the dark man as regards the white'. But it ended up with a sternly proctorial admonition to Indian students, among whom as even one of their 'prominent well-wishers had admitted, were numerous "bounders" – to learn to tell the truth and pay their debts and to show no mercy to those who advocate the dismemberment of the British Empire. No invitations must be given to political demagogues to harangue them in favor of "Freedom or Bloodshed".'

The article's flawed logic was no less noteworthy than its diehard prejudice. Thus, curiously, it singled out, for no apparent reason, the Hindu undergraduates among Indians. Indian students at Cambridge were usually a mixed group of all religions although Hindus were numerically predominant. In any event the religious persuasion of Indian undergraduates could hardly have been regarded as germane to either their academic performance or social conduct and behaviour, except perhaps for dietary restrictions, which, however, were observed by Muslims and Jews no less than orthodox Hindus. More importantly, the proportion of serious students among Indians could justifiably be claimed to have been generally higher than that of 'hearties', considering that the bulk of entrants were on Indian Government (Central and Provincial) or other scholarships (such as those awarded by private foundations, like J. N. Tata or the Aga Khan) which were always highly selective then as now.[11] In point of fact Victorian and Edwardian Cambridge nurtured several Indian undergraduates destined for distinction (see Table 8.1). Moreover, the cult of 'Cyrenaicism' with its philosophy of pleasure was very much the rage in the Cambridge of those days, as Nehru recalls in his autobiography, and Indian undergraduates could not have been unaffected by it.[12]

Table 8.1 Some notable Indians at Cambridge c. 1890–1915

Name	*Remarks*
Sir Basanta Mullick (King's 1887)	Judge, High Court, Patna, first Indian Civil Servant to be nominated to India Council, member of League of Nations Committees.
Aurobindo Ghose (King's 1890)	Double First, Classics; Vice-Principal, Baroda College; founder, Indian Majlis, nationalist leader, philosopher, mystic, author.
(Sir) Atul Chatterjee (King's 1893)	First Indian to head the list in the open competition for the ICS (1896); Member, Industries, Viceroy's Executive Council; High Commissioner for India in London (1925); Member, Secretary of State for India's Council; President, International Labour Office (1933).
Kumar Shri Ranjitsinhji (Trinity 1889–93)	Test cricketer; Jam Saheb (Ruler) of Nawanagar State, India's Representative, first Assembly of the League of Nations.
(Sir) Mohammed Iqbal (Trinity 1907), Ph.D Munich)	Eminent poet-philosopher in Urdu and Persian, National Poet of Pakistan.
(Sir) Shah Muhammed Sulaiman (1906–10, Double First in Mathematics and Law, LL.D Dublin)	UP Government Scholar; distinguished jurist-mathematician, Chief Justice, Allahabad High Court, Judge, Federal Court of India, Vice-Chancellor, Aligarh Muslim University.
Jawaharlal Nehru (Trinity 1907–10)	India's first Prime Minister.
(Sir) Benegal Narsing Rau (Trinity 1908)	Indian Civil Servant, Jurist-diplomat, Constitutional Adviser, Government of India, Judge, International Court of Justice.
(Sir) Manohar Lal (St John's, 1907–08)	Economist, Finance Minister, Punjab Government, 1935–40.
(Sir) Benegal Rama Rau (King's 1909)	Indian Civil Servant, Governor, Reserve Bank of India.

continued on page 156

Table 8.1 *continued*

Name	*Remarks*
(Sir) Ziauddin Ahmed (1909–10)	Mathematician, Vice-Chancellor, Aligarh University.
Sir Vithal Chandavarkar (King's 1908–12)	Vice-Chancellor, University of Bombay, 1933–39.
Sir C. R. Reddy (St John's 1907–10)	Vice-Chancellor, Andhra and Mysore Universities.
Dr. Syed Mahmud (1907–10)	Minister, Bihar Government, 1937–9 and 1946–52; Minister, External Affairs, Government of India, 1954–7.
P. C. Mahalanobis, F.R.S. (King's 1913–15)	Director, Indian Statistical Institute.
Dr L. K. Hyder (King's 1910)	Professor of Economics, Aligarh Muslim University (Member, Royal Commission on Indian Agriculture, 1926–8).
N. S. Subba Rao (St John's 1908–12, McMahon Law Student 1910)	Director of Public Instruction, Mysore, Vice-Chancellor, Mysore University, Head of Department of Economics, Allahabad University, Member, Textile Tariff Board, India, 1926–7, President, Indian Economic Conference, 1929.

Source: Author's compilation from College Reports and other sources.

Such sentiments are a feature of collegiality and high spirits are also a prized part of the ethos of a university. In fact it is well known that traditionally the admissions policies of Oxbridge colleges have aimed at a judicious spread of the undergraduate body over scholars, sportsmen, aesthetes and hearties, following, perhaps unconsciously, the example of Noah's Ark – some of each kind! The Indian hearties in Keynes's day would no doubt have also included a few of the 'bounders' castigated in the *Cambridge Review* article. There was nothing to suggest that their number or proportion was higher than that of any other national group of students, but, given the higher 'visibility' of Indian students, the stray black sheep, not surprisingly, attracted disproportionate attention.[13] Occasionally family connections and status did influence admissions, as in the case of the famous cricketer Ranji (later ruler of Nawanagar State in Western India) – one of the immortals of the game – who never graduated but earned his cricket Blue at Cambridge, and also represented Sussex and England. The following entry concerning Ranji in the Council Minutes of Trinity College bears this out:

> The date is 22 November 1889, and under the heading Tutorial Applications it reads: 'Kumar Shri Ramsinhji and Kumar Shri Ranjitsinhji (one having passed the whole of the Previous Examination and other Part I and the additional subjects), two Indian 'youths of position' to be allowed to enter the College without passing the entrance examination and then reside throughout their course with Mr. Borissow.[14]

Ranji prior to his entry into residence at Trinity (Michaelmas Term 1889 to the Easter term of 1893) was a member of the noncollegiate foundation Fitzwilliam Hall (now Fitzwilliam College). But on the whole, entry from princely India was rather exceptional and was never an issue of concern.

The 'Indian problem' at Cambridge had also attracted attention at the highest levels and no less a person than the 1st Viscount Morley (1838–1923), Secretary of State for India (1905), a liberal intellectual and champion of Irish Home rule, visited Cambridge in March 1909 to confer with the dons on this question following an earlier meeting of masters of colleges and others concerned on the same matter. It is said that one of the resolutions passed by this august conclave 'was one to the effect that no other college should take in an Indian who had been forcibly made to leave his college. The Master of Downing was the only person who objected to this. He told them plainly that if an Indian was expelled through spite and without sufficient reason from his college, he would take him in'.[15] More revealing was Morley's gesture in refusing the invitation for the Majlis dinner in Cambridge on 12 March 1909 which was his best chance of meeting Indian students as a group and to sense their point of view.[16] Following Morley's conference with the dons the number of Indians was limited to three for each college (that is, 54 spread over 18 colleges). It is said that 'Christ's mildly protested against this and Downing refused to have anything to do with it. The other colleges then retaliated by agreeing to take even fewer Indians if Downing took more than three so that the total should not exceed 54.' But this posed a neat arithmetical conundrum since there were at that time 90 Indians in Cambridge and over 30 of them in Downing, and no one knew how they proposed to reduce these numbers. Moreover, as perceptively noted by Nehru, restrictions on admissions to Cambridge would simply have made Indian students go to Continental and other countries, adding that this will be a good thing, as it would then fit them for 'doing something than if they had been to Oxford or Cambridge'. In fact the German universities attracted some of the brightest Cambridge Indians at the postgraduate stage, like Mohammed Iqbal (Munich), Ziauddin Ahmed (Gottingen), and L. K. Hyder (Heidelberg). Another proposal that emerged from Morley's discussions was the appointment of a guardian for Indian students at Cambridge as a paternal overseer who would keep their accounts and also presumably monitor their political proclivities.[17]

The article on 'The Indian Student at Cambridge' evoked a spirited but characteristically cogent, compassionate, yet constructive, riposte from Keynes in the form of a letter to the Editor of the *Cambridge Review*, (20 May 1909, p. 405). Significantly, it did not evoke any support from either dons or undergraduates except for a letter from an Indian student, N. S. Subba Rao, and a close friend of Keynes (*Cambridge Review*, 20 May 1909, p. 404), who cited irrefutable comparative statistics from the *University Reporter* showing that 'Indians have absolutely no reason to be ashamed of themselves as regards examinations'. The percentage of Indians who took honours degrees during 1901–5 (64.8 per cent) was well above the corresponding figure (46.3 per cent) for the University. Keynes regretted that place was found 'for an article so lacking in discernment and good feeling' containing 'the commonplaces of prejudice, which should not have been brought forward anonymously and unsubstantiated'. The *Cambridge Review* as a rule carried signed articles and anonymous contributions were rather exceptional, like the review of Moore's *Principia Ethica* (1903). Keynes added pointedly that it is 'such expressions of opinion which make it easy to understand why we have an "Indian problem" in Cambridge, and why, in the past we have sometimes sent young Indians back to India embittered against us . . . yet it is he and people like him who create the problem as it exists here.' Keynes was, however, perceptive enough to realise that the natural initial phase of 'interested curiosity with which first comers were greeted' was well over in regard to Indian students as a group and had been succeeded by a manifestly 'unsatisfactory state of affairs'. Even this situation which was aggravated by the feelings aroused a few years preceding by the 'bitterly contested elections at the [Cambridge] Union' had subsided and the Indian community was prepared 'on their side with friendlier feelings' reflecting too the 'calmer temper which now prevails in India'.

Keynes characteristically did not rest with mere refutations of allegations but went on to constructive specifics. Thus, while conceding that the idea of distributing Indian students evenly amongst the colleges was the most valuable of all practical suggestions, he thought that the matter would be settled 'if each college would agree to take two applicants a year'. But he was emphatic that the absolute limitation of the total number of Indian students, as suggested by the anonymous contributor, was 'an unwise proposal' because 'it might work indiscriminately' and that to prevent a student from coming to Cambridge was 'not necessarily to dissuade him from coming to Europe' and that life in Cambridge was 'probably much better for him in many ways than in London or Paris'. This was true only up to a point since there were substantial reasons for Indians to study in France and Germany, notably the attractions of the doctoral degree and cheaper living at Continental universities as against the more expensive Oxford and Cambridge who were then known more for their emphasis on and excellence in undergraduate education.[18] Coupled with this was a certain political aversion to study in Britain, as in the case of the Hussain brothers (Dr Zakir Hussain, later the President of India, and his brothers Professors Mahmood Hussain and Yusuf Hussain) who 'unlike their contemporaries, preferred France and Germany to the country of imperialists who ruled India'.[19] Most importantly, Keynes recognised that entry into the All India Services, such as those for the Indian Civil Service (ICS) and the Indian Medical Service (IMS), was 'through examinations held in England on the lines of English education and qualifications for the higher posts in the scientific departments could only be obtained at a European university.' He therefore felt it was 'our duty to give full opportunity to all Indians whose ambitions lie most properly in these directions' and by 'putting obstacles in the way we should create a real and heavy grievance'. Keynes's observations are particularly cogent considering that the All India Covenanted Services like the ICS, the Imperial Police Service and the IMS were attractive careers for talented and ambitious Indian students who were, however, faced with several hurdles. Thus, it was not until 1922 that simultaneous examinations for the ICS were held in England (London) and India (Allahabad and later New Delhi), which was one of the major demands of Indian nationalism. Consequently, aspiring Indian students had perforce to come to England and it was not worth their while to do so solely to sit for the ICS examination. They also sought to obtain a degree at one of the British universities, usually Oxford or Cambridge, prior to taking the competitive examination. Moreover, the reduction of the age-limit for the ICS examination from 21 to 19 in 1879, announced in 1877, was regarded as a deliberate attempt to block the prospects of Indian students who required longer years for graduation because, among other reasons, of the years already spent in Indian educational institutions. The reduction of age limit was the occasion for a huge demonstration in Calcutta organised by the Indian Association.

Keynes welcomed the awakening of the Cambridge colleges to their proper duties and the creation of the advisory committee to ease the task of the admissions tutor. Keynes was of course utterly opposed to any censorship or control of political discussion, hinted at by the anonymous contributor, as being contrary not only to expediency but also 'to the proper spirit of a university', and that 'in any case, suppression of debate or a refusal to grant degrees' was not the right way to dissuade rash undergraduates from their opinions. In any event British rule in India had 'little to fear from free criticism'. Even contemporary undergraduate opinion in Cambridge was in favour of some form of self-government for India, at least judging by the motions passed by the Cambridge Union around 1905–7.[20]

What in fact prompted Keynes's commitment to the cause of a single national group of overseas students so soon after his becoming a don? Undoubtedly, Keynes's exposure to India and Indian public opinion in the course of his work at the India Office was an influential factor. But it was not merely the previous Indian connection that sparked Keynes's involvement in this episode for this was no conventional manifestation of liberalism, much less a remnant of nostalgic bureaucratic loyalties. Rather, it was an expression of Keynes's profound human sensibilities and a passionate sense of justice for the aggrieved, a trait which was to be manifested time and again in his subsequent career. Certainly, Keynes's lone stand on behalf of Indian students seems wholly in character with his later self-confessed credo ('I am not unaccustomed to being in a minority of one').

RELATIONS WITH INDIAN STUDENTS

Keynes's contacts with Indian students were closer and more extensive than with any other national group, as borne out by his activities and the voluminous correspondence with Indian students and Indian economists, preserved in the Keynes Papers. In addition to his appointed role as a University Lecturer in Economics at Cambridge and as a Fellow and supervisor at King's College, Keynes seems to have figured as an honorary moral tutor and father confessor to Indian undergraduates.

Strangely, the Keynes charisma seems to have cast an early spell even on unknown students in India as in the following plaintive letter, dated 28 October 1913, from a student of the BA class in the Madras Christian College, Madras.

3/8 Thambu Chetti St.
Madras
October 28, 1913

Dear Sir,

I shrink from addressing you not only on account of my meagre talents but also on account of my strangeness towards you. . . . I am a poor student, I cannot purchase too many books. . . . You will kindly advise me as to the best way of studying economics. You will with a sympathetic heart, present me with some books, as for instance your book on 'Gold, Currency and Banking in India. [sic]'

I am, Sir,
Yours obediently,

S. Venkatraman

(Source: *Keynes Papers*, King's College)

There is no record of Keynes's response to this letter, which does not necessarily mean that there was none as Keynes was a most scrupulous correspondent and no letter remained unanswered for long.

Keynes's relations with his Indian pupils are best viewed in the perspective of the long and mutually beneficial Indian links of the Cambridge Economics Faculty and of King's College which stemmed both from the intellectual appeal of Indian economic issues to Cambridge economists and the attractions of the prestigious faculty for pupils from the subcontinent. Perhaps the first Cambridge economist to show any unusual interest in India was the economic historian Archdeacon William Cunningham, who visited India (Bombay, Ahmedabad, and Poona) in 1881 and wrote perceptively about its basic socio-political problems.[21] But the long and intimate links of the Cambridge Economics Faculty with the Indian subcontinent date really from the days of Alfred Marshall, the First Professor of Political Economy and the founder of the Economics Tripos whose interest in Indian economic problems dated back to his lectures to Indian Civil Service probationers at Oxford. Marshall's evidence before the Indian Currency Committee (1899) is said to have 'constituted his best account of the theory of money' and 'the parts dealing with specifically Indian problems were supported by many statistical diagrams. . . . He was pleased with his detailed realistic inquiries into Indian problems and the great rolls of Indian charts, not all of which were published, were always at hand as part of the furniture of his study'.[22] But along with the intellectual interest in Indian problems went a deeper interest in Indian students at Cambridge. As Keynes noted, 'He [Marshall] had many devoted Indian (and also Japanese) pupils.'[23] Among these were (Sir) Manohar Lal (St John's, 1907–8, Finance Minister in the Punjab Government, 1935–40), with whom Marshall had an interesting correspondence over the years on Indian economic problems including the vexed question of protection for Indian industry.[24] Another distinguished Indian pupil was (Sir) Jehangir Coyajee, of Gonville and Caius College (1910), who 'received the approbation of all well known teachers at Cambridge', particularly Marshall, 'who made the prophetic statement that Coyajee will add one more to the now not inconsiderable number of natives of India who may claim to rank with the ablest and most thorough students of economics in any country'.[25] Coyajee more than fulfilled Marshall's expectations and went on to serve with distinction not only as a Professor of Economics at Presidency College, Calcutta (as a member of the Indian Educational Service) and the Andhra University, but also as a member of the Royal Commission (Lord Kennet) on Indian Currency (1919), the Fiscal Committee of the Government of India (1928), and the Indian delegations to the Assembly of the League of Nations (1930–32). He wrote several major publications on Indian currency and fiscal problems.

Subsequent to Marshall, and even apart from Keynes, the links between the Cambridge economics faculty and the Indian subcontinent have been fostered through teaching, research and advisory activities of several other members of the faculty, like Sir Austin Robinson, Sir Dennis Robertson, Joan Robinson, Lord Kaldor, and Brian Reddaway. Sir Austin Robinson (Fellow of Sidney Sussex College and later Professor of Economics at Cambridge University) served as a resident tutor (1926–8) to Prince George Jiwaji Rao Scindia, later the Ruler of Gwalior State in Central India.[26] Dennis

Robertson, who was then a lecturer at Trinity College, co-authored with Professor A. L. Bowley (London School of Economics) the pioneering report on 'A Scheme for an Economic Census of India' (1934). But between the Bowley-Robertson Report and the post Indian independence years, there was a visible hiatus in the Indian links of the Cambridge Economics Faculty which is rather hard to explain. Thus, notwithstanding the traditionally strong Indian affinity with the Cambridge economics faculty, the choice of the Government of India as its first Economic Adviser (1937–46) fell on Professor Theodore Gregory (the Sir Ernest Cassel Professor of Economics at the London School of Economics) and a fellow member, along with Keynes, of the Macmillan Committee. These links were revived only much later in the post-independence years when some of the most eminent Cambridge economists visited India in different capacities, like Mrs Joan Robinson as a visiting lecturer, Lord Kaldor, who advised on Indian tax reform and wrote a classic report on the subject, and Brian Reddaway who wrote a highly regarded book on *The Development of the Indian Economy* (1958).

Apart from the consistently prestigious standing of its economic faculty, Cambridge also offered a more specialised education in economics not available in Oxford. Consequently the Economics Tripos at Cambridge (established in 1903) has always been a popular course for students from the subcontinent as well as for probationers of the Indian Civil Service (ICS) in the pre-Second World War era. Not only in numbers but also in quality, the level of Indian students offering economics at Cambridge has been generally not only well above average but even distinguished. As Mrs Joan Robinson observed justifiably, 'in Cambridge, one or two of our best men, in most years, come from the subcontinent. . . . These good men who come to us to be taught (and the not-so-good ones also) go home to teach in their turn, and their pupils too, become teachers and influence thought through other channels.'[27] Much the same sentiment was echoed by Lord Kaldor in his inaugural Sir Chintaman Deshmukh Memorial Lecture at the Reserve Bank of India:

> I am proud that my own University, Cambridge, trained so many of the leading figures of independent India, from Pandit Nehru to C. D. Deshmukh, P. C. Mahalanobis, our Chairman today Dr. V. K. R. V. Rao,[28] as well as the present Governor Dr. Manmohan Singh and many others. Indeed, one of the things the first Indian Governor, C. D. Deshmukh and the present Governor have in

common is that they were both on the top of the firsts of their year in the Cambridge Tripos examination. (I can vouch for the latter since I was Dr. Singh's Examiner in Part II of the Tripos.)

Kaldor might have also added that Cambridge graduates have had a virtual 'corner' on the Governorship (including Acting Governors) of the Reserve Bank since Deshmukh (Jesus) beginning with Sir Benegal Rama Rao (King's), and including thereafter L. K. Jha (Trinity), I. G. Patel (King's), Manmohan Singh (St John's), B. N. Adarkar (Gonville and Caius), and Narasimham (St John's). The post-Keynesian generation of Cambridge Indian economists has more than maintained the traditions of excellence in the highest reaches of analytic economics, looking at the distinguished achievements of Amartya Sen, Jagdish Bhagwati, and Partha Dasgupta. It therefore comes as more than a perverse anticlimax to know that there was at least one Cambridge economics don who did not think much of Indians. Guillebaud, welcoming the young Bhagwati as his moral tutor at St John's, told him frostily: 'You know Indians never do well at Cambridge!' (related to the author by Professor Jagdish Bhagwati).

Although 'in the late sixties and early seventies of the last century St John's was the nursery of Cambridge economics'[29] it has been rightly said: 'Without question Economics has been the academic discipline for which King's has been most famous in this century. It all began with Pigou.'[30] This reputation was enhanced and flourished under Keynes's intellectual banner. Even so iconoclastic a critic of Cambridge economics as Harry Johnson seems to have generally spared King's as a college and Keynes as an economist from the vials of his castigation.[31] Interestingly, even among some Indians there was a subtle notion that King's' general cachet was even higher than its intellectual credentials! for instance, the author recalls the pleasant function at the University Hostel in Bombay (1944) to bid *au revoir* to I. G. Patel and R. C. Desai on the eve of their departure to join King's College. Naturally, there was great excitement at their acceptance by the holy of holies for economics, and a senior resident post-graduate, a pre-Second World War London graduate thoroughly *au fait* with British socio-academic nuances, interposed sagely that admission to King's meant much more than 'entrance' into an intellectual fraternity – a sentiment uncannily echoed by a Trinity man.[32] He recalled that so few Indians had been accepted by King's compared to St John's or Trinity. But regardless of King's' standing, which scarcely needs special pleading, it certainly has had a distinguished Indian roll of honour, particularly among Keynes's pupils, who would perhaps echo the assessment made by A. F. W. Plumptre, a Canadian pupil of Keynes ('In any pedantic sense Keynes was not my best teacher but in terms of impact and influence he was incomparable.'[33]) Keynes's impact and influence were exerted not only through his lectures and tutorials but equally through the deliberations of the Political Economy Club which, however, did not cover any specific Indian economic themes, according to the recollections of active participants like Professor Hans Singer, Sir Alec Cairncross, David Bensusan-Butt, L. K. Jha and I. G. Patel, as communicated to the author. Keynes influenced not only his own pupils but others who did not offer Economics for their Tripos. The most celebrated example among Indians at Cambridge is that of Jawaharlal Nehru, who was said to have been 'drawn by the intellectual liveliness of Bertrand Russell and John Maynard Keynes many of whose lectures he attended although his own university curriculum was scientific and not economic.'[34] It is said that Keynes was one of the three lecturers, besides Bertrand Russell and George Bernard Shaw among visitors, to have exerted a marked influence on Nehru.[35]

It is not commonly known that Keynes, who rarely accepted overseas examinerships, was also the external examiner for two successful doctoral dissertations of the Calcutta University, namely 'Early European Banking in India' (H. C. Sinha) and 'Paper Currency in India' (B. B. Das Gupta).[36] On the other hand, almost as a counterpoint, Keynes's rejection of an Indian candidate's doctoral dissertation on 'India and the Problem of a Central Bank', submitted to the University of Wales, is very revealing of his strong but little known views on research degrees in economics. In his report to the Registrar, 18 May 1932, he remarked: 'It is disagreeable not to be able to say something warmer about an honest and careful piece of work. But there is no real remedy for this sort of thing other than the much deserved abolition of research degrees in economics' (*Keynes Papers,* King's College Library). Keynes thought it was difficult to be original in well traversed fields like central banking in India and that mere competence in research did not merit academic imprimatur.

Interestingly, Keynes's earliest and most sustained contact with Indian students was not with an Indian Kingsman, but with N. S. Subba Rao, a brilliant first in Economics and Law from St John's, who seems to have enjoyed Keynes's special esteem and solicitude, judging by their extensive and intimate correspondence. In his very first letter from Bangalore (28 October 1909) on his return from Cambridge, Subba Rao wrote:

> My dear Keynes,
> . . . I found a good many officers in the Secretariat [in the Mysore State Government offices] had read your paper [in the *Economic Journal* and reproduced in the *Madras Mail*] which surprised me, as we do not pretend to be up to date here . . . I miss Cambridge itself. I did not think I had become so fond of the place. . . . You will not believe me if I tell you how often I am back at Cambridge in my waking thoughts and dreams. With kind regards,
>
> Yours sincerely,
> N. S. Subba Rao
>
> (Source: *Keynes Papers*, King's College)

Subsequently, on 22 June 1910, Subba Rao wrote again to Keynes, after his appointment as a Professor in the Maharaja's College, Mysore, to thank him for sending his name to the India Office for a possible opening which, however, he thought he could neither accept nor use to get a rise as 'the Maharaja [ruler of Mysore] would be displeased' and he was 'beholden to him' for his Cambridge education as well as his present appointment. In another letter (16 August 1911) Subba Rao referred to an animal-skin parcelled by him to Keynes and once again thanked Keynes for 'having made' his Cambridge stay 'very happy'. Subba Rao, who had a distinguished career as a university teacher, member of the Indian Tariff Board, and Director of Public Instruction in Mysore, has been described as 'a good Marshallian of the orthodox sect'.[37]

Among Indian Kingsmen, Keynes's earliest contacts of a sustained character were with J. V. Joshi (1923 – a Double First in Economics and Wrenbury Scholar) whom Keynes regarded as one of his most brilliant students. Those who knew or worked with Joshi will remember him as a touchingly devout Kingsman ('King's or nothing') who enjoyed a very special relationship with Keynes. Joshi was the proud recipient of inscribed copies of Keynes's books. This author, who served under Joshi in the Reserve Bank of India, even recalls a remark of one of Joshi's closest friends that, reportedly, Keynes even wrote to the concerned Indian authorities to say that if there was no suitable position for Joshi one will have to be created! In the event Joshi served in India successively as Assistant Secretary in the Finance Department of the Government of India and Director-General of Commercial Intelligence and Statistics before being appointed in the pre-independence days as the first Economic Adviser (1945) of the Reserve Bank of India to head its newly-created Research and Statistics Department. Joshi's approach to economic research and intelligence was properly Cambridge and Keynesian, with more emphasis on facts and issues than on abstract reasoning. His thought style could not inaptly be described as Marshall and Keynes served with Indian curry, rather like Findlay Shirras's treatise on Public Finance ('Bastable served with Indian Curry' as remarked by Hugh Dalton). It was a variant of Keynes's recipe: 'Know your principles (Marshall) and follow the markets (the city columns of *The Times*)'.

Another notable Indian pupil of Keynes at King's was Professor B. P. Adarkar (Benares and Allahabad Universities, and later Indian High Commissioner, Hong Kong) the author of several major works on Indian monetary and fiscal policy, a pioneering study of federal finance and the architect of the first social insurance scheme for India (1944). Adarkar – the only candidate to obtain a First Class in Part I of the Economics Tripos in his year – was the recipient of special congratulations from Keynes: 'So nice to see a Kingsman in solitary splendour in the First Class.' (Information provided by Priya Adarkar of Bombay, Copyright King's College.) Keynes, supporting Adarkar's application for a Professorship at Benares Hindu University, wrote to the selectors as follows:

> he is unquestionably of first class quality . . . a most learned economist and extremely well-fitted for research work in modern economic theory. . . . I consider him to be the most promising Indian student of economics, as far as original work is concerned, who has been in this country. (Letter from Keynes 21 June 1932, *Keynes Papers*, King's College)

Adarkar recalls Keynes as follows:

> I myself had an interesting experience of his helpfulness and meticulous care as an editor of the [Economic] 'Journal'. I had written a note for the 'Journal' in 1931, just after graduation. He spoke in encouraging terms about it and made it part of a Symposium [on 'Saving and Usury', *Economic Journal*, March 1932] allowing me to rub shoulders with two or three senior and quite eminent economists (including Edwin Cannan). He called me for a discussion and suggested some slight amendments, cut a joke about my abilities as a typist (said I could earn my living as a typist if I ever failed as an economist!) and handed to me the type-script

> which I found corrected by him to the smallest comma and prepared for the press. I think that was my first lesson in the preparation of manuscripts for the press. . . . Owing to his practical contact with City finance and his theoretical upbringing under the masters at Cambridge, he was able to delve very deep here and his mastery to us students was simply breath-taking. ('Lord Keynes of Tilton – A Tribute,' *Eastern Economist*, New Delhi, 10 May 1946, pp. 780–81)

Outside King's, the two most notable Indian student contacts of Keynes at Cambridge, both through the Political Economy Club, were V. K. R. V. Rao (Caius) cited in Chapter 6 and L. K. Jha of Trinity College (ex-Governor, Reserve Bank of India and ex-Ambassador to the USA). The following communication to the author from Jha is very revealing of the impact of Keynes on Indian students.

> I first came in contact with Keynes as an undergraduate at Cambridge when I heard him expounding his General Theory in a series of lectures and a few months later the book came out. It was a fascinating experience because Keynes was unquestionably a brilliant lecturer. . . . I also had occasions to join in the discussions on this subject – and indeed on many others – that took place every week in his rooms in King's College in an after-dinner session. Most of the participants in it were dons or post-graduate students. A few undergraduate students, who had done well in their exams or were well spoken of by their supervisors, were also included in what was officially known as the Political Economy Club, but always referred to as the Keynes club. I believe, Sir Dennis Robertson, who was my supervisor, had suggested to Keynes that I should be inducted in this circle though Robertson himself rarely put in any appearance there.

During the last years of his life, when Keynes returned to King's after completing the negotiations for the Anglo-American loan, there were very few Indian students at Cambridge. One of them was I. G. Patel, a Baroda State scholar and pupil of D. Ghosh (Gonville and Caius – later Professor of Economics, Baroda College), who was at King's 1944–9 and is now an Honorary Fellow of King's. Patel followed up an outstanding academic career at Cambridge (First in the Economics Tripos, Wrenbury Scholar, and Adam Smith Prize) with a singularly distinguished record of public service as Secretary and Chief Economic Adviser to the Government of India, Deputy Administrator of the United Nations Development Programme, Governor of the Reserve Bank of India, and currently as the Director of the London School of Economics. Although Patel's supervisors at King's were the late Gerald Shove and Pigou, he came into contact with Keynes when he (Patel) was Secretary of the Political Economy Club. Patel's personal impressions of Keynes in the following communication to the author are of exceptional interest as revealing some characteristic facets of Keynes's personality as a preceptor and teacher and his singular rapport with undergraduates.

> Keynes's return to King's after the war and after completing the negotiations for the Anglo-American loan was naturally a great event for our small community of economists at King's and at Cambridge. We were all anxious to find some excuse for meeting him, and mine came when Robertson, who had just taken over from Keynes the stewardship of the Political Economy Club, suggested to me that, as the Secretary of the Club, I should call on Keynes and request him to come and speak to the members. Keynes agreed to my request most readily and asked me a few questions about myself to make me feel at ease. As a mere undergraduate, I was much too dazzled by the experience to remember what we discussed then. But I do remember an exchange which took place after Keynes had completed his exposition of the Anglo-American loan at the Political Economy Club in Robertson's rooms at Trinity. The loan agreement contained two rather contradictory provisions about the treatment of sterling balances. At one place, the agreement implied that the loan was intended to enable the UK to honour the obligations arising from the accumulation of sterling balances. At another point, the agreement implied that the UK would take suitable steps to strengthen its balance of payments position including, if necessary, scaling down the sterling balances or restricting their use. As an Indian student vexed by the current talk in the UK of the case for (and against) the scaling down of these balances, I was naturally anxious to know on what side the Americans were trying to throw their weight. As soon as I asked Keynes which of the two interpretations he read into the Loan Agreement, Robertson intervened to say that he too was puzzled by the ambiguity and was glad that I had raised the point. Keynes raised his voice in mock anger, I believe, to avoid giving straight answer and admonished Robertson instead:

> 'Dennis, I can understand Patel asking such a question. But I am amazed that you should ask me for clarification. At Bretton Woods we always turned to you when we wanted a form of words that could satisfy all the parties and you never let us down. Now you are telling me that I am so poor at this game that even young Patel has found me out.' The answer, of course, was there. But it was instructive to see how deferential even Robertson was to Keynes and how Keynes could be rough with his colleagues but not with the students.

Against this backdrop of Keynes's relations with Indian students, it seems a stark anticlimax that two of the most comprehensive recent biographies of Keynes should have placed a wholly disproportionate emphasis on Keynes's involvement with an Indian undergraduate of Clare College, Bimla Kanta Sarkar, to the total exclusion of any other aspect of Keynes's varied and more enduring intellectual, official and social relationships with a truly distinguished group of Indian students.[38] Perhaps the rather extensive correspondence in the Keynes papers, between Keynes, Sarkar and his father, Kumudini Kant Sarkar, and concerned dons and British officials, may have biased Keynes's biographers into inflating this peripheral episode in Keynes's life. The precise origins of Keynes's involvement with Sarkar are obscure. The only clue, and a cryptic one at that, is a letter from Sarkar to Keynes (6 January 1912 from York House, Eastbourne Royal Parade).

> No one introduced me to you – yourself you have taken me under your kind protection – and I hope you would not leave me because I am unable to pay my way at Cambridge. Your unfortunate and obedient pupil, Bimla Kant.

Sarkar arrived in Cambridge (around 1911) in a thoroughly impecunious condition – his father having refused to pay his growing debts – seeking entry into Trinity or King's. Keynes had him admitted into Clare from where Sarkar had to withdraw after his father refused to send him money. His interests were said to have been wholly literary and he even wrote a long essay on Marlowe and Shakespeare for Keynes's perusal. In fact Keynes gradually became not only his friend and philosopher but also his financier for quite a while. The grateful Bimla confided to Keynes all his personal problems and worries including the racial slurs he had to suffer in Cambridge.[39] Keynes did support Sarkar for several months but thereafter expressed his inability to continue his assistance while volunteering to help him with his passage back to India. But whatever the extent of Keynes's involvement with Sarkar, it is scarcely plausible to even suggest that Keynes 'was diverted from probability by a new adventure involving an Indian called Bimla Sarkar',[40] considering that very soon after an Easter (1914) reading party at Asheham to which he had invited Sarkar, Keynes wrote to his parents: 'I am now very deep in Probability and enjoying myself.'[41] Above all, given Keynes's intrinsic and sustained intellectual interest in Probability and his professional involvement in policy issues of Indian finance, it is a little grotesque to say that 'Keynes's continuing interest in Indian finance went beyond the affairs of Bimla Sarkar.'[42] Hession claims that in his 'study of Keynes's life, much attention has been given to the nature of his sexuality and its relationship to his creativity' (p. 362), and that 'Keynes saw the economic world differently from his more orthodox colleagues', 'not least' because 'his homosexuality . . . made him sceptical of the conventional way of looking at reality'. Is this somewhat excessive dilation on a small part of Keynes's psyche and his emotional involvements really germane to even the most in-depth appraisal of so seminal an intellect? Whatever the role of androgynity in intellectual creativity and of Keynes's membership of what Isaiah Berlin called the 'Homintern', the Sarkar episode is best regarded as wholly peripheral to any assessment of Keynes's life and work.

More interesting is the fact that notwithstanding his intense intellectual involvement with Indian students Keynes never had the same social relationships with Indian students as E. M. Forster, who with his intimate associations with the subcontinent, virtually kept open house at King's for at least select Indian undergraduates, a type of hospitality which Forster extended generally to 'the better known or bred undergraduate'.[43] There was no Keynesian counterpart to the celebrated afternoon tea for invited Indian students in Forster's rooms at King's. But such absence of convivial sociability with Indian students was not unusual for Keynes who by nature and disposition seemed to have had little time or inclination for small talk or social activities.[44]

THE APOSTLES: INDIANS NOT ACCEPTABLE

Keynes, who was one of the most prominent members of the Apostles, Cambridge University's elite society (founded around

1820), never sponsored any Indian for its membership, although he and Lytton Strachey had a large share in netting new members ('embryos') for the Apostles. It is difficult to analyse the reasons for Keynes's lack of interest in fostering Indian membership of the Apostles given the traditional secrecy of the criteria and conventions of the Apostles. It is said that one requirement was 'One must be very brilliant and extremely nice' (according to Sir John Sheppard, later a Provost of King's).[45] It also came to be the custom 'to choose members for their good looks even more than for their brains' and 'if the prospective new members' also came from 'good families, so much the better'. But since its inception, the Apostles, who have grudgingly admitted a few Europeans (the Austrian Wittgenstein, the Italian Sraffa, and the Hungarian Franc Bekassy), Americans (Michael Straight) and Canadians (Harry Johnson), have not elected any Asian or African members. Neither Keynes, who was so appreciative of the talents of Indian students, nor his fellow Apostles, seemed to have found a single Indian with the right credentials to sponsor for membership from among a student body which has consistently produced Double Firsts, Blues, Nobel Laureates, and Fellows of the Royal Society. Indians figured in the annals of Keynes's Political Economy Club but they were presumably not clubbable enough for the Apostles. Yet one more of Keynes's paradoxes. But then, as Lord Annan has so rightly pointed out: 'The Apostles have never claimed to be a super Phi Beta Kappa, electing to their society all the brightest students. They simply enjoy discussing general ideas; and that bores many brilliant savants.'[46] Even many brilliant Cambridge intellects like Pigou the economist and Karl Pearson the statistician were not elected. The criteria of clubbability – is he 'sound' enough? – are necessarily much more subjective than those for college admissions, on which Keynes was so supportive of Indians. Perhaps Keynes too felt that Indians were meritorious but not 'clubbable' enough for the Apostles, rather like the Oxford don who turned down Kenneth Boulding for a college fellowship ('a very bright young chap, but not really one of us').[47] Merit can be measured like the regulation First or good Upper Second, an implicit condition of entry to Keynes's Political Economy Club, but clubbability is hardly amenable to definition. Regardless of such speculations, it also seems as though there have been hardly any recorded moves for greater catholicity of membership of the Apostles, with the possible exception of a suggestion of Harry Johnson: 'If one were reforming the Society today, one would select perhaps two people from Cambridge or Oxford, one from Manchester, one from Aberdeen, and one from India or Africa or even from a remote college in the United States. There are people all over the world who have the true apostatic [sic] spirit.'[48] But then curiously even Johnson did not ask the more basic question: Why even among those *in statu pupillari* at Cambridge no one other than Europeans, (and the very occasional North American) made it to the sanctum of the Apostles despite at least two such cosmopolitan members like Forster and Leonard Woolf, given their close rapport with Indians and Ceylonese? The published evidence also seems to suggest that generally British students could be chosen as Apostles even as students whereas the non-British had to distinguish as teachers or fellows at Cambridge before they could be admitted. One hesitates to be critical of any voluntary affinity group and an outside observer of a secret society like the Apostles is particularly prone to all varieties of conspiracy theories. Nevertheless it is hard not to feel a curious bafflement at the spectacle of an intellectual and aesthetic group like the Apostles, excluding particular national groups. Such exclusion, it would seem, was not wholly peculiar to the Apostles. An American economist, Walter Salant, wondered whether his exclusion from the avowedly academic Political Economy Club of Cambridge, which always had a good sprinkling of Indian members, was due, not so much to his having been a research student for one year, who had come on very short notice, but that 'he came from a country that was not in the Empire'.[49] Salant, in a communication to the author, wrote:

> As reported there [in Patinkin and Leith], I wondered whether my not being invited to the Political Economy Club was explained by my not coming from a country in the Empire and was assured that it was certainly not. What is not in the book is that the assurance came from Austin Robinson, who said it must have been because my supervisor did not get me invited. But I note that Henry Villard, another American, also was not a member. I suspect that although what I put forward tentatively as a possible explanation may not be the whole one, there is more truth in it than Austin Robinson, in all good faith, could bring himself to believe. The book reports me as having said 'it might be interesting to find out whether any non-empire students were members, I still think that would be interesting to know.

THE MORAL TUTOR

Perhaps even more intriguing is the fact that despite his interest in Indian students, Keynes never got around to purvey to them the type of sage didactic advice which his mentor Alfred Marshall was so fond of reiterating.

> For twenty years I have been urging on Indians in Cambridge to say to others: 'How few of us, when we go to the west think of any other aim, save that of our *individual culture?* Does not the Japanese nearly always ask himself in what way can he strengthen himself to do *good service* to his country on his return? Does he not seek real studies? Does not he watch the sources of western power? Is not that the chief reason for Japan's quick progress? Can we not imitate her? Do we need any other change than, like the Japanese, to think of our country in the first place and ourselves a long way behind?' (emphasis provided; Alfred Marshall to Mukherjee, ibid, p. 472.)

Nor did Keynes have the same sustained intellectual correspondence on Indian economic affairs with Indian students or even Indians, as Marshall, who did not miss a chance to comment in his letters to Indian correspondents on burning policy issues like Indian industrialisation, tariff and currency policy. In fairness to Keynes it could be argued that he did not feel specially called upon to give any specific advice to Indian students about the use of their Cambridge education, considering that he always envisioned the role of the economist as providing an essential element in the possibility of social betterment, a message which comes through resoundingly in his citation from Marshall's inaugural lecture at Cambridge (1885).

> It will be my most cherished ambition . . . to increase the numbers of those whom Cambridge, the great mother of strong men, sends out into the world with cool heads but warm hearts, willing to give some at least of their best powers to grappling with the social suffering around them; resolved not to rest content till they have done what in them lies to discover how far it is possible to open up all the material means of a refined and noble life. *Collected Writings*, Vol X, pp. 224–25.

Keynes was deservedly regarded as a true 'guru' in the best Indian traditions by generations of devout and admiring Indian students. Keynes's interest in Indian students emerges as a more sustained and extensive manifestation of an exquisite sensibility which he displayed later no less in his courageous defence of English conscientious objectors during the First World War, in his concern for the milk-starved children of Austria, in his esteem for Dr Melchior, the leader of the German Financial Delegation, in his remonstration against the discrimination against women at Cambridge (1921). In the same spirit Keynes during the Second World War strove manfully to alleviate the pathetically ironic lot of European economists like Piero Sraffa, Erwin Rothbarth and Hans Singer, who despite being refugees from Italy and Germany long before the Second World War, were interned in England. Certainly, Keynes was not afflicted by the 'Undeveloped Heart' syndrome, so often lamented by his fellow Kingsman, Forster, for he never failed 'to connect'.

Notes

1. C. R. Reddy to S. S. Campion (British lobbyist for the Indian National Congress), 2 March 1905, cited in B. R. Nanda, *Gokhale* (Oxford University Press, 1977), p. 196.
2. As India's first Prime Minister, Nehru (Trinity College, 1907–10) recalled fifty years later: 'I was . . . an Indian nationalist desiring India's freedom and rather inclined to the more extreme wing of it as represented then by Mr. Tilak. I felt like any average Indian student would feel. There was nothing peculiar about it.' (To Michael Brecher, *Nehru: A Political Biography* (Oxford University Press, London, 1959), p. 49. But Nehru's official biographer regards Nehru's political extremism as being confined to his letters to his father. See Sarvepalli Gopal, *Jawaharlal Nehru, (A Biography)*, Vol. 1, 1889–1947, (Oxford University Press, Delhi, 1975), p. 22.
3. M. C. Chagla, *Roses in December* (An Autobiography) (Bharatiya Vidya Bhavan, Bombay, 1978 p. 34.) Chagla, after a distinguished career at the Bombay Bar, became the Chief Justice of India and later Minister for External Affairs. A leading lawyer of Bombay, S. G. Velinker, even asked Chagla to 'see that Vasant [his son] does not join that seditious body – the Oxford Indian Majlis', ibid., p. 35.
4. '"Do not go near the Majlis, or the Native Club, or whatever it is called", Motilal warned Jawaharlal . . . the warning was not heeded. "I went the other day to a meeting of the Majlis, came the answer, just to see if they were as bad as they were painted. I failed to discover anything reprehensible in it. And as for the Native Club, Jawaharlal reported that there was one in Cambridge but it was eating natives"'. B. R. Nanda, *The Nehrus* (Oxford University Press, Delhi, 1962), p. 89.
5. Syed Mahmud, 'Jawaharlal Nehru as I knew him', Islamic Institute files, cited by S. Gopal, ibid., p. 23.

6. 'The Indian Majlis was an active body in which I took great interest and of which in due course I rose to become President. Just prior to this I recall taking part in a debate on Lord Sinha's speech as President of the Congress (1916–17). I led the side criticizing him vigorously. . . . Since popular sympathy was with the extremists, our side won hands down . . .'. C. D. Deshmukh (Indian Civil Service and later first Indian Governor of the Reserve Bank of India and Finance Minister, Governmen of India) in his autobiography, *The Course of My Life*, (Orient Longman, New Delhi, 1974), p. 42. K. P. S. Menon, an Oxford graduate, and later Secretary for External Affairs, Government of India, describes the Oxford Majlis of his undergraduate days as a 'forum for letting off steam'. 'The inconsistency between the making of anti-British speeches and the attempt to enter the ICS which was the mainstay of the British Government in India did not strike us.' *Many Worlds Revisited*, An Autobiography (Bharatiya Vidya Bhavan, Bombay, 1981), p. 54.
7. Chagla, *Roses*, op. cit., p. 42.
8. Ibid.
9. The *Cambridge Review* (founded 1879) is a magazine of 'University Life and Thought'. See *The Cambridge Mind: Ninety Years of the Cambridge Review 1879–1969*, (ed.) Eric Homberger, William Janeway and Simon Schama (Little, Brown, and Company, Boston, 1979).
10. *Cambridge Review*, 13 May 1909, p. 385.
11. The J. N. Tata Endowment financed many brilliant Indian students at Cambridge, like B. N. Rao, the jurist and the noted economists Jehangir Coyajee and V. K. R. V. Rao. 'In 1924 it was calculated that out of every five Indian I.C.S. officials, one was a Tata scholar', R. M. Lala, *The Creation of Wealth* (the Tata Story) (IBH Publishing Company, Bombay, 1981), p. 132.
12. 'I enjoyed life [at Cambridge] and I refused to see why I should consider it a thing of sin . . . work and games and amusements filled my life, and the only thing that disturbed me sometimes was the political struggle in India.' *Toward Freedom: The Autobiography of Jawaharlal Nehru* (New York, 1941), p. 34.
13. Hugh Dalton, who was at King's during those troubled times, recalls one incident at the Majlis, the society of Indian students, when 'a Sikh student drew a knife on a Moslem, and we had to separate them', *Call Back Yesterday (Memoirs 1887–1931)*, (Frederick Muller, London, 1957), p. 52. Jawaharlal Nehru attended a meeting of the Majlis (31 October 1907) 'just to see if they were as bad as they were painted' but 'failed to discover anything very reprehensible in it. It is curious how the Cambridge Indians have got a bad name on account of the doings of a very small number of gentlemen', *Selected Works of Jawaharlal Nehru*, Vol. 1, General Editor S. Gopal (Orient Longman, 1972, p. 36).
14. Alan Ross, *Ranji (Prince of Cricketers)* (Collins, London, 1983), p. 41.
15. Nehru's letter to his father from Trinity College, 12 March 1909, *Selected Works of Nehru*, ibid., p. 65.
16. 'His answer, of course, was that he was too busy.' Nehru's sarcasm will not be lost on the reader. Ibid., p. 65.
17. 'A certificate of loyalty would also be necessary', Nehru, ibid, p. 66.

18. The costs of a Continental university education seem to have been historically low compared to England. For example, 'On May 15, 1785, Daniel Mathus writing to his son Robert then at Jesus, said that he thought 100 pounds a year a reasonable price for the university expenses of ordinary folk. . . . At Leipzig, he added, it could be done for 25 pounds. The letter is quoted in Dr. Bonar's *Mathus and His Work*, p. 408.' Keynes in a letter to the editor of the *Cambridge Review*, 25 February 1933, in *The Collected Writings of John Maynard Keynes*, Vol. XXVIII, Social, Political and Literary Writings (Macmillan, London, 1982), p. 421.
19. Salman Khurshid, *At Home in India, A Restatement of Indian Muslims*, (Vikas Publishing House, New Delhi, 1986), p. 27. The author is a grandson of Dr Zakir Hussain.
20. *Selected Works of Nehru*, ibid, p. 38.
21. 'Letter from India' (reprinted from *Cambridge Review*) in *The Cambridge Mind* (*Ninety Years of the* Cambridge Review, *1879–1969*), (ed.) Eric Homberger, William Janeway and Simon Schama (Little Brown & Company, Boston, 1969), pp. 21–5.
22. J. M. Keynes, 'Alfred Marshall, 1842–1924', in *Memorials of Alfred Marshall*, (ed.) A. C. Pigou (Macmillan, London, 1925) p. 53.
23. Ibid., p. 53.
24. Marshall wrote warmly to Manohar Lal: 'I am very glad to know of the excellent work you are doing', *Memorials*, op. cit., p. 458.
25. Sir Atul Chatterjee, 'Obituary: Jahangir Cooverjee Coyajee', *Economic Journal*, Vol. 53, No. 212, December 1943, p. 454.
26. His *Structure of Competitive Industry* in *The Cambridge Economic Handbook Series VII*, General Editor, J. M. Keynes (Nisbet and Co. Ltd., London, Cambridge University Press, 1943), has the following charming reference to Gwalior: 'The same locomotive crew works the thousand-ton train of the Twentieth Century Limited and the fifty-ton Shivpuri express of the Gwalior Light Railway', p. 32.
27. Joan Robinson, 'Teaching Economics: A Passage to India', *Collected Economic Papers*, Vol. III (Basil Blackwell, Oxford, 1965), p. 1.
28. Austin Robinson refers to 'that astonishing vintage of 1934 [in Cambridge] which included Brian Reddaway, V. K. R. V. Rao, and T. W. Hutchinson, as well as Bob Bryce and Lorie Tarshis', 'Keynes and his Cambridge Colleagues' in *Keynes, Cambridge and 'The General Theory'* (ed.) Don Patinkin and J. Clark Leith (Macmillan, London, 1977), p. 33.
29. Keynes on 'Herbert Somerton Foxwell' in *Collected Writings*, Vol. X, *Essays in Biography*, 1972, p. 267.
30. L. P. Wilkinson, *Kingsmen of a Century, 1873–1972* (King's College, Cambridge, 1981), p. 222.
31. 'I had not been forethoughted enough to stipulate King's College, which shows something of my lack of understanding of economics at the time, since King's was where A. C. Pigou was and General Shove was and J. M. Keynes still had rooms; in short, where the action was.' Harry Johnson, 'Cambridge in the 1950s'. *The Shadow of Keynes* (Basil Blackwell, Oxford, 1978), p. 128.
32. 'It [King's] had a special aura about it and King's always gave the

impression of having been, like the twelve chosen', Raymond Leppard, in *My Oxford and My Cambridge*, edited by Ann Thwaite and Ronald Mayman (Taplinger Publishing Company, New York, 1979), p. 309.

33. A. F. W. Plumptre, 'Maynard Keynes as a Teacher' in *Essays on John Maynard Keynes*, edited by Milo Keynes (Cambridge University Press, 1975), p. 252. This sentiment finds an echo in the interesting symposium 'Keynes as Seen by his Students in the 1930s' by Robert Bryce, Walter Salant, and Lorie Tarshis, who recalls 'Keynes's influence on students was striking. Most of us became zealous. . . . it was intoxicating and doubly so because we felt we were a part of the revolution' (p. 51) in *Keynes, Cambridge and 'The General Theory'*, (ed.) Don Patinkin and J. Clark Leith (Macmillan, London, 1977).
34. Frank Moraes, *Jawaharlal Nehru (A Biography)* (Macmillan, New York, 1956), p. 42.
35. Michael Brecher, *Nehru: A Political Biography* (London, Oxford University Press, 1959), p. 48.
36. Letter from B. B. Das Gupta (Faculty of Commerce, Lucknow University, 8 June 1927) to Keynes, forwarding a revised copy of the dissertation for publication (*Keynes Papers*).
37. Austin Robinson in his review of Subba Rao, *Some Aspects of Economic Planning* (Bangalore Press, 1935), *Economic Journal*, Vol. 46, September 1936, p. 531.
38. Skidelsky, *Keynes*, op. cit., pp. 260–61, 272, and 285; and Hession, *Keynes*, op. cit., pp. 79–80.
39. '. . . in some of the streets – people from the windows remark to my hearing, small black man . . .' (Letter to Keynes from 5, All Saints Passage, Cambridge, 6 September 1911). *Keynes Papers*, King's College.
40. Skidelsky, *Keynes*, op. cit., p. 260.
41. ibid., p. 285.
42. Skidelsky, ibid., p. 272.
43. 'The literary jewel in Kings' crown was E. M. Forster who was kind to the better known or bred undergraduates, and used to give parties and occasional readings of chapters from his overtly homosexual novel, "Maurice",' Raymond Leppard, *My Cambridge*, op. cit., p. 310.
44. 'With Pigou, I could and did gossip about the latest Agatha Christie, cricket, or climbing, or a dozen other trivialities; but I never remember gossiping with Keynes in that sort of way . . . he had . . . no interest in sport . . . he rested with a book that most of us would regard as serious . . . his frivolities were half-serious frivolities.' Austin Robinson, in Milo Keynes (ed.), *Aspects of Keynes*, op. cit., p. 22.
45. See Richard Deacon, *The Cambridge Apostles* (Farrar, Straus, and Geraux, New York, 1986), p. 38.
46. See Noel Annan's review of *The Red and the Blue: Intelligence, Treason, and the Universities* by Andrew Sinclair (Weidenfeld & Nicholson), in *Observer*, 15 June 1986, p. 24.
47. G. C. Harcourt, 'A Man for All Systems: Talking with Kenneth Boulding', *Journal of Post Keynesian Economics*, Vol. VI, No. 1, Fall, 1983, p. 147.

48. Deacon, ibid., p. 175.
49. Walter Salant, 'Keynes as Seen by his Students in the 1930s' in Don Patinkin and J. Clark Leith, *Keynes, Cambridge, and the General Theory* (Macmillan, London, 1977), p. 44.

9 Keynes Politicus: The Indian Question

'The key to India is in London.' *Benjamin Disraeli*
'But what is this India Home Rule Bill?' *Winston Churchill*

Keynes's political philosophy as a lifelong but never an uncritical Liberal and even more his espousal of a variety of fashionable causes like the German problem, pacifism, conscription, women's suffrage, divorce reform, birth control, and public subsidy to the arts, prompts the question:[1] What in fact was Keynes's attitude to the Indian Question which historically has figured along with the Irish and Eastern Questions as one of the great perennials of Britain's imperial policy from Disraeli to Churchill and Attlee. Keynes too did not think that 'as regards the empire' there was 'any important problem except in India'.[2] But his liberalism did not extend at least publicly to the advocacy of self-government for India and the colonies after his Cambridge Union speech (1905) in support of Gokhale's resolution on popular government for India.[3] This hiatus in Keynes's liberalism certainly did not stem from any lack of political sensitivity on the part of one who so eloquently affirmed that 'civilization and liberty are a fairer cause than the integrity of our possessions'.[4] There could not have been a more unequivocal expression of Keynes's anti-imperialist stance and it is a grotesque misrepresentation to claim that 'his only major contribution as a British official involved a clear case of imperial-colonial exploitation' designed 'to prevent the Indian peasant from becoming unwarrantedly affluent'.[5] This charge has been made solely because Keynes, as Secretary of the British Cabinet's Wheat Committee (1915), organised government purchases of Indian wheat at below world market-price. But this measure – made possible by the embargo on private exports of Indian wheat – was in fact inspired by Keynes's former supervisor, Sir Thomas Holderness.[6] The more intriguing question is why Keynes never really followed Indian politics despite his close association as a Director and as a frequent contributor to the *New Statesman and Nation*, a periodical noted for its sustained espousal of India's independence. Perhaps the only exception to Keynes's public indifference to Indian political matters was the famous Meerut conspiracy case (1929) of the Government of

India against thirty-one communists, including two Englishmen, Philip Spratt and Ben Bradley, who were charged with conspiracy to deprive the King-Emperor of sovereignty over British India. Keynes took issue with Kingsley Martin, the editor, on his description of the case as a 'frame up' and his comparison of the Meerut trial with the Russian trials under the communist regime. Keynes pleaded for a better understanding of the efforts towards constitutional reform in India.[7] Even much later Keynes continued to adopt a wholly conventional approach to India's political problems as evidenced by the following personal letter (9 February 1943) to Kingsley Martin which was provoked by an article of H. N. Brailsford, the noted British journalist, on 'Famine in India' (*New Statesman and Nation*, 23 January 1943).

> Heaven knows that few can have a lower opinion of the Government of India today than I have, nor is there anyone more conscious of how it has muddled this and most other matters. But the article contained some fantastic misrepresentations of fact, largely inconsistent with its own, perfectly correct, diagnosis of hoarding, and then when it came to its proposed remedy for hoarding overlooked the fact that the greater number of the Viceroy's Council are Indians. The conclusion Brailsford ought to have drawn is that, since the Indianisation of the Viceroy's Council, the once prized efficiency of the I[ndian] C[ivil] S[ervice] and the Government, at any rate on the administrative side, has largely disappeared, which is a sad forecast of what will happen when we have entirely withdrawn our hands. Personally, I am so fed up with India, that I should like to clear out on any terms and at the earliest possible moment. But probably, if I was nearer the facts, I should not have the heart to follow my inclinations literally; and then, I suppose, I should become a victim of Brailsford's raving on the matter.[8]

This letter has a strange unKeynesian flavour of cynicism, political prejudice, and, more surprisingly, of *non sequitur* logic, particularly in equating Indianisation of the Viceroy's Executive Council with increasing inefficiency of the Indian Civil Service. Could a former civil servant and an astute political observer like Keynes have been really unaware that the Indian members of the Viceroy's Council were powerless official nominees in the emergency regime of an Imperial dependency, or that the overwhelming bulk of the Indian members of the civil service were entrants through a highly competitive examination common to Indian and English candidates? Likewise, Keynes's diagnosis of the Great Bengal Famine as a hoarding phenomenon reflected a rather simplistic and uncritical acceptance of the official line. The famine was in fact a culmination of more basic causes, most notably of some egregious bureaucratic failures, which led to a cumulative decline in exchange entitlements (that is, the purchasing power and market access) of the most vulnerable classes like landless labour, rural artisans and craftsmen. These aspects were well-known to contemporary observers and have been subsequently confirmed by authoritative research.[9]

It would, however, be misleading to attribute Keynes's lack of interest in Indian politics to the belief that he was 'the most unpolitical of men' or that 'he had no taste for politics'.[10] Such labels in any event scarcely fit so leading a protagonist – Principal Treasury Representative – of the Paris Peace Conference and the author of such politically influential tracts as *The Economic Consequences of the Peace* and *The Revision of the Treaty*. A more plausible, albeit unconscious, clue to Keynes's lack of interest in Indian politics is to be found in Keynes's memorable description of his mentor, Edwin Montagu, as 'an Oriental, equipped, nevertheless, with the intellectual technique and atmosphere of the west' and one who was drawn 'naturally to the political problems of India' which 'allowed an instinctive, mutual sympathy between him and its peoples'.[11] Keynes might have felt that he lacked precisely these attributes in understanding Indian political aspirations. This also explains why, unlike his fellow Bloomsberries, Leonard Woolf and Forster, who showed such perceptive understanding of the social and political nuances of nationalism in Ceylon and India, Keynes was never provoked to examine the human, social and political aspects of British rule in India or even its exploitative economic aspects. Keynes's image of British rule in India was that of a paternalistic regime which protected the Indian peasant against the grasping middleman-moneylender and the urban businessman; gave India a sound monetary system; brought moral and material progress with law and order; and, in short, introduced good government. Given his staid view of British rule in India it is all the more remarkable that Keynes's radical suggestion for abolition of the salt tax in India (c.1907) was so far ahead of contemporary Indian nationalist opinion which was more concerned with the abatement of the tax rather than its outright abolition. If implemented Keynes's suggestion would have removed what was to prove later a major prop of Indian nationalism under the leadership of Gandhi, whose famous eleven points of political demands to Lord Irwin, the Viceroy (1930–31), included the abolition of the salt tax, reduction of land revenue, and the introduction of prohibition. True, the salt-tax agitation was in a sense a symbolic movement which could hardly be expected to undermine the financial foundations of British rule, considering that the salt tax accounted for about 3–4 per cent of the Government of India's revenue. In the event, Gandhi's salt *satyagraha* (non-violent agitation) initiated with the dramatic long march from Sabarmati to Dandi in the Gujerat region, had a marked effect on salt sales and revenue only in the Bombay Presidency. But its political significance was certainly far out of proportion to its fiscal impact.

In any final assessment it is far more important to remember that whatever his views on Indian politics Keynes never wavered in support of India's vital national interests. Thus, he was totally averse to any semblance of political huckstering which might seek to link up any British concessions on the question of India's sterling balances to the more basic issue of political freedom for India. His steady advocacy of a politically dependent India's case for an adequate quota in the International Monetary Fund and India's due place among the Big Five on its Board of Directors certainly went far beyond any call of duty.

Nevertheless, Keynes's somewhat lackadaisical attitude to Indian politics poses a different but equally interesting conundrum. Did it at bottom reflect his cultural insularity, a trait noted by widely disparate commentators like his fellow Bloomsberry, Clive Bell, and the High Priests of Cambridge (Massachusetts), Schumpeter and Paul Samuelson? Bell thought that Keynes was a 'provincial' of 'limited culture' unable to see a foreign country from inside.[12] Schumpeter thought that 'barring some of his artistic tastes, he was surprisingly insular, even in philosophy, but nowhere so much as in economics [this is debatable]' and that his patriotism although 'quite untinged by vulgarity' excluded 'full understanding of foreign (also American) viewpoints, conditions, interests, and especially creeds'.[13] Samuelson too has remarked on 'the paradox that Keynes the cosmopolitan was at the same time the most provincial of British patriots', who 'never really cared for Americans'.[14] Although caring for Americans can scarcely be a yardstick for measuring Keynes's cosmopolitanism, there is arguably an element of substance in such statements. Keynes's Indian Connection too provides a not untypical example of his attitudes, which were never articulated, to other societies and cultures. The Renaissance Man of Bloomsbury and Cambridge and the connoisseur of the civilising arts, was also wholly oblivious to the rich artistic and cultural heritage of India. Interestingly, Keynes, never an avid reader of fiction, is on record as having enjoyed that classic of Anglo-Indian literature, Ackerley's *Hindoo Holiday*, which in fact, as he himself noted, is a 'fragment of memoirs'.[15] There is no evidence of Keynes's reactions to the other and even greater classic of Anglo-Indian literature – Forster's *A Passage to India*. But such speculations risk the charge: Can one judge even Keynes by standards not applied to others? As rightly pointed out by Sir Roy Harrod, 'How many distinguished living Englishmen would be exempt from the charge of provincialism. . . . Would the number be about half a dozen? I should find it difficult to name so many'.[16] Even the Bloomsbury group – the most distinguished intellectual coterie in Britain – of which Keynes was such a shining light, was at best Eurocentric with the possible exceptions of Leonard Woolf and Forster.[17] Cultural provincialism is not peculiar to any particular society and even intellectuals should be allowed their artistic and cultural blindspots without inviting the charge of prejudice or philistinism. A hard core of ethnocentrism seems to persist even in the most cultivated savants. One cannot therefore read too much into Keynes's lack of interest in Indian culture or in one of his very rare reactions to Eastern art.[18] At least Keynes's cultural parochialism and indifference to Indian art and culture did not spring from any lack of understanding or respect for Eastern civilisation. Even the callow Etonian wrote in a College essay:

> we see the reason why the East formed the great civilizations of the past and why it is incapable of further advance. It could arrive at great dogmas which are true for the mass . . . but it is altogether lacking in that initiative and invention which can emanate only from the individuals and without which further progress is impossible. . . . If history is to be taken as the basis of prophesy . . . it is difficult to find reasonable grounds for hoping that the mainlines of difference between the East and the West will be erased by the agency either of space or time. ('The Differences between East and West: Will they ever Disappear?' Early Composition, Eton, November 1900 in *Keynes Papers* (pages 1–19), King's College)

Three decades later, a maturer Keynes articulated a different worldview justifying economic and financial nationalism while wholeheartedly approving cultural and social internationalism.[19] Paradoxically, Keynes was also reproached by Winston Churchill as too much of a suprapolitical and international economic statesman who 'only understood the necessities of world economy but did not understand political necessity'. But the fact remains that Keynes's cultural parochialism never blurred his vision of a just world order. As he eloquently remarked at the Executive Plenary Session of the United Nations Monetary and Financial Conference (21 July 1944):

> It is with some emotion that I find myself today collaborating . . . to bring to birth an institution which may play a unique part in restoring the devastation of a second war and in bringing back to a life of peace and abundant fruitfulness those great European and Asiatic parents of civilization to which all the world owes so much of what is honorable and grand in the heritage of mankind. (*Proceedings and Documents*, Vol. II, p. 1217)

The humanist international economic statesman had truly advanced well beyond the horizons of the Etonian.

Notes

1. Keynes wrote to the press under the pen name 'Politicus' on political issues such as conscription (p. 160) and the German problem (p. 183), *Collected Writings of John Maynard Keynes, Vol. XVI*, Activities 1914–19: The Treasury and Versailles (Macmillan, London 1971).
2. In his speech 'Am I a Liberal?' to the Liberal Summer School, Cambridge, August 1925 reproduced in *The Collected Writings of John Maynard Keynes*, IX, Essays in Persuasion (Macmillan, London, 1972), p. 301.
3. It is noteworthy that the most systematic discussion of Keynes's political philosophy ('Keynes: His Political Ideas and Their Influence' by Maurice Cranston in Thirlwall, (ed.) *Keynes and Laissez Faire*, op. cit. does not have any reference to self-determination for India or the colonies.
4. In a letter to the *New Statesman and Nation*, 3 April 1938, reproduced in *The Collected Writings of John Maynard Keynes*, Vol. XXVIII, Social, Political and Literary Writings, (ed.) Donald Moggridge (Macmillan, London, 1982), p. 110.
5. Harry Johnson, 'Keynes and Development' in *The Shadow of Keynes* by Elizabeth S. Johnson (Basil Blackwell, Oxford, 1978), p. 227.

6. Montagu Papers, Trinity College, 86(1) Holderness to John Maynard Keynes, 3 February 1915.
7. '. . . the Russian trial had nothing whatever to do with the question of suppressing dangerous opinion . . . even if one were to admit your alleged parallels, I do not remember you writing a leader about the Meerut trial, telling the Indians not to excite themselves too much, because what is going on is no worse than what regularly happens in Russia . . . the Indian White Paper [on The Future Form of Government for India (Cmd. 4268)] is broadly speaking the utmost progress which can be made at this stage; yet you are quite ready to inflame, rather than pacify, Indian grievances against it'. Letter to Kingsley Martin, 23 April 1933, *The Collected Writings of John Maynard Keynes*, Vol. XXVIII, Social, Political and Literary Writings, (ed.) Donald Moggridge (Macmillan, London, 1982), p. 18.
8. *Collected Writings*, Vol. XXVIII, p. 188.
9. Cf. Ian Stephens, the British editor (later a Fellow of King's College) of the Calcutta newspaper, the *Statesman*, wrote in his book on wartime India, *Monsoon Morning* (Ernest Benn, London, 1966), that 'India had a surplus in commodities, which had the [Food] Department then existed, could have been purchased by government, as provision against the rainy day which has now found India unprepared', p. 183. According to Amartya Sen, 'food availability decline seems to fail altogether in explaining the famine. . . . There seems to have been sharp movements in exchange entitlements with respect to food in Bengal in 1942 and 1943 . . . indicating a growing cause of starvation for several occupation groups' ('Starvation and Exchange Entitlements, A General Approach and Its Application to the Great Bengal Famine', *Cambridge Journal of Economics*, Vol. 1, March 1977, p. 55).
10. Joseph A. Schumpeter, 'John Maynard Keynes, 1883–1946', *American Economic Review*, Vol. XXXVI, No. 4, September 1946, p. 497.
11. *The Collected Writings of John Maynard Keynes*, Vol. X, Essays in Biography (Macmillan, London, 1972), p. 41.
12. 'In such discussions [about French or Italian ways of thinking, feeling and living] one could not but be struck by Maynard's inability to see a foreign country from inside. France, Italy, America even, he saw them all from the white cliffs of Dover, or, to be more exact, from Whitehall or King's combination room. Compared with (say) Roger Fry, who was often of the company, he seemed ludicrously provincial. And that may be what I had in mind when I called his culture limited'. Clive Bell, *Old Friends, Personal Recollections* (Chatto and Windus, London, 1956), p. 60.
13. Schumpeter, 'Keynes', op. cit., p. 505.
14. Paul Samuelson, 'Sympathy from the Other Cambridge', *The Economist*, 25 June 1983, Vol. 287, No. 7295, p. 20. But as rightly pointed out by Singer, 'Samuelson's sole explicit evidence for calling Keynes "the most provincial of British patriots" is that "he never really cared for the Americans. Is not this perhaps an example of American provincialism?"' H. W. Singer, 'Relevance', op. cit., p. 423 (fn 10).
15. 'I do not much care for them [contemporary novels] when I am lazy and

relaxed; nor yet when I am contemplative and serious' (p. 329). 'Even two out of the few recent novels I have read and enjoyed, J. R. Ackerley's *Hindoo Holiday* and David Garnett's *Beany Eye* are, in fact, fragments of memoirs. It is a mixed lot you see. But they have splinters of truth and life in them'. *Collected Writings*, Vol. XXVIII, p. 331. Keynes cites Forster's *A Room with a View* (not *A Passage to India*) as a good example of 'pleasant easy reading', ibid, p. 330.

16. R. F. Harrod, 'Clive Bell on Keynes', *Economic Journal*, Vol. LXVII, December 1957, No. 268, p. 694.
17. For instance, 'Bloomsbury found it difficult to despise the Germans, for they thought more often of Goethe and Bach than of Kaiser Bill; this pro-Germanism was purely cultural', Paul Levy, 'The Bloomsbury Group' in Milo Keynes (ed.), *Aspects of Keynes* op. cit., p. 67. Once, when Keynes returned from one of his visits to the USA, he remarked: 'When I come home I don't come home to England. I come home to Europe'. Cited by Mary Glasgown, *Keynes and the Bloomsbury Group*, (ed.) Crabtree and Thirlwall, op. cit., p. 108.
18. 'He [Keynes] found some of the Egyptian temples rather boring' (letter of 20 March 1913 to Neville Keynes, cited by Skidelsky, *Keynes*, op. cit., p. 274). This type of selective reaction is essentially a matter of taste and not uncommon in relation to all categories of art.
19. 'Ideas, knowledge, art, hospitality, travel – these are the things which should of their nature be international. But let goods be homespun whenever it is reasonably and conveniently possible; and, above all, let finance be primarily national'. National Self-Sufficiency (Yale Review, Summer, 1933), *Collected Writings of John Maynard Keynes*, Volume XXI, Activities 1931–39, 1982, p. 237.

10 Epilogue and Apotheosis: Keynes Indophilus

'India is full of such wonders . . . To have done good work is something and I don't the least doubt that I have done some.' *E. M. Forster*

'He achieved that rare and coveted combination of 'Lakshmi' (the Goddess of Wealth) and 'Saraswati' (The Goddess of Learning) in his own life . . . he added the celestial gift of an 'Urvashi' (The God Indra's Dancer) to it by marrying Lydia Lopokova.' *B. P. Adarkar* (*Lord Keynes of Tilton – A Tribute*)

The strength, variety and continuity of the Indian Connection in Keynes's writings and activities, prompts 'the really interesting question' which as Lytton Strachey said 'is always the particular one'. How did the Indian Connection contribute to the making of Keynes the foremost monetary economist, policy adviser extraordinaire, international economic statesman, and the revered guru? What in the final analysis did India and Indians really mean to Keynes? Which, in the interface between Keynes and India, was more decisive and significant, the impact of India on Keynes, or of Keynes on India?

Keynes's contributions and achievements must be seen in the light of his early and highly opportune institutional exposures. It is hard to conceive of an alternative experience comparable to his service in the India Office, his membership of the Royal Commission (Chamberlain) on Indian Currency and Finance (1913) and his role as a star witness before the Babington Smith Committee on Indian Exchange and Currency (1919) and the Hilton Young Commission on Indian Currency (1926) in the formation of Keynes's mind-set as an applied economist and economic statesman. The British Treasury certainly would not have afforded him the same variety of exposure to issues and personalities and above all to the art of coping with bureaucrats as well as non-officials which was to prove so invaluable in his later career. Keynes's early Indian encounters doubtless honed up a hard core of workaday talent without which even genius cannot flourish in a policy-orientated subject like economics. Keynes the economist and the economic statesman could not have been fashioned so well as in the bureaucratic crucible of the byzantine India Office, his most formative spell as a serving civil servant. While it would be too much to claim that contemporary policy measures were adopted because of Keynes's advocacy, his superiors showed a lively appreciation of his expertise and intellectual inputs in all official decisions and policies.

It is well known that Keynes chose the India office not out of any special interest in India but only because it was then one of the two top home departments of the British Government. His entry into the India Office, and even more the internal transfer from the Military Affairs to Revenue and Commerce Departments, was therefore a most happy accident for his own career and the history of the subject to which he made such signal contributions. What would Keynes's career have been like if Sir Otto Niemeyer had decided to stick to his first choice in the Civil Service – the India Office – and let Keynes go to the Treasury? Sir Roy Harrod provides part of the answer:

> Had he gone to the Treasury, he probably would not have come out after two years. Would he as a permanent, and not a temporary, Civil Servant have resigned at Paris in 1919? What would have been the balance of good? Rising towards the top of the Treasury in the inter-war period, would he have achieved a better conduct of British finances? We can hardly doubt that Mr. Churchill, the innocent victim, as Chancellor of the Exchequer, in the crucial years (1925–29), of the old orthodox school at the Treasury and the Bank of England, would have found in Keynes a man after his heart's desire. We may guess that Keynes would have influenced the mind of Benjamin Strong of the Federal Reserve Bank of New York. Could he and Strong's successors between them have availed to mitigate the great slump of 1929–32? Then the Nazis would not have come into power. . . . But then, although no doubt he would have written books – and possibly on economics – they would inevitably have been of a different character. Valuable analyses we might have had, but the strong undercurrent of rebellion could hardly have been present, and without that, would his works have had comparable influence?[1]

In the 1920s Otto Niemeyer was regarded as the prime architect and codifier of the Treasury View against which Keynes fought so strenuously in the interwar years. 'What would have happened had Keynes gone into the Treasury rather than Niemeyer? Would he have been tempted to make a career in government service – with possibly profound influence on British economic policy in the 1920s? Probably not. Maynard was far from ready in 1906 to disappear into Whitehall'.[2] One could add other counterfactuals to these. Would Keynes have been able to complete his famous dissertation on Probability in the much busier and more humdrum atmosphere of the Treasury? Above all, would he have got involved in the problems of the gold exchange standard and central banking without exposure to the Indian currency and financial system?

Likewise, Keynes's association with the Royal Commission on Indian Currency and Finance (1913) was productive not only in terms of his own substantial contributions to its work and Report, but also in enlarging and strengthening Keynes's peculiar intellectual *métier* – the perfect blend of cogent economic analysis with institutional, administrative and practical details. This Commission also brought Keynes into the rarefied personal orbits of influential figures in government, business and finance like Austen Chamberlain, Robert (later Lord) Chalmers, Lord Kilbracken, Lord Faber, and Basil Blackett of the Treasury, who became his close lifelong friend. These intimate early contacts undoubtedly contributed to his subsequent self-confidence and assurance in moving in the highest policy-making circles. But it is totally beside the mark to say that Keynes's career in the India Office 'as a member of one such elite [superior class of administration] shaped his attitude to policies for the rest of his life'.[3] Keynes was too much of a maverick civil servant to have developed rigid attitudes whether in economics or politics.

Keynes's India Office service was also instrumental in strengthening the most crucial formative influence in his early career – Edwin Montagu, Secretary of State for India, to whom Keynes – as he graciously acknowledged in private – owed 'nearly all my steps up in life',[4] an aspect which is hardly noticeable from Keynes's published obituary of Montagu.[5] As President of the Cambridge Union (1902), Montagu picked Keynes out in his first term as a freshman to give him 'a place on the paper' (roster of speakers). The first electioneering Keynes ever did (1906) was on behalf of Montagu. It was Montagu as the Secretary of State for India (1913) who nominated Keynes to the Royal (Chamberlain) Commission on Indian Currency when Keynes was relatively unknown outside Cambridge. This was Keynes's first entry on to the public stage. It was Montagu who got Keynes called to the Treasury in 1915, took him to Paris in February of that year for the first inter-Allied Financial Conference and thus established him in his war work. Montagu, as the Minister to whom Keynes was responsible during the first part of the Peace Conference, got him invited to the private gatherings of Cabinet secretaries and chief ministers during the early years of the war to discuss its big problems. Likewise, Montagu introduced Keynes to the great ones like Lloyd George, McKenna and Margot Asquith and nominated him as the Vice-Chairman of the Indian Fiscal Commission (1921). Subsequently, Montagu invited Keynes to join a special mission to Brazil in 1923. Keynes records feelingly: 'Thus for more than 20 years I had reason to be grateful to him; and there was a certain affectionate relation between us'. Montagu's role in Keynes's career, together with Keynes's links with the governing classes, suggests that even a genius like Keynes could not have had public scope without a powerful and influential mentor and access to the establishment and the corridors of power. But then how many geniuses like Keynes would be found to record their gratitude even in private to mentors and benefactors? At a more technical level, Keynes always regarded Lionel Abrahams of the India Office as his mentor on Indian Finance, a relationship which he constantly reiterated and cherished. Significantly, Keynes's two principal mentors each had a strong India Office affiliation.

The contribution of practical experience to the intellectual development of savants is a perennially absorbing theme in the sociology of knowledge. The role of his India Office experience in the making of Keynes the applied monetary economist could be paralleled by similar illustrious examples like Gibbon, who believed that his captaincy in the Hampshire Grenadiers had helped in the writing of his history, or of Macaulay who too thought that his experience as Secretary at War in Melbourne's Ministry had sharpened his historical perceptions. Adam Smith's service as a Commissioner of Customs was not without influence on his economic writings. Perhaps economics too would be a richer discipline if only more economists had sustained exposure like Adam Smith and Keynes to the world of affairs. As Kenneth Boulding once remarked picturesquely in a lecture at the London School of Economics, 'Every sociologist is necessarily born in a family but few economists are born in a firm'! In retrospect, Keynes's service with the India Office should be seen not as a 'brief interlude in his life which had nothing to do with a particular interest in India or in poor colonies in general'[6] but as an invaluable apprenticeship to his work and achievements as an economist and as a public figure. Likewise, in any final assessment of the interface between Keynes and India the impact of India on Keynes emerges as perhaps more decisive and significant than the influence of Keynes on India even though in the long run most of his ideas did find their way into India's monetary and banking arrangements. Keynes's significant early achievements as an economist which established him in public esteem and won him academic acclaim were all related to his involvement in Indian matters. The Indian Connection was thus crucial to the making of not only the Early Keynes but even more to the Classical and Institutionalist Keynes. Judging alike by his writings and activities India was the one country other than Britain which figured most consistently and prominently in Keynes's life. No other economist of such stature thought and wrote as much about the problems of another country and made significant contributions to the subject. All this leads us naturally to ask: Could Keynes, given the strength of his Indian connections, be also cast as an Indophile in what seems to be the historical dichotomy of Cambridge intellectuals – some might even say of Anglo-Saxons – into Indophiles (Forster, Malcolm Darling, Percival Spear, and Nicholas Kaldor) or Sinophiles (Arthur Waley, Lowes Dickinson, Bertrand Russell, and Joseph Needham). Some like Joan Robinson could justifiably be said to straddle both.[7] Yet others like Archdeacon William Cunningham remained clinically detached and even self-critical after an extended visit to India.[8] Where would Keynes have fitted into such a typology? It is difficult to be dogmatic in the case of Keynes who never judged or expressed himself on India as a country and society or Indians as a people and never visited the country. Nevertheless, it is fascinating to conjecture how Keynes would have reacted to India and Indians if he had visited the country and articulated his impressions. Would he have shared Bertrand Russell's experience after his travels in Germany and America which he found 'were useful in curing [him] of a certain Cambridge provincialism'?[9] Or else would he like Lowes Dickinson have felt 'Indian art, Indian religion, Indian society, to be "alien and unsympathetic" and "never found in Indian society either the happiness or the peacefulness which have made my own [Forster's] visits to the country so wonderful"'[10] Perhaps rather than the gently emotional Indophilia of Forster, Keynes the meliorist Liberal may well have developed the eminently constructive interests in Indian economic and public affairs of his fellow Kingsman, Malcolm Darling, the archetypical British Indian civil servant. How then would Keynes, ever obsessed by the 'Benthamite worm' have viewed India the classic home of applied Utilitarianism? He may well have conceded the validity of Benthamism in the Indian milieu, if, as argued by his pupil, 'the Benthamite version of human nature had much to be said for it . . . so long as the vast majority of the population are in or near conditions of gross material want, with their simplest needs completely satisfied, and living in a society with a simple economic organization', where 'material needs predominate' and 'are largely uniform'.[11] This is a perfect description of Indian society and a perceptive nuance of Benthamism eminently in consonance with Keynes's concerns with the 'condition-of-the-people' problem in India which were so well manifested in his India Office and early Cambridge years and his consistent solicitude for the Indian peasant as against the businessman and exporter. But would such pristine Benthamism have survived the subsequent revolution of rising expectations in so complex and plural society as India where paradoxically relative poverty poses even greater problems than absolute poverty and deprivation? On the other hand, as one who felt that 'the failures of the nineteenth century democracies to maintain the grandeur and dignity of the State was at least one of the seeds of their decay', Keynes the romantic aesthete might have found the pomp and circumstance of the British Viceroyalty and the quaint courtliness and old-world manners of Princely India not altogether uncongenial. However such conjectures should not be pressed too far if only because empathy, like its obverse, prejudice, seems to belong more to the caverns of the unconscious than to the rational self. Even Forster found it hard to explain his attachment to India ('I love this country [India] though I don't know why or how' – to Jack Sprott, 1945). True, what drew Keynes to India was not the country or the people but the sheer intellectual challenge of the uniqueness and complexity of India's monetary experience and problems. His approach to India was basically issue-and-policy orientated, unlike Forster's, which was so essentially personal and emotional. Yet there is enough to suggest that the Indian Connection in Keynes's life and work was not wholly intellectual. There was perhaps somewhere deep down in the Keynesian psyche a subtle undefined Indian element. Strangely, his extramural contacts and correspondence with Indian pupils were largely personal – more like a moral tutor than a don – unlike those of Alfred Marshall which were wholly intellectual and academic. Alike in his concerns and relations with Indians he showed a rare sensibility. He did not sponsor any Indian for the Society of the Apostles, but like a true guru he rallied to the support of Indian students in Cambridge, and spoke up for an aggrieved low-level official in the

Rangoon stamp office. Which other Englishman of his stature in the heyday of the Raj would have so graciously agreed to serve under an Indian Chairman of an official Commission? In sum, Keynes's Indian Connection stands out as possibly the longest saga of its kind for any economist in time and space – *pianissimo* from the 'prentice years at India Office and the spirited defence of Indian students at Cambridge to *fortissimo*, the principled support for a still-dependent India's concerns at Bretton Woods and Savannah. The Keynes charisma cast an uncanny spell over Indians even as India and Indians exercised a subtle yet palpable influence on *Keynes Indophilus*. A fitting epitaph to an eventful life which fulfilled so admirably the Indian ideal of a synthesis of the material, the intellectual, the moral, and the aesthetic. Nonetheless, there will always remain a poignant hiatus in Keynes's rich and memorable involvement with India.

> Like an anthropologist, Maynard was a fieldworker; to be chairman of an insurance company was necessary for his theoretical work. *The pity of it is that he was never a fieldworker in India.* [emphasis provided] Would he have become a development economist had he set eyes on rural India? After all he loved farming. (Polly Hill to author, 1 May 1987).

The rolling countryside around Ooty in the Nilgiri Hills may well have reminded him of his beloved Sussex Downs. We shall never know.

Notes

1. Harrod, *Life*, op. cit., p. 120–21.
2. Skidelsky, op. cit., p. 175.
3. Maurice Cranston, 'Keynes: His Political Ideas and their Influence' in Thirlwall (ed.), *Keynes and Laissez Faire* op. cit., p. 114.
4. Keynes to Lydia Keynes, 16 November 1924, *Keynes Papers*, King's College.
5. *The Collected Writings of John Maynard Keynes*, Vol. X, Essays in Biography (Macmillan, London, 1972), pp. 41–2.
6. A. P. Thirlwall (ed.), *Keynes and Laissez Faire*, op. cit., p. 7.
7. '. . . she and Austin Robinson went to live on in India for two-and-half years in Gwalior. . . . That was her first experience of the Raj and the beginning of her love of India. [She thought "India is a great melting pot. Human nature is the same everywhere, but in India it is more so".] But in China, as in India, Joan felt at home'. Sita Narasimhan, Joan Robinson, 'In the Radical Vein: A Laywoman's Homage', *Cambridge Journal of Economics*, 1983, 7, pp. 217–18.

8. '. . . one realizes the entire incompatibility of Eastern and Western civilization. . . . We cannot appear as benefactors to the people of India . . . we really are nihilists overthrowing the institutions of society, and helpless to develop anything in their stead—', letter from India, 8 March 1882 in Homberger, Janeway and Schama, *The Cambridge Mind*, op. cit., p. 24.
9. Bertrand Russell, 'My Mental Development' in *The Basic Writings of Bertrand Russell, 1903–1959*, (ed.) Robert E. Egner and Lester E. Denton (Simon and Schuster, New York, 1961), p. 43.
10. E. M. Forster, *Goldsworthy Lowes Dickinson* (Harcourt Brace Jovanovich, New York, 1973), p. 137 and p. 141, 'The Chinese amused and charmed him in a way in which Indians did not' and he confessed, 'Clearly I'm Chinese and not Indian, though I believe I was Indian from the age of twenty to twenty-five and would have become an ascetic with the smallest encouragement' (ibid, 145).
11. D. M. Bensusan-Butt, 'Thoughts About the Benthamite Worm', *On Economic Knowledge (A Sceptical Miscellany)* (Australian National University, Canberra, 1980), pp. 118–19.

Keynes's Writings on India

Book

Indian Currency and Finance (1913) *Collected Writings of John Maynard Keynes* (see p. 199) (CW) Vol. I (1971).

Other Writings

(All reproduced in CW Vol. XV unless otherwise indicated)

Articles and Papers

'Great Britain's Foreign Investments' (*New Quarterly*, February 1910), pp. 44–59.

'India During 1907–8' (review of report on 'Moral and Material Progress and Condition of India' *The Economist*, 3 July 1909, pp. 34–8.

'Recent Developments of the Indian Currency Question' (paper read to the Royal Economic Society, 9 May 1911), pp. 67–85.

(Those below are all from CW XI)

'Recent Economic Events in India', *Economic Journal*, March 1909, pp. 1–22.

'Trade of India in 1913–14', *Economic Journal*, December 1914, pp. 36–40.

Reviews

Engelbrecht, Von Th. H. *Die geographische verteilung der gertreeidpreise in Indien von 1861 bis 1905* (Berlin, Paul Parey) 1908 *Journal of the Royal Statistical Society*, March 1909), pp. 22–23.

Jevons, H. Stanley, 'The Future of Exchange and the Indian Currency', *Economic Journal*, March 1923, pp. 42–8.

Memorandum and Statistical Tables relating to the Trade of India with Germany and Austria-Hungary, *Economic Journal*, December 1914, pp. 36–40.

Morison, Sir Theodore, 'The Economic Transition in India', *Economic Journal*, September 1911, pp. 27–33.

Report upon the Operations of the Paper Currency Department of the Government of India during the Year 1910–11, *Economic Journal*, March 1912, pp. 33–6.

Review of the Trade of India in 1913–14, *Economic Journal*, December 1914, pp. 36–40.

Shirras, G. Findlay, 'Indian Finance and Banking', *Economic Journal*, September 1920, pp. 40–48.

Webb, M. de P., 'The Rupee Problem, a Plea for a Definite Currency Policy for India', *Economic Journal*, September 1910, pp. 23–6.

Memoranda, Draft Memoranda, Notes and Comments

Comment on Abrahams's State Bank Memorandum (1 July 1913) pp. 133–7.

Covering Note for Keynes's State Bank Memorandum (addressed 'To the Members of the Royal Commission', (19 November 1913) p. 145.

Criticism of Draft Reserves Proposal (December 1913) pp. 240–42.

Gold Currency: Draft Conclusions (December 1913) pp. 232–4.

Gold in Internal Circulation (December 1913) pp. 223–31.
Gold Standard Reserve, The: Draft (December 1913) pp. 234–6.
Memorandum by Mr J. M. Keynes on the Commission's Paper Currency Proposals (3 February 1914) pp. 258–63.
Note on Purchase of Silver (December 1913) pp. 266–7.
The Paper Currency Reserve and Gold Standard Reserve (regarded as a joint fund, from the Report of the Royal Commission on Indian Currency and Finance, March 1914) pp. 264–5.
Paper Currency: Revised Draft (December 1913) pp. 243–50.
The Position of the Jute Trade (19 March 1907) pp. 5–11.

Proposals for the Establishment of a State Bank in India pp. 151–211
Introductory, 151–3.
Outline constitution, so far as concerns the relation of the Bank to Government, the powers of the shareholders, and decentralisation, pp. 153–6.
Discussion of the outline constitution, pp. 156–65.
Capitalisation of the bank and division of profits, pp. 165–72.
Regulation of the note issue, pp. 172–84.
The London Office and Remittance, pp. 184–90.
Other functions of the bank, pp. 190–92.
General advantages of a State Bank, pp. 192–200.
Some adverse criticisms, pp. 200–202.
Appendices, pp. 202–11.
A. The relation of state banks to their governments, pp. 202–8.
B. State banks and private capital, pp. 208–10.
C. The division of the profits of the Reichsbank, pp. 210–11.

Some Aspects of Recent Events (affecting Indian banking, latter part of 1913) pp. 146–7.
State or Central Bank (from the Report of the Royal Commission on Indian Currency and Finance, March 1914) pp. 148–51.
Evidence
To the Indian Exchange and Currency Committee (1919) pp. 273–98.
Minutes of Evidence
Memorandum of Evidence for the Royal Commission on Indian Currency and Finance, 19 March 1926 (CW XIX, Part II) pp. 477–9.
Minutes of Evidence, Royal Commission on Indian Currency and Finance, 22 March 1926 (CW XIX, Part II) pp. 480–524.
Minutes
To Holderness, Mr (Thomas), 19 March 1907 (with draft memorandum on the jute trade) pp. 4–5.
To Holderness, Sir Thomas, 9 February 1908 (appointment of a Director of Statistics, India) pp. 11–12.
Published Letters
To the *Cambridge Review*, 20 May 1909 (Indian students at Cambridge) pp. 31–3.
To *The Times*, 26 October 1912 (Indian currency system) pp. 88–90.
To *The Times*, 14 November 1912 (Indian currency system) pp. 91–4.

Select Bibliography

Books

C. Bell, *Old Friends* (London: Chatto and Windus, 1956).
A. G. Chandavarkar, 'Money and Credit, 1858–1947', Chapter IX in Dharma Kumar (ed.) *The Cambridge Economic History of India, Vol. 2: c.1757–c.1970* (Cambridge University Press, 1983).
D. Crabtree and A. P. Thirlwall (ed.) *Keynes and the Bloomsbury Group* (London: Macmillan, 1980).
M. Cranston, 'Keynes: His Political Ideas and their Influence', in A. P. Thirlwall (ed.) *Keynes and Laissez-Faire* (London: Macmillan, 1978).
R. Deacon, *The Cambridge Apostles* (New York: Farrar, Strauss, and Gevaux, 1986).
C. D. Deshmukh, *Central Banking in India* (Poona: Gokhale Institute of Politics and Economics, 1948).
———, *The Course of my Life* (New Delhi: Orient Longmans, 1974).
P. J. Grigg, *Prejudice and Judgement* (London: Jonathan Cape, 1956).
R. F. Harrod, *The Life of John Maynard Keynes* (London: Macmillan, 1951).
C. H. Hession, *John Maynard Keynes: A Personal Biography of the Man who Revolutionised Capitalism* (London: Macmillan, 1983).
H. G. Johnson, 'Cambridge in the 1950s'; 'Keynes and Development'; 'The Early Economics of Keynes', in E. S. Johnson and H. G. Johnson (ed.) *The Shadow of Keynes* (Oxford: Basil Blackwell, 1978).
R. F. Kahn, *The Making of Keynes's General Theory* (Cambridge: Cambridge University Press, 1954).
The Collected Writings of John Maynard Keynes (London: Macmillan).
Vol. I *Indian Currency and Finance* (1913) [1971].
Vol. IV *A Tract on Monetary Reform* (1923) [1971].
Vol. VI *A Treatise on Money: The Applied Theory of Money* (1930) [1971].
Vol. VII *The General Theory of Employment, Interest and Money* (1936) [1973].
Vol. IX *Essays in Persuasion* (1931) [1972].
Vol. X *Essays in Biography* (1933) [1972].
Vol. XI *Economic Articles and Correspondence: Academic* [1983].
Vol. XII *Economic Articles and Correspondence: Investment and Editorial* [1983].
Vol. XIV *The General Theory and After, Part II: Defence and Development* [1973].
Vol. XV *Activities 1906–14: India and Cambridge* [1971].
Vol. XVI *Activities 1914–19: The Treasury and Versailles* [1971].
Vol. XIX *Activities 1922–9: The Return to Gold and Industrial Policy* [1981].
Vol. XX *Activities 1929–31: Rethinking Employment and Unemployment Policies* [1981].

Unpublished Letters
To Abrahams, Lionel, 1 July 1913 (Abrahams' State Bank memorandum) p. 132.
Vol. XXI *Activities 1931–9*: *World Crisis and Policies in Britain and America* [1982].
Vol. XXII *Activities 1939–45*: *Internal War Finance* [1978].
Vol. XXIII *Activities 1940–43*: *External War Finance* [1979].
Vol. XXIV *Activities 1944–6*: *The Transition to Peace* [1979].
Vol. XXIX *The General Theory and After*: *A Supplement* [1979].
Vol. XXV *Activities 1940–44*: *Shaping the Post-War World*: *The Clearing Union* [1980].
Vol. XXVI *Activities 1941–46*: *Shaping the Post-War World*: *Bretton Woods and Reparations* [1980].
Vol. XXVII *Activities 1940–6*: *Shaping the Post-War World*: *Employment and Commodities* [1980].
Vol. XXVIII *Social, Political and Literary Writings* [1982].
Milo Keynes (ed.) *Essays on John Maynard Keynes* (London: Cambridge University Press, 1978).
D. E. Moggridge (ed.), Keynes: *Aspects of the Man and His Work* (London: Macmillan, 1974).
D. E. Moggridge, 'Keynes and the International Monetary System 1909–46' in J. S. Cohen and G. C. Harcourt (ed.) in *International Monetary Problems and Supply-side Economics* (London: Macmillan, 1986).
K. N. Raj, *Monetary Policy of the Reserve Bank of India* (Bombay: National Information and Publications, 1948).
——— 'Keynesian Economics and Agrarian Economies', in C. H. Hanumantha Rao and P. C. Joshi (ed.), *Reflections on Economic Development and Social Change (Essays in Honour of Professor V. K. R. V. Rao)* (Delhi: Allied Publishers, 1979).
A. Robinson, 'Keynes and his Cambridge Colleagues', in D. Patinkin and J. Clark Leith (ed.), *Keynes, Cambridge and The General Theory* (London: Macmillan, 1977).
R. S. Sayers, *Central Banking after Bagehot* (Oxford: Clarendon Press, 1957).
R. Skidelsky, *John Maynard Keynes*, *Vol. I: Hopes Betrayed*, *1883–1920* (London: Macmillan, 1983).
E. Stokes, *The English Utilitarians and India* (Oxford: Clarendon Press, 1959).
A. P. Thirlwall (ed.), *Keynes and International Monetary Relations* (London: Macmillan, 1978).
——— (ed.), *Keynes and Laissez-Faire* (London: Macmillan, 1978).
——— (ed.), *Keynes and Economic Development* (London: Macmillan, 1987).
——— (ed.), *Keynes as a Policy Adviser* (London: Macmillan, 1982).
L. P. Wilkinson, *Kingsmen of a Century, 1873–1972* (Cambridge: King's College, 1981).
D. Worswick and J. Trevithick (ed.), *Keynes and the Modern World (Proceedings of the Keynes Centenary Conference)* (Cambridge: Cambridge University Press, 1983).

Articles

B. P. Adarkar, 'Lord Keynes of Tilton – A Tribute', *Eastern Economist*, 10 May (1946).
A. G. Chandavarkar, 'Keynes and India', *Economic and Political Weekly*, XVIII (1983).
———, 'Keynes and Central Banking', *Indian Economic Review*, XX (1985).
——— 'Was Keynes a Development Economist?', *Economic and Political Weekly*, XXI (1985).
E. A. G. Robinson, 'John Maynard Keynes', *Economic Journal*, LVII (1947).
——— 'John Maynard Keynes: Economist, Author, and Statesman', *Economic Journal*, Vol. 82 (1972).
R. S. Sayers, 'The Young Keynes', *The Economic Journal*, Vol. 82 (1972).
J. A. Schumpeter, 'John Maynard Keynes, 1883–1946', *American Economic Review*, XXXVI (1946).

Archival material

Edwin Montagu Papers, Trinity College, Cambridge.
Keynes Papers, King's College Library, Cambridge.
Grigg Collection, Churchill College, Cambridge.
Malcolm Darling Papers, Centre of South Asian Studies, Cambridge.
India Office Records, London.
International Monetary Fund (Washington, DC) Archives.

Index